RELIGIOUS LIBERTY

With the compliments
of Woodstock

[signature]

RELIGIOUS LIBERTY

CATHOLIC STRUGGLES
WITH
PLURALISM

John Courtney Murray

Edited by J. Leon Hooper, S.J.

Westminster/John Knox Press
Louisville, Kentucky

Book design by Susan E. Jackson

First edition

This book is printed on acid-free paper that meets the American National Standards Institute Z39.48 standard. ∞

Published by Westminster/John Knox Press
Louisville, Kentucky

PRINTED IN THE UNITED STATES OF AMERICA

9 8 7 6 5 4 3 2 1

Library of Congress Cataloging-in-Publication Data
Murray, John Courtney.
  Religious liberty : Catholic struggles with pluralism / John
Courtney Murray ; edited by J. Leon Hooper.—1st ed.
        p.   cm.—(Library of theological ethics)
  Includes bibliographical references and index.
  ISBN 0-664-25360-1 (pbk. : alk. paper)

  1. Freedom of religion.   2. Religious pluralism—Christianity.
3. Freedom of Religion—United States.   4. Religious pluralism—
Doctrines.   I. Hooper, J. Leon.   II. Title.   III. Series.
BV741.M88001993
261.7′2—dc20   92-17829

CONTENTS

LIBRARY OF THEOLOGICAL ETHICS

GENERAL EDITORS' INTRODUCTION

The field of theological ethics possesses in its literature an abundant inheritance concerning religious convictions and the moral life, critical issues, methods, and moral problems. The Library of Theological Ethics is designed to present a selection of important texts that would otherwise be unavailable for scholarly purposes and classroom use. The series will engage the question of what it means to think theologically and ethically. It is offered in the conviction that sustained dialogue with our predecessors serves the interests of responsible contemporary reflection. Our more immediate aim in offering it, however, is to enable scholars and teachers to make more extensive use of classic texts as they train new generations of theologians, ethicists, and ministers.

The volumes included in the Library will comprise a variety of types. Some will make available English-language texts and translations that have fallen out of print; others will present new translations of texts previously unavailable in English. Still others will offer anthologies or collections of significant statements about problems and themes of special importance. We hope that each volume will encourage contemporary theological ethicists to remain in conversation with the rich and diverse heritage of their discipline.

ROBIN W. LOVIN
DOUGLAS F. OTTATI
WILLIAM SCHWEIKER

ACKNOWLEDGMENTS

Acknowledgment is made to the Maryland Province Archives Committee, Society of Jesus, Maryland Province, to reprint the following copyrighted material by John Courtney Murray, S.J.:

"De argumentis pro iure hominis ad libertatem religiosam." In A. Schönmetzer, ed., *Acta Congressus Internationalis de Theologia Concilii Vaticani II* (Rome: Vatican, 1968). English translation copyright © 1993 Westminster/John Knox Press.

"The Issue of Church and State at Vatican II." *Theological Studies* 27 (December 1966): 580–606.

"Leo XIII and Pius XII: Government and the Order of Religion." Murray Archives, 1955: file 7-536.

The Problem of Religious Freedom. Westminster, Md.: The Newman Press, 1965.

General Introduction

J. Leon Hooper, S.J.

John Courtney Murray's name had assumed near-mythic, even Promethean, undertones long before his death in 1967. Enshrined on a 1960 cover of *Time* magazine,[1] Murray's thoughtful smile and uncompromising Roman collar appeared to capture and bind into a dynamic unity several social and personal forces that polarized his Roman Catholic Church and American society. Murray was simultaneously Catholic and American, scholar and priest, committed to tradition and to modernity, possessed of an otherworldly piety and a this-worldly *savoir faire*. While many opted for the minimal peace of mutually assured destruction or the isolation of the ghetto, Murray attempted internally to unite these and other polarities and expected, in fact demanded, their unity in public civil and religious life. By the publication of his *We Hold These Truths: Catholic Reflections on the American Proposition*[2] in 1960 (hereafter *WHTT*), in word and print Murray had tackled most of the public moral debates that had preoccupied America and American Catholics since 1945. With intelligence, concern, and humor, he dealt with post–World War II reconstruction, the difficulties of intercredal cooperation in religiously pluralistic America, censorship, aid to private education, constitutional law, the morality of cold war strategies, and the loves that flourish (or ought to flourish) at the heart of American public life.

In the seven years that remained to him between his appearance on *Time*'s cover and his death in 1967, this Jesuit did not rest on his secular laurels. He became an American Catholic hero at the Second Vatican Council, writing extensively on Trinitarian doctrine, doc-

trinal development, contemporary atheism, and the church's adjust-
ment both to the modern world and to its own internal diversity. He
revisited the issues that had given him national recognition, assuming
in tone and substance the role of a wise, elderly statesman who had
advanced beyond partisan politics. He commented favorably on the
Catholic commission majority report that, to Pope Paul VI's chagrin,
had recommended that the church adjust its stance toward artificial
birth control. As a member of a governmental commission that stud-
ied selective conscientious objection, he recommended the allowance
of a selective conscientious objector classification in the face of the
growing conflict in Vietnam.

On all these issues Murray would rightly be classed as a progressive—as one who thought that present doctrinal and policy formulations more often than not needed revision—but no more so than on
the issue of religious freedom. On this "most American of issues" he
wrote thirty-eight articles before 1962, then another thirty during
and after the Council. He worked closely with the American bishops,
writing many of their conciliar interventions, and drafted two versions of what eventually became the conciliar decree on religious
freedom.

This volume presents four distinct arguments for civil religious
freedom, all written by Murray. He completed the first in 1955,
therein concluding ten intensive years of research, writing, and po-
lemics. By 1955 he had developed a complex, coherent, and historically sophisticated defense of religious freedom. However, in getting
to that argument he had united Catholic traditionalists in both the
United States and Rome around the fear that his argument seriously
undermined Catholic faith and morals. Although this first article was
slated for publication in *Theological Studies,* it never advanced beyond
galley pages. His church and his religious order suppressed its publication and instructed Murray to cease writing on the issue. The second article contained in this volume was published in 1964. After
being invited to the second, but not the first, session of the Council,[3]
Murray fashioned an earlier version of this argument that was then
distributed to all participants in the Council. Finally, in response to
what the Council had to say about religious freedom and church/
state relations, Murray wrote the last two articles of this collection.

The Council, in its declaration entitled *Dignitatis Humanae Personae (The Dignity of the Human Person),* clearly endorsed civil religious
freedom. This reversed long-standing Roman Catholic opposition to
the separation of church and state and to the freedom of religion

(and freedoms of speech, assembly, and press). As alternatives to the freedoms of liberal society, the church had insisted upon the establishment of Catholicism as the religion of the state and coercive intolerance toward non-Catholic religious expression. These endorsements of establishment and intolerance received their most vitriolic expression in the condemnations of Pope Pius IX (1856–1878) and their most systematic endorsement in the writings of Pope Leo XIII (1878–1903).[4]

The religious freedom that Pius IX and Leo XIII condemned and the Council endorsed is not evangelical freedom—the power given in Christ Jesus to conquer sin and death, to live in the power of the Spirit. It is not an empowerment. Civil religious freedom connotes immediately a personal immunity from state-directed coercion and secondarily an immunity from those more subtle forms of coercion that result in economic or educational disadvantage. Pius IX and Leo XIII held that the state ought to suppress the public expression of heretical and atheistic belief. The Council claimed that neither internal commitments to religious (or atheistic) beliefs nor the external actions that are judged by believers to flow necessarily from those beliefs ought to be subject to political or social coercion.

These arguments, then, signify a major shift in Roman Catholic social teaching, a shift that Murray facilitated. Yet many of Murray's own comments suggested that the church's December 1965 endorsement of religious freedom verged on the inconsequential. Earlier that year, with the Council's acceptance of *Dignitatis* assured, he wrote that "the Church is in the unfortunate position of coming late, with the great guns of her authority, to a war that has already been won, however many rearguard skirmishes remain to be fought" (1965j, p. 43). For the previous two decades Murray had argued that the institution of civil religious freedom had achieved the status of international consensus. It was accepted and affirmed throughout the world, to the point that even the totalitarian Soviet state had to give it lip service. In 1965 the church was simply playing a game of catch-up. At its best, the church's endorsement of religious freedom was an act of humility on the part of the church, since the church had done little to develop the institution (1966b, pp. 566–67). In fact, it had fought against the religious and other civil freedoms that were developed outside of, and independently of, the church.

Nor did Murray think much of the three or four justifications that *Dignitatis* advanced for its endorsement of civil religious freedom. As we will see in the fourth chapter in this volume, he claimed that what is doctrinal about the declaration is its positive endorsement of the institution, not the arguments that it advanced for that endorsement. By doctrinal he meant a judgment in which the full church concurred and to which all Catholics must give assent. The justifications advanced by the decree did not fall under the doctrinal. Now the church must formulate better arguments.

The Social Importance of Theoretical Justifications

If the Roman Catholic Church, in Hilaire Belloc's sympathetic portrayal, was once again "arriv[ing] on the scene a little breathless and a little late," why did Murray insist that the church develop better, more coherent and consistent arguments for civil religious freedom? The short answer is that Murray was responding to a deep-seated commitment within his own religious tradition, namely, to a religiously grounded sense of responsibility for the public, civic forum. As we will see, Murray argued that the church in the past had fulfilled its responsibility in multiple ways, responding in each historical period to differing political forms and differing configurations of moral authority. When he turned to contemporary social problems, he found that the development of complex, democratic societies placed on the state, on the church, on other intermediate institutions, and on the people new demands that were in part different from those that shaped earlier responses. What had changed? Murray answered that the moral role that the people at large played in determining social policy and general social commitments had changed. Two examples from Murray's time might highlight some of those distinctively contemporary moral forces that the church now faces and the ways in which, according to Murray, the church ought to engage them.

Beyond Realpolitik in the International Order

The first social issue that Murray addressed was the reconstruction of the international order after World War II. He was responding to Pius XII's call for cooperation among "all men of good will," Catholics and non-Catholics, in a task that far exceeded the resources of the Roman Church alone. He was also responding to the formation of the United Nations, in which he saw the potential international order of law that had so preoccupied his Pope.

In 1948 the United Nations shaped and ratified the nonbinding Universal Declaration of Human Rights.[5] That declaration was later followed by the International Covenant on Economic, Social and Cultural Rights and the International Covenant on Civil and Political Rights. When Murray wrote of a growing international consensus on religious freedom that forced even the most totalitarian states to justify their oppression, he was speaking of the gradual acceptance of at least the second covenant. Internationally the burden of proof was shifting against those who would violate the religious rights of others. The public was learning to be shocked by torture for the sake of religious orthodoxy. Murray judged this consensus to be a moral good, not simply a concession to bourgeois decorum. As we know from a 1945 memo to then Archbishop Edward Mooney, Murray first broached the issue of religious liberty precisely to facilitate national and international cooperation (1945e).

In his depreciating comments about *Dignitatis* and the Roman Catholic Church's role in the development of the rights traditions, Murray suggested that only "many rear-guard actions remain to be fought." Yet as Amnesty International has documented, people continue to suffer persecution and imprisonment as "prisoners of conscience." Why these violations, given the increasing international pressure to respect civil and religious rights? Why our ongoing difficulties at clarifying what our commitments to religious freedom entail in significantly different cultural and economic situations?

Some voicing of respect for religious freedom is certainly hypocritical and can be challenged as such. But there do exist more difficult and potentially more fruitful situations in which the affirmations are sincere, but their background justifications radically differ. How might a Muslim, with a weak appreciation of individual rights but a strong appreciation for collective rights, understand religious freedom? How might a strict Calvinist, within the doctrine of predestination and with an abiding sense of God's providential guidance, construct a society that houses both the saved and the damned? What might a Latin American Catholic, shaped by the Roman Catholic common good tradition while living in societies of deep impoverishment, say about the importance of civil rights? One is led to question the contours of the universe within which others, and we ourselves, situate claims for religious freedom. That is, one is led to the philosophies, theologies, and political theories that support these affirmations.

At issue here are not mutual commitments to commonly held beliefs, only cross-cultural understanding of where in our and others' moral universes our policy proposals find their grounding. Understanding how deeply those justifications reach into the moral and religious commitments of a people does not require adoption of those commitments, nor does it automatically establish trust. We might find that the affirmations by some citizens have no deep rooting in what we or they hold dear. But understanding is a beginning toward the establishment of trust, as the search for understanding rests on a commitment to establish trust between peoples.

For Murray, the common goods of civil society ranged far beyond the brute survival or economic utility of *realpolitik*. To establish discussions of those goods required an environment that was shaped by public trust, not public suspicion. If the church could shape justifications for its policy choices that were rooted deeply within its own philosophical and theological commitments, it was obliged to do so. Public trust, as the condition for the possibility of public moral discourse, required those better arguments.

The Problem of Trusting Catholic Political Intentions

With the Second Vatican Council's 1965 promulgation of *Dignitatis,* American Catholics breathed a collective sigh of relief. For the first time in their three-hundred-year history, Catholics could publicly, unequivocally, and loudly proclaim the virtues of civil religious freedom without raising distrust among other Americans or condemnation by their church.

The problem was not of the practical order. From the initial founding of the Catholic Maryland colony, most Catholics had prudently argued for the church's accommodation to religious freedom and the separation of church and state. As the numbers and strength of the Catholic community grew, practical arguments for Catholic acceptance of First Amendment protections gained force. The church thrived on the new American soil of civil freedom.

Rather, the difficulty lay more at the level of theory, at the level of the justifications that Catholics gave for their accommodation to religious freedom.[6] By the end of the nineteenth century the Roman Church had boxed itself into what was considered a permanent commitment to the establishment of Catholicism as the religion of the state. This commitment was forged in the European religious wars that ended with the treaty of Westphalia (1648), strengthened in reaction to the French Revolution and the 1908 French laicist laws, capped by the First Vatican Council's declaration on papal infallibility (1870) and condemnations of Americanism (1899) and Modernism (1907), and codified in the manuals by which the church supervised its seminary and university training. A body of political and ecclesiological theory emerged that appeared to allow at best only a grudging acceptance of civil religious freedom. Within that theory, Catholic establishment was considered the "thesis" or ideal of Catholic social expectations; religious freedom remained the "hypothesis" or a prudent strategy until an approximation to the ideal could be effected.

Pragmatic or practical justifications were not able to counteract public reactions against this theory. As late as 1940 the otherwise progressive priest and social theorist John A. Ryan asserted that Catholics, if they could, were obliged to establish Catholicism as the religion of the United States.[7] He immediately attempted to assuage non-Catholic fears of Catholic totalitarianism by asserting that the possibility of doing so was so remote that non-Catholics should be able to rest easy. However, non-Catholics did not rest easy. Ryan's assessment of the practical impossibilities of Catholic establishment was not sufficient to stave off torrents of anti-Catholicism that surfaced then and again during John Fitzgerald Kennedy's presidential campaign.

At play here was the impact that even the most private religious arguments can have on American public debates. Murray initially counseled against bringing the church's internal theological justifications to public discussions.[8] Non-Catholics, however, refused to ignore the church's internal theological arguments. Was this refusal an arrogant attempt to submit the church's theological arguments to Protestant or atheistic challenge, an attempt that the church ought to fiercely resist? Or did it rightly suggest that America was in fact a religious nation and that the church, as much as the government, was obliged to recognize the social impact of its own religious arguments on American society? As we will see, Murray eventually suggested a limited type of theological discussion within the public school system.

Common to both these international and national considerations is a concern with what is variously called public consensus or public opinion.[9] For Murray the engagement of that consensus, as the moral center of civil society, required reasoned public argument. He found that commitment to reasoned argument rooted in both his philosophy and his faith.

Three Reasons for Better Justifications

Murray offered two reasons for a better argument for religious freedom, both of which presume that civil society is a forum for the moral discussion and determination of social goods. From his later comments about public education in the United States, we can infer a third reason that addresses some of our present concern with the role of theological languages in public discourse.

Murray's first reason for a better argument concerned the church's credibility. Given past Catholic opposition to civil freedoms, the church must demonstrate that its affirmation is not simply a concession to superior force, to human weakness, or to sinful social institutions.[10] The church is not merely caving in to religious freedom because all other practical alternatives are worse. If the church's affirmation of religious freedom is not publicly seen to be rooted in its own deeper commitments, non-Catholics will continue to suspect that Catholics will curtail those freedoms wherever and whenever they get the chance. In such an atmosphere, all else that the church has to say about a just social order (and even about the love of God) will be ignored. For the sake of the church's redemptive mission, better arguments must be developed.

Murray's second reason was directed toward the church's mission to the temporal order. Granted that, in their earliest historical incarnations, the institutions of religious freedom and the separation of church and state received secularistic, even atheistic, justifications (1966b, p. 570). Because those arguments were anti-Catholic and anti-God, Christian peoples rejected them. Now, Murray argued, for the sake of those civil freedoms, Catholics must demonstrate that moral and religious thought can offer similarly strong, or even stronger, foundations for them. The arguments that the Catholic might offer can advance or retard the future of those freedoms throughout the world. Since those freedoms are social goods, and since the church has a God-given responsibility toward the temporal order, it must develop better arguments.

A third consideration arises out of something Murray said about public education in the United States. For Murray, the public educational establishment was not simply a creature of the state, nor of the churches, nor even of the family (see 1962b; *WHTT,* pp.134–39). Public education is a forum in which the hopes and aspirations of civil society come to expression and within which the family, the churches, and the state each have a legitimate voice. While the state in its own proper sphere must remain neutral concerning the people's faith commitments, it must not suppress expressions of the American faiths within the educational forum, any more than it may suppress faith expressions in civil society at large. Murray strongly endorsed the teaching of America's faiths by believers within public schools and universities.[11] The state has no right to impose a neutrality of silence in the schools, much less actively to impose a secularistic or atheistic belief on students. Students and citizens have a right to bring their beliefs to bear on public moral problems.

So far Murray's call for religious education rests on the rights of families and churches. Yet he had more in mind than simply the citizen's right to address, from the perspectives of faith, moral questions that arise in civil society. The people, he claimed, must learn to appreciate the various "logics" of America's faiths. By "logics" he meant the manner by which believers moved from their expressed theistic beliefs to policy recommendations. He was not yet calling for full-scale ecumenism, that is, for argument on the theistic content of those faiths. Murray was after a public discussion of how religious beliefs lead to policy choices. About this time he was confronting the presupposition that religiously based commitments (Catholic and Protestant) entered the public forum only by force, as irrational assertions that cannot be argued.[12] Murray's confidence in the moral sophistication and adequacy of his own church's theory of policy formation was at play here. He wanted religious languages in the public forum; he also wanted America's religions to answer for their own tendencies to positivism, legalism, and ecclesiological and scriptural fundamentalism. He thought the manner in which his church moved from belief to policy could stand the test of public argument.

Why teach the "logics" of faith in public schools? We are back to a democracy's need for what are here called theoretical discussions, for presentation of the justifications of particular policy decisions in the public forum. Citizens must be able to perceive why and how deeply a policy commitment reaches into the moral universe of others. Without those discussions that forum remains simply an arena in which force, not truth, determines public policy.

We are now discovering something that Murray always seemed to know: that even postmodern societies do not function solely under the rubrics of pragmatic survival and economic utility. Religion remains important. People continue to be willing to fight and die for social goods that are much richer than our normal calculus of utility can reach. Our very ignoring of those commitments itself represents a failure to address the core requirements for a just society.

Murray attempted to ground the church's affirmation of civil religious freedom in what the Roman Catholic Church holds dear. Yet he moved slowly to the principled arguments contained in this volume. He himself began with a Roman Catholic equivalent of the American pragmatic argument (while he fought against the latter). Over time, as I outline below, he had to reshape layer after layer of the theoretical argument that had supported the church's endorsement of establishment and intolerance. Readers of these articles, as moral actors in democratic societies, can question whether Murray and the Catholic Church have in fact grounded their commitment to religious liberty in what they hold most dear, namely, their understanding of God in Christ Jesus and their own sense of election by God. If they have not, is the grounding they offer sufficient for effective social trust?

For those readers unfamiliar with how Scholastic thought relates policy decisions and theory, faith and reason, even what I have said so far must appear alien. Since Murray's own arguments presuppose much of that Scholasticism, in the remainder of this introduction I will briefly attempt definitions of the key terms that the following articles presuppose. By filling in some of Murray's moral universe, we might better understand why he demanded better arguments and where he looked for those justifications. Then I will outline Murray's movement beyond Catholic practical or pragmatic arguments to the arguments presented here. Finally, I will close with a discussion of where these arguments have moved since Murray's death in 1967.

Some Initial Concepts

Murray's call for better justifications of civil religious freedom itself presupposed a complex image of the moral universe. In this sense his religious liberty arguments and his call for better arguments are theoretical—they appeal to theories and images of what it means to be human, to live in human society, to interact with a God who chose to become human. Here I move from the types of arguments he looked for to the type of freedom he affirmed.

Types of Arguments

In the mid-1940s Murray divided the first of his discussions on religious liberty according to a three-part division of human knowing. He claimed that any defense of religious freedom must contain (1) a prudential, practical, or (in a loose sense) pragmatic component, (2) a philosophical component, and (3) a theological component. All these manners of human knowing were open to public discussion, challenge, and correction. That is, all three were areas of argument in which assertions could be tested and corrected. Although he would later expand and differentiate the manners of human knowing that are relevant to a religious liberty argument, these traits of publicness and distinctiveness remained constant throughout his writings.

The major dividing line within these three arguments lay between the prudential and the theoretical. The prudential applied the principles that had been developed in the theoretical realms to the real world. It was practical reason shaping the institutions, laws, and procedural methods by which social living is governed. Murray never subscribed to a philosophical or biblical legalism, a belief that the lawmaker could apply a theory directly to the construction of social institutions. Human intelligence had to prudently weigh the issues, forces, and values at stake in each specific historical situation, if the moral possibilities of each situation were to be realized.

The theoretical foundations for prudential judgments could be found in nature and/or in revelation, in natural law philosophy and/or in Catholic theology. Those theories were not simply value-free, mechanical models. Each offered principles that expressed generalized value commitments. These value commitments were themselves grounded in God-given, human drives toward personal and social betterment. Both natural law and theology directed the human person to recognize the values that were nascent or potential in specific historical situations, values that might be missed without sufficient theoretical guidance. Theory in this sense was a form of wisdom.

Philosophy and theology, while both theoretical, differed in what they accepted as the source for the principles that they formulated. Natural law philosophy began with an examination of the human person, while it methodologically ignored any insights that might derive from revelation. This examination discloses the human person's complex individual, social, physical, and spiritual aspects. Theology began in the revelation of God as definitively given in the Incarnate Word,

Jesus Christ. Philosophy gained access to the normative pattern of human existence that was established in God's act of creation. Theology gained access to that pattern as it had been altered by God's act of redemption.

Throughout his life, Murray maintained that these two theoretical images of God,[13] the human person, and society could not in principle contradict each other. God was both Creator and Redeemer. To admit any irreconcilable contradiction between creation and redemption, between the civic community and the redeemed community, would be to assert a fundamental contradiction in God.

These different ways of knowing gave Murray a basis for a positive evaluation of at least one type of pluralism—an evaluation that appears necessary for any full affirmation of religious or moral freedom. Practical judgment was thought to be the preserve of the laity, granting them some independence from philosophers and from the clergy. While he granted primacy to the theological argument (based as it was on God's special revelation), he also maintained that revelation would not, and could not, contradict the principles of natural law. This granted a relative autonomy or independence to natural law and, later, to philosophies developed outside the borders of the church. His (initial) three realms of human knowing, then, had important implications for the respect that is necessary for social living.

Finally, by the mid-1950s, Murray clearly held that the church's argument for establishment/intolerance was actually two distinct arguments. One started from the premise that "the Catholic Church is the true church" and concluded to the establishment of Catholicism as the religion of the state. The other started from the principle that "error has no rights" and concluded to coercive intolerance. As I will mention in section IV of this introduction, questions have arisen whether the Catholic Church has fully dismantled the first, though not the second, argument.

The Temporal/Eternal

In approaching Murray's arguments for religious freedom, we find (initially) three distinct realms of argument, each with its relative autonomy and its relatively autonomous practitioners. Again in 1945, Murray characterized the practical/theoretical distinction by the further distinction between the temporal and the eternal. The world of practical judgment (including the formation of civil and constitutional law) was thought to be an expression of the impermanent, the contingent, that which is always caught in the flux of history. The theoretical worlds were thought to be permanent, unchanging, even though the human community might yet have more to clarify about the human person or the revelation offered in Christ Jesus.

The development of Murray's religious liberty argument is at its core a story of Murray's recognition that first the philosophical argument, then at least in part the theological argument, were open to change, to development and decline. In the process he would distinguish several other types of arguments, all necessary for an understanding and affirmation of religious liberty, that were open to historical development (see p. 173 of "The Problem of Religious Liberty" and pp. 238–39 of "The Argument").

The Church/State/Society Distinctions and Moral Agency

Who are the major actors involved in the establishment/religious liberty question? The tradition that Murray inherited, and out of which he first argued, held that the two most significant actors were the state and the church. Both had concern for the collective, common good. The state was obliged, as was no other temporal institution, to protect and encourage the common welfare. The church was obliged to preach the gospel and to aid the secular order in making the social sphere receptive to the gospel. The state's natural law obligation and the church's mission to the temporal order made harmonious activity between them necessary and possible. Again, in principle there could be no fundamental, irreconcilable contradiction between the natural and the supernatural.

Through his historical studies Murray was forced to ask who stands at the moral center of the contemporary social order. In past social arrangements it was fairly easy to identify the social actors who occupied the moral center. With highly centralized civil and ecclesiological institutions, the top leadership of each could be isolated and their obligations defined. In turning from the seventeenth to the twentieth century, however, Murray found moral authority and action diffused throughout society among many different actors and intermediate institutions. The older, centralized model of moral authority no longer applied.

Better yet, Murray reclaimed a Thomistic theory of social moral authority in what is called the "authorization principle." To the question of where moral authority resides in temporal society, Thomas Aquinas answered that it ultimately resided with the people. The people—not the king himself, not the upper classes, not even the church—judge, correct, and direct the king's justice. Murray could then recast civil society as the primary moral agent in the temporal order, with both the church and the state in a service role toward that moral center. More, he could then accept a restriction placed on the state that confined its role to the protection of public peace and welfare, giving over concern of the full common good to civil society. The moral sense of the people, claiming their rightful role as public moral agents, has placed legitimate restrictions on the proper concern of the state. The Anglo-American restriction on the range of state activity was a "dictate of reason," an emerging requirement demanded by the natural law, as the people assumed some form of social, moral maturity. Civil freedoms (including religious), rather than establishment/intolerance, were moral requirements based on the proper moral role of the people.

At this point Murray was moving beyond civil freedom as a practical institution created by the prudential wisdom of the legislator, and even beyond the notion that it is a simple, structural immunity. Here was an assertion of a change in the theoretical, philosophical order that was effected by moral agents outside the Roman Church. The moral sense of the people shaped a new social and political theory as well as structures to which the church must be attentive.

Laws and Constitutions

From the beginning, civil law was for Murray coercive and external. It constrains or restrains particular actions of individuals and groups. Blunt instrument that it is, it can never legitimately encroach on internal beliefs. Civil law is the product of practical, prudential reasoning.

The term "law" in "natural law" has nothing immediately to do with civil law, though indeed civil law ought never contradict natural law. As discussed above, natural law is theoretical reasoning exposing and thematizing the created drives of the human person, yielding principles that then direct our attention to morally significant factors in any specific situation. The moral agent, in Murray's view, then moves from natural law to civil law by way of prudential judgment. Any forms of personal and social living that contradict those creative drives carry with them their own punishments (i.e., failures in human potential and development). But in themselves they are not immediately matters of civil punishment. Murray asked, "Should there be a law?" to which he answered, "Only sometimes."[14]

The "Christian constitutionalism" (also called Gelasian Dualism or the Gelasian Dyarchy[15]) to which Murray appeals in each of the following articles resides in the realm of theory, but again theory that has real-world significance. It is in fact a principle that is rooted in Catholic faith. It claims that in this world there are two sources of moral authority. Early on these were for Murray the state and the church, or, more generally, the natural law and revealed law. Later they became civil societies and religious communities, or the secular and the sacred. Each of the two orders is differently based (in creation and redemption) and is directed toward different ends (civic friendship and eternal beatitude). Each can legitimately claim its own autonomy. Here was a second basis for a permanent pluralism that Murray accepted. Those who seek, from the secular or the religious sides, to reduce social reality to a "Monism" are violating Christian constitutionalism. Yet the principle by itself cannot determine what the proper institutional arrangement between these two orders must be. Prudential evaluation of each historical, social context must intervene to determine that proper arrangement.

American constitutional law, or political constitutionalism generally, presented Murray with a special problem. Constitutional laws are usually written with extreme care and achieve some type of specificity. They take form within a particular historical society, grounded in all the particularity of that society. Yet they also embody some of the general value commitments that a people hold, commitments that are then used by the courts to judge the consistency or inconsistency of specific civil legislation. In Murray's own work on American constitutional law (a concern that permeates *WHTT*, though only alluded to in the following articles), he highlighted what he thought were the general value commitments that grounded the American Constitution, then demonstrated that those value commitments were compatible with the commitments involved in Christian constitutionalism. That is, the moral orientation at the heart of a secular political philosophy was compatible with, though not identical to, the moral orientation at the heart of the Roman Catholic mission to the secular order.

Political Tolerance Versus Religious Liberty

Murray's adopted tradition had allowed that Roman Catholics could practice religious tolerance. In the context, the term meant permitting an evil to exist in society for the sake of some greater or more fundamental good. Catholics might not suppress heretical or

atheistic public expression, lest they thereby destroy the minimal conditions of public peace that make social living possible. Tolerance was
a virtue that accepted the lesser of two evils, though tolerance itself
was not considered an evil. One did not sin by being tolerant. One
just operated virtuously within a less than perfect world.

Tolerance can also connote a sensitivity on the part of the agent, a
refusal, say, to be brutal in the public forum. This moral sensitivity is
not the tolerance that the church accepted. By itself visceral repug-
nance at political repression could suggest an excessive individualism,
a concern with personal feelings, that is blind to one's social responsibilities. Each person ought to be concerned that the truth govern
society, just as the truth ought to govern the life of the individual.
The Catholic should be concerned that Catholic social doctrine shape
all social institutions. To the degree that Catholic social doctrine does
not shape social institutions, to that degree a society is evil. The instrument that disallows the full impact of Catholic social doctrine on
civil society, namely separation of church and state with its religious
freedom, is itself a social evil.

Tolerance can also embody the belief that all moral systems and
religions are equally true or equally false. That is, they are equally
relevant or irrelevant to social living. Under the label of "indifferentism," tolerance in this form collided with a Catholic faith assertion.
Catholics claimed that Catholicism offered the best set of principles
for ordering a just society. Similarly, tolerance could be based on a
claim that religion ought to be kept private, kept out of the public
forum, because it was politically dangerous or socially inadequate.
Again, Catholics could not accept tolerance in this form.

The church accepted tolerance in the first sense as a virtue, though
religious liberty itself remained the lesser of two evils. Tolerance in
this sense is an attitude taken for the sake of the common good. On
the other hand, religious liberty as discussed here is an institution.
Yet behind Murray's defense of religious liberty is a moral attitude
that is taken toward modern societies and contemporary peoples.
Murray argued that civil religious freedom was a social institution
that emerged out of the quickening moral sense of contemporary
peoples. The formation of the institutions that support religious freedom was itself an act of social virtue. What is that virtue that parallels
the tolerance of the canonical position? As we will see, he called this
virtue a presupposition of equality or respect in public argument.

Why does religious freedom presuppose attitudes of equality or respect? Again, for Murray, the common goods of civil society range far beyond the brute survival or economic utility of *realpolitik*. To establish those goods requires an environment that is shaped by public trust, not public suspicion. If, then, the church could shape justifications for its policy choices that were rooted deeply within its own philosophical and theological commitments, it was obliged to do so. Public trust, as the condition for the possibility of public moral discourse, required those better arguments. I will now outline the ways in which his arguments moved toward those deeper commitments.

The Development of Murray's Arguments

Of Murray's 166 published works and manuscripts, 68 deal with the problem of civil religious freedom. These religious liberty articles further divide into (1) internal Roman Catholic arguments for civil religious freedom and (2) arguments concerning the practice of religious freedom in the United States—the latter shaped by American constitutional concerns with a primary focus on public aid to Catholic schools. Here I discuss only internal Roman Catholic arguments for religious liberty.

Of the intrachurch articles, the majority attempt to define and justify civil religious freedom. Some postconciliar articles, while taking up civil religious freedom and *Dignitatis Humanae Personae*, actually revolve around the larger question of the development of Roman Catholic theological doctrine.

Murray's developing civil religious liberty argument can be sorted into eight different stages. In the following brief outline I cite articles that make up each stage in his argument.

The Canonical Argument (1945–1947)

- 1945a: "Current Theology: Freedom of Religion." *Theological Studies* 6 (March):85–113.
- 1945b: "Freedom of Religion, I: The Ethical Problem." *Theological Studies* 6 (June):229–86.
- 1945e: "Notes on the Theory of Religious Liberty." Memo to Archbishop Mooney, April. Murray Archives, file 7-555.
- 1962a: "Le droit à l'incroyance." *Relations* [Montréal] 227 (April):91–92.

After commenting favorably on a Federal Council of Churches' statement on religious freedom (1945a), Murray outlined a three-part Roman Catholic argument for religious liberty (1945e). He did so at the request of Edward Mooney, Roman Catholic archbishop of Detroit (1937–1958).

Murray's outlined argument remained within the methods and terminology that had dominated most turn-of-the-century Catholic thought and that had reached codification in Catholic moral manuals and in the 1917 code of canon law. As mentioned earlier, he divided the argument into three subarguments: an ethical argument, a theological argument, and a political argument. The ethical argument proceeded from premises that were accessible to unaided reason, from premises of natural law. In the Catholic thinking of the time, all people of good will could arrive at these premises. The theological argument would follow from Catholic revealed principles. This argument was not accessible to people outside the Catholic faith. If they wanted, non-Catholics could develop their own theological arguments from their own understanding of Christian faith.

From either or both of these theoretical realms, one could then move to a political (practical) argument for religious freedom. Yet Murray judged that the faith differences between Catholics and Protestants were so vast that no common theological argument could be forged between them. He initially recommended that the church stick with its natural law argument, since mutual theological comprehension between the churches was impossible.

The general structures and terms of this argument can be found in the second article of this collection, in its first section. There Murray presents the canonical or manualist argument as a counter-position to his own. Here it is sufficient to note that only the first, the philosophical argument, was published in *Theological Studies* (1945b). Murray abandoned the promised theological and political arguments when he found that the methodological approach of the Roman Catholic canonical tradition could yield little beyond political tolerance. His presupposition that the contingency of civil law alone would allow Catholic abandonment of establishment and intolerance as ideals proved to be false.

The last article cited above accompanied a 1962 translation and reprint of 1945e. One might suspect that this later publication, along with 1962a, was meant to support the tolerance position just as the conciliar debate was heating up.

The Historical Series (1948–1950)

- 1948c: "Government Repression of Heresy." In *Proceedings of the Third Annual Convention of the Catholic Theological Society of America*, pp. 26–98. Bronx, N.Y.: Catholic Theological Society of America.
- 1948i: "St. Robert Bellarmine on the Indirect Power." *Theological Studies* 9 (December):491–535.
- 1949b: "Contemporary Orientations of Catholic Thought on Church and State in the Light of History." *Theological Studies* 10 (June):177–234.
- 1949c: "Current Theology: On Religious Freedom." *Theological Studies* 10 (September):409–32.

The collapse of the canonical argument moved Murray to examine the history of church/state relations. Only a year previously he had castigated Protestants for concentrating on the historical record, for not paying sufficient attention to the "natures" of the human person, the state, and civil law (see 1945a, 1945e ("Review of *Religious Liberty: An Inquiry*," by M. Searle Bates), and 1946d). When he turned to the history of his own church's theoretical arguments, he found social and historical factors that shaped and distorted the church's *philosophical* arguments. Murray still allowed a certain timelessness and constant clarity to the church's *theological* argument. Yet he now acknowledged some movement in the theological argument by insisting that the philosophical argument was always a component of the church's argument and that that philosophical argument, as a creature of the temporal order, was constantly on the move. He pulled philosophy from its eternal pantheon, recognizing that it is always shaped by what a people in each historical period are capable of imagining.

During this examination he firmed up his notion of the contingency of human law (legislative and now more clearly constitutional, since he had found a realm of general value commitments that could develop and decline). Pivotal to this argument was his notion of a "mature" state, that is, one that could effectively monopolize coercion within a delimited territory for the sake of justice. Given the political anarchy of the early Middle Ages, the church rightly exercised its concern for the temporal order by filling in the power vacuum created by the collapse of the Roman Empire. But this was a temporary concession to contingent disorder. The mature state is an "intention of nature" or "dictate of reason," that is, a requirement of natural law. With the rise of the mature state, "the Pope, for all the fullness of his apostolic authority, would not have the slightest shadow of a right to 'crown' so much as a third-class postmaster" (1948i, pp. 535–36). The state could assume its own proper autonomy. Similarly, the church could renounce its use of temporal means, that is, coercive governmental power. The means proper to the church in the fulfillment of its mission are the spiritual means of persuasion and argument. The church's taking up of coercive means to suppress heresy/treason was then understood to be a contingent, nonideal right, no longer existent in a mature state.

The Catholic University Series (1951–1952)

- 1951b: "The Problem of 'The Religion of the State.' " *The American Ecclesiastical Review* 124 (May):327–52.
- 1952b: "For the Freedom and Transcendence of the Church." *The American Ecclesiastical Review* 126 (January):28–48.

The principal American proponents of the canonical tradition taught at the Catholic University of America and wrote for the *American Ecclesiastical Review*. Fathers George Shea, Francis J. Connell, C.S.S.R., and Joseph C. Fenton provided Murray with an opportunity to exercise his considerable polemical skills. At one point, Murray accused Connell of subjugating the church to absolute state control. More to the point, these heated exchanges forced Murray into the church/state/society distinction that was to guide his work from this point on. Murray focused on the weak underbelly of the canonical argument, namely, the vague notion of a Catholic majority. If, it was argued, the Catholic people of a nation were in the majority, then they were obliged to establish Catholicism and suppress heretical expression. After Murray gleefully pointed out the ambiguous notion of a Catholic majority that permeated such arguments, he then outlined a notion of a "people" that opened the way to his effective use of the society/state distinction.

The Leonine Series (1952–1956)

- 1952a: "The Church and Totalitarian Democracy." *Theological Studies* 13 (December):525–63.

- 1953b: "Leo XIII on Church and State: The General Structure of the Controversy." *Theological Studies* 14 (March): 1–30.
- 1953c: "Leo XIII: Separation of Church and State." *Theological Studies* 14 (June):145–214.
- 1953d: "Leo XIII: Two Concepts of Government." *Theological Studies* 14 (December):551–67.
- 1954b: "Leo XIII: Two Concepts of Government: Government and the Order of Culture." *Theological Studies* 15 (March):1–33.
- 1955c: "Leo XIII and Pius XII: Government and the Order of Religion." Murray Archives, file 7-536.

In this long, complicated analysis, Murray at times promised to develop the argument in one direction, only later to abruptly shift to another. Here he applied the society/state distinction he had honed in response to the Catholic traditionalists, reinterpreted Leo XIII's church/state theory in terms of church/society, and extended his argument to the writings of Pius XII. The last article of this Leonine series is the first article included in this collection.

Just as he had pivoted his earlier, historical discussion on the notion of a "mature state," here he pivoted his argument on the notion of a "mature people." Murray did judge that contemporary peoples were better educated and thereby better able to assume their rightful responsibilities toward the collective good. But his argument did not rest solely there. Particularly within the Anglo-American political tradition, structures that could support the direct participation of the people in shaping the common good had in fact, for the first time, emerged. These included written constitutional limitations placed on government and the institutions that supported free public argument.

Social Monism Argument (1954–1957)

- 1954c: Notes to Murray's *Ci Riesce* Talk at Catholic University. March 25. Murray Archives, file 5-402.
- 1954d: "On the Structure of the Church-State Problem." In *The Catholic Church in World Affairs,* edited by Waldemar Gurian and M. A. Fitzsimons, pp. 11–32. Notre Dame, Ind.: University of Notre Dame Press.

- 1957a: "Church, State and Political Freedom." *Modern Age: A Conservative Review* 1 (Fall):134–45.

This stage in Murray's argument should perhaps be considered only an aspect of the preceding one, since Murray's study of Pius XII in the last Leonine article includes much of the analysis treated here. Yet there is a strong polemical element in this argument, again directed at the traditionalists or manualists, that moves beyond the close historical analysis of the Leonine series.

In March of 1953 Alfredo Cardinal Ottaviani, then working for the Sacred Congregation of the Holy Office, had presented the canonical argument as if it were the present position of the church, including Pius XII. Pius XII himself spoke on the issue of religious tolerance with Italian jurists on December 6, 1953. Murray took Pius XII's address (the talk was entitled *Ci Riesce*) as a repudiation of Ottaviani's argument and authority. Unfortunately all we have from Murray's talk are notes taken by a now unknown auditor (see 1954c). Besides numerous polemical comments on the fate of the cardinal (e.g., "Significance caught in Rome: '*exit auctoritas Emissimi*,' ") Murray apparently argued that a clearer notion of the juridical order (as opposed to the more abstract moral order) allowed Pius XII to move beyond the thesis/hypothesis (ideal) argument to a clear notion of the contingent, nonideal nature of all institutions that regulate interactions between church and state (established, concordatory, or separated). He also argued that in 1954 Pius XII clearly viewed the question of national establishment within the larger question of the church's international position. Within this international perspective, Pius XII recognized that the church is best served by a condition of nongovernmental interference in the internal life of the church(es) or in the mission of the church to national and international societies (peoples). He concluded the talk with a reference to the thesis/hypothesis position as a form of "Catholic Jacobinism."

Murray was silenced soon after giving the address, the publication of the last Leonine article was suppressed, and Murray was instructed to call back the distribution of 1954d, "On the Structure."

Strongly positioned within the principle of Gelasian social dualism, Murray now developed a style that would carry over into the conciliar documents: a sharp contrast between the Catholic tolerance view and his own civil religious liberty argument. He forcefully suggested that totalitarian monism can develop from the ecclesiastical as well as from the secular sides.

Interim Arguments (1958–1960)

- 1958b: "Church and State: The Structure of the Argument." Murray Archives, file 6490.
- 1959d: "Unica Status Religio." Murray Archives, file 7-558.

In 1958 Murray wrote and sent to his Roman censors an argument in which he contrasted a "disjunctive" and a "unitive" theory of church/state relations and attempted to provide a properly theological grounding for his theory of religious liberty (1958b). The article was rejected. The next year he again sent basically the same argument, this time augmented by Latin and Italian quotations (1959d), again receiving a rejection. One theological grounding he provided was the notion of the providential care of God for this world, in which both good and evil exist side by side. (He also continued to rely heavily on the social and legal dualism premise, itself, as I will later argue, a theologically based principle.) In both articles he suppressed the notion that the church might have something to learn from developments in Anglo-American politics and political philosophy, namely, from specifications in the authorization principle and from the correlative notion of the people's active moral agency.

The Conciliar Argument (1963–1965)

Between 1962 and 1966 Murray's attention shifted as swiftly as did the conciliar debate on civil religious freedom. I have subdivided the following articles according to the areas of the debate on which they focus.

Preliminaries

- 1963i: "On Religious Liberty." *America* 109 (November):704–6.
- 1965h: "Religious Freedom." In *Freedom and Man*, edited by John Courtney Murray, S.J., pp. 131–40. New York: P. J. Kenedy.
- 1965j: "This Matter of Religious Freedom." *America* 112 (January 9):40–43.

During the council, Murray published in *America* two comments on early drafts of the religious liberty declaration and on the politics of the Council. The first article dealt with, by Murray's count, the first two drafts, and the second with the third or fourth draft (the ones for which Murray was the "first scribe"). The third article here described the counter-positions of the Council.

The Main Argument and Analysis

- 1964e: *The Problem of Religious Freedom*. Woodstock Papers, number 7. Westminster, Md.: The Newman Press.
- 1966e: "The Declaration on Religious Freedom: Its Deeper Significance." *America* 114 (April 23):592–93.
- 1966h: "The Issue of Church and State at Vatican II." *Theological Studies* 27 (December):580–606.
- 1966i: "Religious Freedom." In *The Documents of Vatican II*, edited by Walter M. Abbot and Joseph Gallagher, pp. 673–98. New York: America Press.
- 1967c: "Declaration on Religious Freedom: Commentary." In *American Participation at the Second Vatican Council*, edited by Vincent A. Yzermans, pp. 668–76. New York: Sheed & Ward.

During the Council Murray wrote, for conciliar distribution, a three-part "statement of the question" of religious liberty. This was then published in a briefer form in *Theological Studies* and in an expanded form as *The Problem of Religious Freedom*. The second article of this volume is a reprint of the Newman Press argument. In it, the influence of Jesuit systematic theologian Bernard Lonergan[16] is apparent. The notion of "changing states of the question," along with the contingency and emergence of even theoretical (political) formulations, were brought to mature formulation. At this point Murray was comfortable with what Lonergan called the "historicity" of at least philosophical arguments.

Most of Murray's conciliar argument was based on the principle of Gelasian dualism, now formulated as the realms of the sacred and the secular. He took great pains to demonstrate that parallel arguments toward similar affirmations were emerging from within the secular order and from within the sacred order. Both operated semi-autonomously out of their different foundations (in creation and redemption) with a view to their different ends. These two arguments from two distinct societies were "converging" on the common judgment that religious freedom is a social good.

This line of argument was continued after the Council in the other works cited above, and especially in 1966e,"Its Deeper Significance," now augmented by a near-Parsonian sociological notion of "social differentiation." For Murray's best comparison and contrast of the argument of *Dignitatis* and the roots of American constitutionalism, see 1967c, "Commentary."

His 1966h, "The Issue of Church and State," is a detailed analysis of how *Dignitatis* and *Gaudium et Spes* ("The Church in the Modern World") deal with the relationship between church and state. This article highlights Murray's disagreements with both documents. The article is included as the third chapter in this volume.

Doctrinal Development

- 1966a: "Conference on the Development of the Doctrine of Religious Liberty." In *Council Day Book,* edited by Floyd Anderson, pp. 14–17. Washington, D.C.: NCWC Press.
- 1966c: "The Declaration on Religious Freedom." In *War, Poverty, Freedom: The Christian Response,* pp. 3–10. New York: Paulist Press.
- 1967i: "Religious Liberty and Development of Doctrine." *The Catholic World* 204 (February):277–83.
- 1967m: "Vers une intelligence du développement de la doctrine de l'Église sur la liberté religieuse." In *Vatican II: La Liberté Religieuse,* edited by J. Hamer and Y. Congar, pp. 111–47. Paris: Cerf.

In the above articles Murray explored why and how the church had in fact shifted positions on the religious liberty issue. Here he tried to argue that the Council had sanctioned a distinct way of thinking, the historical, which he held to be on a par with the Nicene Council's endorsement of the "dogmatic" mode of thought. He contrasted this historical mode or "historical consciousness" to the "classicist consciousness" that had dominated the preconciliar church. The notion of a shifting mode of knowing is a continuation of Murray's use of Lonergan's Trinitarian analysis. Lonergan was himself developing the classicist/historical consciousness distinction during the Council. For those wishing to explore the systematic theological background of this analysis, see "On the Structure of the Problem of God" (1964c) and "The Status of the Nicene Creed as Dogma" (1966j). Murray also tried to interpret past Catholic opposition to artificial contraception in terms of his classicist/historical consciousness distinction (see "Murray Says Church Was Too Sure," 1967g).

The Social Position of the Atheist

- 1965a: *Acceptance Speech.* New York: Unitarian-Universalist Association. Pamphlet of a talk given on receipt of the Second Annual Thomas Jefferson Award, March 22, 1965.
- 1970: "La liberta religiosa e l'ateo." In *L'ateismo contemporaneo,* pp. 109–17. Torino: Società Ed. Internazionale.

It can be argued that early Murray's reliance on the notion of a natural law state allowed no legitimate social position for the atheist in public discourse. Since natural law entailed a theistic premise, those who denied the existence of God were not among the "men of good will." Here Murray asserts that the new argument for religious liberty does recognize the civil freedom of the atheist. The last article in this collection ends with a recognition of the atheist's social legitimacy. For the theoretical underpinnings of this new affirmation, see "The Declaration on Religious Freedom" (1966c) and "The Unbelief of the Christian" (1969).

Moral Agency Arguments (1965–1967)

- 1966b: "The Declaration on Religious Freedom." In *Vatican II: An Interfaith Appraisal,* edited by John H. Miller, pp. 565–76, 577–85. Notre Dame, Ind.: Association Press.
- 1966d: "The Declaration on Religious Freedom: A Moment in Its Legislative History." In *Religious Liberty: An End and a Beginning,* edited by John Courtney Murray, S.J., pp. 15–42. New York: Macmillan & Company.
- 1968: "De Argumentis pro Jure Hominis ad Libertatem Religiosam." In *Acta Congressus Internationalis de Theologia Concilii Vaticani II,* edited by A. Schönmetzer, pp. 562–73. Rome: Vatican.

In response both to the reduction of his historical and juridical arguments to secondary positions within *Dignitatis Humanae Personae* and to European, primarily French, critiques of his argument (they called it "superficial"), Murray developed the notion of active moral agency, present but not fully developed in his conciliar argument, as a positive foundation for religious liberty.

Particularly, the last article cited here, which is included in this volume, is of interest. During the Council Murray had argued that the principle of "as much freedom as possible and as much coercion as necessary" had grown primarily out of Anglo-American political experience (with the society/state distinction and the notion of limited government) and was understood to be subsequent to notions of the human person and the limited state. Without denying such historical rooting, Murray here takes the notion of human dignity, expands it beyond any potential hint of individualism, and predicates the principle of "as much freedom as possible" on both the individual and the social aspects of human dignity (making freedom a principle prior to the political and jurisprudential principles). According to my reading, he was moving toward a constructive, empowering role for the state that remained consistent with, yet moved beyond, the notion of the limited state that he argued before and during the Council.

The Ongoing Argument

Does Murray present a convincing case that the Roman Catholic church can and ought to affirm civil religious freedom? On the surface, it would seem fair to examine only the philosophical adequacy of the argument, given especially Murray's claim that his and *Dignitatis*'s major arguments were philosophical or based in natural law. However, given some challenges that have been directed at Murray's work since his death and our own present concern about the depth out of which various peoples affirm religious freedom, the problem of the theological adequacy of his arguments does deserve some attention. To conclude this introduction, I will discuss (1) the theological premises that support Murray's natural law argument, (2) recent American Catholic discussions of religious freedom that abandon Murray's understanding of civil law and/or his notion of developments in natural law, and (3) the possibility that the Roman Catholic Church has not abandoned the argument that supported establishment (which is not the same as saying that the magisterium wants establishment). Here I question how deeply the church's justification of religious freedom reaches to what it holds most dear.

Since the Council, Roman Catholics have been far more willing to bring theologically grounded perspectives to discussions of public moral goods. It is now thought that theology does not simply motivate social concern, but that it also highlights and shapes substantive values that are at stake in secular society. Questions concerning the theological adequacy of Murray's and the church's affirmations, therefore, fall within this broader willingness to bring a theological perspective to public moral discussions.[17]

How Natural Are Murray's Arguments?

Murray claimed that the first, larger argument in *Dignitatis* was based on nature; only the last, shorter section attempted a theological grounding for religious liberty. There is a sense in which his claim is accurate and another in which it is inaccurate.

The claim is accurate insofar as the argument relies on a sense of human dignity that developed within the secular order. Murray's original 1945 natural law argument was absorbed and transformed by his study of Western constitutionalism. He came to understand the best of Western constitutionalism as a development of medieval natural law theory, transforming an earlier notion of natural law that was individualistic, asocial, and ahistorical into a philosophy that continues to develop (or decline) within historical societies. What he had claimed were permanent "dictates of reason" in that 1945 argument (definitions of the state, law, conscience) were replaced by emerging "dictates of reason" (involving the notions of the mature, then the limited, state and of the mature peoples). Insofar as the major argument of *Dignitatis* relied on this notion of a developing philosophical tradition, it was, in Murray's changing understanding of natural law, grounded in natural law insights.

However, the emerging notion of the moral state and the moral people was only one line of the argument that we find in "The Problem" and *Dignitatis*.The other was the argument that arose within the church concerning the church's freedom to preach the gospel and the community's responsibility to bring the insights born of faith to public moral issues. This second line is, of course, theological, though not biblical. It is grounded in a Christian affirmation that God intervened in human history in the person of Jesus of Nazareth.

That civil society and the church can and ought to develop their relatively independent arguments is itself premised on Murray's notion of Christian constitutionalism. Further, that those two arguments can and ought to converge on similar policy conclusions rests on his understanding of the compatibility of nature and grace. We find at the heart of his, and *Dignitatis*'s, so-called "natural" arguments, then, substantive theological premises. They are theological arguments in a sense far broader than simply that they were written for internal Catholic consumption, to move the argument within the church toward an adequate affirmation and defense of civil religious freedom. The Declaration's argument that was offered to "all men of good will" reaches into core Catholic understandings of how the person and human society are transformed by the Incarnation.

Murray could have offered a natural argument that might have concluded to a position near where he did end up. If he had chosen, he could have argued to civil freedom from the natural law principle of subsidiarity—from the notion that many social groups within society by right ought to be allowed the freedom to pursue their own good and even to contribute to the common good. But he did not choose this strategy. His overarching argument, then, remains structured within theological premises, despite his own disclaimers. Christian constitutionalism spelled out its overall structure. Murray's presuppositions about nature and grace, reason and revelation, natural law and divine law, spelled out its possibility and limits.

Recent Appeals to Murray

American Catholics continue to appeal to Murray's various arguments in their discussion of religious freedom. However, their focus has not been on the adequacy of those arguments in support of civil religious freedom. Rather, their dominant concern has been with the development of church doctrine. That is, they have been struggling with an explicitly theological problem.

In a fitting way, recent appeals to Murray's thought dialectically demonstrate what he himself discovered, namely, that the church's argument has to move from the practical to the theoretical and from the philosophical to the theological. At issue here is just how timeless are the church's policy statements (establishment versus religious freedom), philosophies (canonical versus historical natural law), and theologies (the one true church versus the ecumenical church). By attempting to freeze the church's argument in any of its past policy, philosophical, or theological positions, the affirmation of religious freedom collapses into a conditional acceptance of tolerance. The philosophies and theologies that the church held in the nineteenth and twentieth centuries allowed little else.

Those who interpret *Dignitatis* as simply a continuation of the canonical, prudential argument end up endorsing religious tolerance, not religious liberty. By not allowing that the "changing state of the question" has invalidated the "error has no rights" argument, some conclude that the Declaration in fact did not invalidate intolerance; it actually strengthened its affirmation of establishment.[18] This and similar attempts to preserve the canonical tradition suggest that it is impossible to endorse religious freedom if one does not admit a philosophical shift between *Libertatis*, much less the *Syllabus*, and *Dignitatis*.

What of those who interpret *Dignitatis* as involving a philosophical but not a theological shift? Not surprisingly, those who accept Murray's claim that the natural law tradition underwent a legitimate development within secular society have little difficulty recognizing that the church has abandoned the bias toward intolerance.[19] Granted that the state has matured and that the people are assuming their rightful moral control over the state and society. Granted also that our understanding of the limits of civil, coercive law have become more sophisticated. Within these understandings of contemporary philosophy, religious freedom can be unequivocally affirmed. Or can it?

A Problem Within the Argument for Establishment

Concern over the sincerity of the church's affirmation arises from two different directions. Both touch the religious liberty argument only tangentially.

Several authors have recently appealed to Murray in their discussions of American secularism.[20] Using particularly the Murray of *We Hold These Truths*, it can be argued that Anglo-American constitutionalism is based on, or parallel to, Christian constitutionalism, that America will lose its soul if it settles into a secular monism. If then it is judged that Supreme Court treatments of religion are based on hostility to religion, not on incompetence in religious matters, then the alleged militancy of this monistic secularism can be perceived as an occasion for a Christian crusade to reclaim the Christian constitutional roots of the republic. By itself even this reading of civil society need not concern non-Catholics, if it is kept within Murray's discussion of the limits of civil law and of the means that are proper for social transformation. But sometimes it is not.

Further, the Murray of the 1950s found several grounds for tolerating the atheist in the latter's Enlightenment, Marxist, or American pragmatic forms. As mentioned above, his earlier natural law analysis began with the corollary that no person of good will could deny God's existence. Staying with the Murray of *WHTT*, then, one searches in vain for a principled grounding for the atheist's voice within the natural law state.

Note here the language of the argument. If what I have said above about the theological roots of Murray's religious liberty argument is accurate, then this argument is also theological, not simply philosophical. By masking as a philosophical argument, it leaves unexamined the roots of contemporary atheism and, for that matter, the "unbelief of Christians." Murray himself moved to these studies in the last years of his life, and his discussions of them were theological, not simply philosophical (1966c, 1969, 1970).

A second source of concern arises from an internal church debate that again appears to be only tangential to the affirmation of religious liberty. The church does claim to embody the fullness of Christian revelation and, thereby, the truth of human existence. What is the relationship of this truth to the truths found outside the church? The Council affirmed that legitimate moral goodness emerges beyond the church's borders. Even more, it claimed that non-Catholic and non-Christian religions contain elements of truth that are salvific. This was, as almost everyone grants, an advance over previous Catholic teaching. But the question now can be put: How does the Roman Catholic Church understand the salvific truths that it affirms and the salvific truths held by other churches and religious peoples? And what are the social, not just the political, implications of this understanding?

Recent papal documents (e.g., *Centesimus Annus*[21]) use a quantitative metaphor to describe this relationship, that of a whole to a part. The Roman magisterium encompasses the "fullness" of redemptive truth granted in Christ Jesus; other Christians and other faiths "participate" to varying degrees in that truth, possessing fragments of that truth. What might these terms "fullness" and "participate" mean for ecumenical relations and for the defense of human freedoms?

At this point the Catholic claim to the fullness of redemptive truth might, as someone has described it, simply be an "ecumenical inconvenience," an internal self-understanding not to be brought up in mixed company. More serious difficulties arise, however, when these quantitative images of truth are combined with the further claims that Roman Catholicism is the "one true church" and that "the truth shall make us free." The claims were at the heart of the canonist argument. As Murray describes in the following articles, the canonists

ran two distinct arguments: one from the principle of Catholic freedom in the truth to the policy of Catholic establishment, and a second
from "error has no rights" to intolerance. In the last portion of "Leo
XIII and Pius XII" Murray argues that the church can, and ought to,
dismantle both arguments. Why do both arguments need disman-
tling?

The short answer is that the principal foci of these two arguments
are different and that they raise overlapping but distinct sets of concerns. Both have to be dismantled to get at the moral forces that are
necessary for social living. The second argument concentrates on the
narrow arena of "public order," normally thought to be the preserve
of the mature but limited state. The discussion of establishment,
while it might reach codification in civil law, is more properly an expression of a society's understanding of the full social (common)
good, of the larger social order within which, and by which, we live
out our moral and religious lives. By abandoning only the intolerance
argument, one has not yet taken account of the moral and spiritual
center of human society, namely, a group of people "locked together
in conversation."

The church has clearly endorsed civil religious freedom in the
sense of immunity from state-sponsored restraint and constraint. It
has embraced the rightfulness of noncoercive means in social transformation, to the point that it has problems with any judgments supporting a "just war" or a "just revolution."[22] Can the church,
however, grant to participants within morally and religiously pluralistic societies the presuppositions of dignity, respect, and equality that
the later Murray discovered to be conditions for the possibility of
moral and theological discourse? Within the quantitative metaphor
for faith, granting much more than paternalistic care appears difficult.

It might well be that Roman Catholics will have to bear the cross of
their understanding of the truths they hold, if they are to remain
consistent with the faith given them in Christ Jesus (as Cardinal Ottaviani counseled them to bear with political intolerance as a Catholic
ideal). In that case, Murray's and *Dignitatis*'s renunciation of coercive
means would rule out political intolerance, but Catholics would need
to continue what has been called dogmatic intolerance. However, alternatives do exist to a renunciation of Catholic faith or a carrying of
that particular social cross. Murray himself offers some clues to at
least one of those alternatives.

The claim of freedom in the truth reaches deeply into Roman

Catholic understanding of the way in which its Lord of History guides and ultimately redeems the people of God. By the grace of God humans are freed and empowered. Murray gradually peeled away an elitist political theory and a paternalistic reduction of the people to a childlike status from his faith that the Lord of History continues to act in human history. He found that what he called the "dialectic removal of inconsistencies" was in fact presently required by that very faith. Might the current debate be conceived in terms of a similar dialectic?

The Roman Catholic debate on truth and freedom appears to revolve around what is normally called a cognitional theory, that is, on a way of visualizing the truths that make us free. When those truths are conceived in what Murray called a classicist manner, they are thought to be permanent, complete, immutable, and immediately present to the privileged knower. The truth of what the rest of us hold is measured by the relationship, the correspondence, between what we claim and what the privileged knower knows. We are free to the degree that the correspondence approaches the absolute. Within this understanding of the relationship, the moral and religious truths that the church possesses can only be conceived as immediately and completely at hand to the magisterium at all times and in all places, while the truths that others hold are only partial at all times and in all places. At no point does the theory allow, in principle, that new moral and theological insight might arise outside its borders, because the theory allows no room for substantive development of redeeming truth. The classicist in matters of faith need not deny, on an ad hoc basis, that goodness sometimes arises outside the explicit faith community. In fact, the classicist can sometimes be exceedingly humble in his or her recognition of the goodness of the stranger. Yet, by having no theory by which they can understand the occurrences of new insight into God and God's creation or understand redemptive sacrifices that put many Christians to shame, they likewise have no basis on which to construct virtues and structures that would encourage the emergence of redemptive power, much less full Catholic cooperation with it.

If our understanding of the relationship that is freeing is shifted from an abstract order of truth to an ongoing interaction with the Lord of History, and if it is admitted that an Incarnate God can effect redeeming insight and goodness anywhere in creation, then a theoretical grounding can be laid for the virtues that Murray described as necessary conditions for civil and religious living. That which is salvifically freeing, then, is a relationship to a living Lord, sometimes entwined in interaction with the stranger and the alien. The believer must develop virtues that allow the recognition of that Lord. By and in that interaction we are made free.

These competing notions of freedom as correspondence and freedom in interaction equally rest on a promise, the promise that Christ will be with his people until the end of time. The classicist believer looks for the fulfillment of that promise in an abstract, atemporal realm of concepts; the historically minded believer searches the tangles of human living. In Murray's and Lonergan's terms, the choice between these approaches is a matter of dialectics. Believers and communities of believers must somehow explore and decide which competing theory best preserves and deepens their common faith. Even the notion that the fullness of redemptive truth resides in the Catholic church might be preserved within a framework of the church's God-given ability, over time, to sift the good from the bad, no matter what the source of redemptive insight and good will might be. At any rate, the twisting point of the present Catholic argument concerning redemptive freedom appears to be at the level of cognitional theory, not at the level of faith in their redeeming Lord.

This last discussion has moved beyond Murray's terminology and methods. It is, however, in line with Murray's postconciliar call to search out a better grounding for the affirmation of religious liberty. In praise of Pope John XXIII, Murray wrote "The symbol for [John XXIII] might well be the question mark—surely a unique symbol for a Pope" (1963f, p. 108). Murray himself left several question marks. How completely, compellingly, and deeply have he and his church situated their arguments for civil freedoms and human dignity within what they hold most dear? How might they better do so? I hope a reading of the following essays will help the ecumenical church answer the first question and work toward a fulfillment of the second.

If nothing else, Murray's thoughtful smile and his intricate arguments both remind us that we live in a complex world of competing interests, fears, faiths, and aspirations. Many competing faiths and hopes, with their accompanying anxieties, went into the gathering of this collection. My thanks go out to Tom Field, who helped transfer two of these articles from the written page to electronic bits and bites, and to the staffs of Lauinger Library (Special Collections) and Woodstock Theological Library, both at Georgetown University. In an age of shaky financial expectations, we at the Woodstock Theological Center have greatly appreciated a grant from Lilly Endowment, Inc., for both the work behind this collection and a conference on Murray's legacy that Woodstock and the University of Notre Dame will jointly sponsor. Sr. Jeanne Knoerle of the Endowment deserves special thanks for her faith in Roman Catholic commitments to civil discourse. As I mentioned above, ecumenism came late to Murray, but he did begin to trace through some of its implications. So it is fitting that Westminster/John Knox Press is publishing these arguments that might lead to a deeper ecumenism. My thanks, then, to Davis Perkins, Danielle Alexander, and other anonymous editors at the Press for their help and patience in editing this collection, and to the general editors of the Library of Theological Ethics for allowing a Roman Catholic within the ranks of American religious classics. And finally, I am grateful to the staff and fellows of Woodstock Theological Center and to James L. Connor, S.J., the director of the Center. They more than others have borne the heat of the day and have done so with a graciousness that some of them experienced with Murray at Woodstock College, Maryland.

Notes

1. "City of Man and God," *Time* 76 (December 12, 1960):64–70 and cover. Throughout this introduction and in the reprints of Murray's own texts that follow, I have observed the following conventions: Citations of Murray's works are by year/letter (and sometimes page) and correlate with the bibliography of Murray's works. Citations of secondary sources are by author name, year/letter, and page and correlate with the bibliography of works about Murray. Bibliographic information for materials that are not listed in either of the two bibliographies will be given in the notes. I have left all Murray's own citations in the form that he used and only rarely expanded their content.

2. *We Hold These Truths* (1960c) is a collection of essays, most of which Murray wrote and published between 1950 and 1958. During that period, Murray's understanding of the natural law philosophical tradition underwent considerable development. A reader of *WHTT* can trace that development, if aware of the order in which the articles were written and the amount and type of editing they underwent. See the bibliographical entry accompanying 1960c for the prior publication of those essays.

3. For a brief discussion of the various sessions of the Council, their dates, and secondary source material on Murray's role in the Council, see the introduction to the second essay of this volume, pp. 127–28.

4. Murray's own articles will cite the appropriate Pian and Leonine texts. For a thorough background discussion of those texts, see Dionne, 1987.

5. For a discussion of the United Nations declarations and Catholic responses to them, see David Hollenbach, *Claims in Conflict* (New York: Paulist Press, 1979). For recent discussions of developments in rights studies within the United Nations context, see Cindy Cohn, "The Early Harvest: Domestic Legal Changes Related to the Human Rights Committee and the Covenant on Civil and Political Rights," *Human Rights Quarterly* 13, no. 3 (August 1991): 295–311, and Edy Kaufman, "Prisoners of Conscience: The Shaping of a New Human Rights Concept," *Human Rights Quarterly* 13, no. 3 (August 1991): 339–67.

6. Throughout this discussion I will use the term "theory" to cover any rational system or image that address questions of ultimate meaning or of the general makeup of the moral universe. Murray was a firm believer in the validity of theoretical thinking, especially in its more conceptual, systematic modes. Here I purposely use the term to apply to any manner of describing or presenting general human value commitments. My reason for doing so can be found in "Types of Arguments" in my introduction. It is based on Murray's own understanding of the differences between policy determinations and the justifications that we advance for those policies.

7. For a discussion of John A. Ryan and the continuing impact that Catholic theory had on U.S. public arguments, see Curran, 1982, pp. 26–91. Ryan's original text was written with Moorhouse F. S. Miller, S.J., with the title *The State and the Church* (New York: The Macmillian Co.), released in 1924 and reprinted in 1930 and 1934. The section that non-Catholics and many Catholics had difficulties with was pp. 32–38. In 1940 it was revised for classroom use with Francis J. Boland, C.S.C, as *Catholic Principles of Politics* (New York: The Macmillan Co.), this latter reprinted in 1950. *Catholic Principles* included portions of Leo XIII's *Libertas* and *Immortale Dei*, along with a commentary that defended the establishment position (pp. 310–21).

8. In a review of arguments supporting intercredal cooperation, Murray dismissed attempts to find a residue of Christian symbols or doctrine that might serve as a basis for cooperation (see 1942b, 1943a). This echoed a claim he made while in theological studies that the break caused by the Reformation was so severe that there did not exist a basis for even analogical theological conversation between Catholics and Protestants (1933). Throughout much of his life Murray offered only natural law philosophy as a common ground. But then the natural law itself began to change, and concerns with the church's theological arguments would not go away.

9. In keeping with Murray's own usage, I refer to public opinion as agree-

ment over policy issues and public consensus as agreement over the general value commitments or principles that ought to inform policy determination.

10. As reported by Pelotte (1976, p. 79) in a letter to Archbishop Joseph Sheehan.

11. The endorsement first arose in correspondence with Robert MacIver (1954a). MacIver and Murray worked together on a project that tried to address the question of controlling Communist propaganda within the public university while preserving free speech. Murray was uncomfortable with talk of excluding communistic expression. He countered with the need for the public presentation of religious beliefs.

12. See 1949b, 1955a, 1955d, and 1959a for his comments on Catholic conventionalism. For Murray's concern with what he perceived to be an American Protestant propensity toward irrationalism, see 1960a and 1961d.

13. Murray's natural law philosophy contained a theistic premise. As will be discussed further, this meant that some form of theism was open to all people of good will. Within this understanding of human natural drives, atheism is a revolt against the God of nature as well as the God of revelation.

14. See his discussion of the limits of civil law in WHTT, chapter 7, "Should There Be a Law?," pp. 155–74.

15. Named after Pope Gelasius I (492–496), who insisted, in a letter to the emperor Anastasius (492), that "two there are, august emperor, by which this world is chiefly ruled, the sacred authority of the priesthood and the royal power." For the Gelasian text, see Gelasius I, "Letter to the emperor Anastasius," in Brian Tierney's The Crisis of Church and State (Englewood Cliffs, N.J.: Prentice-Hall, 1964), pp. 13–15.

16. Murray had adopted Lonergan's approach to Trinitarian doctrinal development in 1958 and led a discussion of the latter's Insight at the Jesuit Theological Society meeting that year. For a discussion of Murray's gradual adoption of much, but not all, of Lonergan's cognitional analysis, see my discussion in Hooper, 1986, pp. 121–25.

17. These concerns entered Murray studies in the mid-1970s (see Hollenbach et al., 1979). A debate has swirled around the question of just how "natural" were the various arguments that Murray weaved through WHTT, or how natural they now ought to be. The dispute has focused on public issues such as war and peace, not on religious liberty. Among both the politically right and left, some assert that theologically based languages ought to be kept out of public discourse. The church is under obligation, it is argued, to use languages that can be understood and accepted by those outside the Catholic faith. For the sake of the public good, then, religious premises should remain cloistered within the church's internal arguments. Others, in-

cluding myself, suspect that there is more theology in Murray's argument than is usually conceded, and, as I mentioned above, that the church's theology is important for public argument.

18. See Marshner, 1983, and Most, 1983.

19. Kossel (1984) offers a good demonstration of accepting philosophical development while leaving the eternality of theological truth claims unexamined. He does clearly recognize that those philosophical changes render intolerance unacceptable.

20. See the various Weigel and Neuhaus citations in the bibliography. Less militant approaches can be found in the works of McElroy and Canavan.

21. See particularly paragraph 46; also 17, 29, and 47.

22. It can be argued that the source of the magisterium's present disdain for any coercive action is grounded in a deeper appropriation of pacifist New Testament commands than in Murray's political theory of limited government, dual orders, and appropriate means. If the roots of this disdain are exclusively biblical, with an accompanying further disdain for Western decadent democratic theory, then some Catholic confusion concerning political forms might be understandable. One is fairly hard-pressed to find limitations on government to public order goods or affirmations of general moral empowerment within the biblical record.

1

Leo XIII and Pius XII: Government and the Order of Religion[1]

As mentioned in the general introduction, this was the last of six distinct articles written between 1952 and 1955. Throughout the series Murray tackled the problem of Leo XIII. Leo XIII had encouraged the church's reappropriation of Thomism with Thomas's distinction between the natural and the supernatural orders and his recognition of the relative independence of the natural order. This notion of relative independence had been, and would remain, important to Murray's argument. The entire series, and particularly this last article, was based on the principle of Gelasian dualism or Christian constitutionalism.

Yet Leo XIII was a problem because he had also endorsed establishment and intolerance, giving them a more systematic and thereby more compelling grounding than had Pius IX. Here Murray attempted to separate Leo XIII's reclaimed focus on social dualism from his endorsement of establishment and intolerance.

The entire series offers an intimate look at the way Murray's mind worked—its probing, testing, exploring, rejecting, deepening. The first articles set out in directions that were eventually rejected. Much of the material that Murray had earlier touched upon he later transformed within newer perspectives.

For the clarity of Murray's argument, however, the article included in this volume stands in its own. In it Murray pulled together his distinctions between Continental and American liberalism, church/state/society, and the people as an inert mass versus morally active agents. My edited notes to this text, included with Murray's notes, offer references to themes that Murray developed in his earlier articles.

The difficulty inherent in the present subject, which concerns the relation of religion to government and to the order of human law, is apparent at first glance. There is no doubt that the care of religion stands high among the functions and purposes of government. However, the mode of action proper to government in the pursuit of all its purposes is the mode of law. And human law is, in St. Thomas' definition, "the discipline that is coercive through fear of penalty" (*disciplina cogens metu poenae*) (I-II, q. 95, a. 1 c). Law is indeed a form of moral discipline, directed to a moral end, which is civic virtue. But law is also a social discipline, directed to the common good of the body politic, which is primarily "the unity which is called peace," in St. Thomas' phrase. More specifically, law is a coercive discipline, whose specific mode of action is "through force and fear" (*per vim et metum*). Hence the question arises, what is the full body of principle which governs the use of legal coercion and constraint in the service of religious truth and moral action? How are these principles to be applied in practice—under what safeguards, to what extent, within what limitations? This is the general question.

The more concrete question concerns a particular legal institution—the institution of "establishment," as it is usually called in English—whereby Catholicism is erected by human law into "the religion of the state." The specific juridical significance of this legal institution lies in the fact that it furnishes the premise of legal intolerance of dissenters.[2] That is to say, the institution of legal establishment creates a juridical situation within the state, in which it follows by logical and juridical consequence that the force of law is to be used to "exterminate" all manner of dissent from the official state religion.

Whether dissent is to be "exterminated" by forcibly thrusting dissenters beyond the horizons of physical life, as in the days of the Spanish Inquisition; or by forcibly inviting dissenters to depart from the territorial boundaries of the state, as in the practice of the *ius emigrationis* in postWestphalian Europe; or by more gently, but still forcibly, outlawing manifestations of dissent from the order of public existence and confining them to the order of private life, as in the practice of present-day Spain—these are secondary questions. They merely concern the lengths to which penal law in its various historical stages of development is prepared to go in the process of "extermination." In all these cases, and in other conceivable intermediate cases, the substantive issue is always the same. It is the issue of legal intolerance and of its juridical premise, the legal institution of a "state religion."

Leo XIII's Polemic Intentions

It is no derogation of the authority of Leo XIII's encyclicals to say that they were, rather importantly, tracts for the times. And in situating his teaching within the historical conditions of its utterance one is not diminishing its import; one is—such is the hope—simply trying to make its import clear. A historical fact therefore calls for some brief preliminary consideration. The fact is that Leo XIII fashioned his doctrine in the face of sectarian Liberalism, an ideology that was a burning issue chiefly in the historic "Catholic nations," so called, in Continental Europe. This fact fixed Leo XIII's polemic intentions; and these intentions influenced to a considerable degree the contours of his doctrine.

The essence of sectarian Liberalism, as Leo XIII lengthily analyzed it, consisted in two related doctrines. They were put forward by the sectarians as proper dogmas, ultimate truths, universal in their import. They were also put forward as the foundations of a "new order, the progeny, they say, of an age come to adulthood, born of the progress of freedom" (*Immortale Dei*). The new dogmas inspired and were embodied in political and legal institutions, especially in the institutions of "freedom of religion" and "separation of state." These institutions were proclaimed to be "the highest glory of our age and the necessary basis of the constitution of civil societies, in such wise that, if they were to be missing, the ideal government (*perfectam gubernationem*) could not even be conceived" (*Libertas*).

The first dogma was a piece of religious philosophy, the theory of *conscientia exlex*, the absolutely autonomous individual conscience which recognized no law higher than its own subjective imperatives.[3] This philosophy of the "free conscience" inspired the legal institution of "freedom of religion," whose conscious and deliberate purpose was to effect a complete divorce between society and traditional religion. This law embodied, and enforced upon society, the theological judgment that religion is a purely subjective and private matter; that all religions are inherently equal in value; that religious faith and worship are "alien and of no interest" (*Immortale Dei*) to society; that, whatever private value the name of "God" might or might not have for the individual, for society God does not exist.

The companion dogma was a piece of political philosophy, the theory of *principatus sine modo, sine lege,* government as subject to no law higher than the will, itself lawless, of the Sovereign People. This concept of government as "a master whose power knows no limits" (*Im-*

mortale Dei) was the political projection of the concept of the individual conscience as itself *sine modo, sine lege,* a power of subjective decision unlimited by any measure or law. This philosophy of government inspired and was embodied in the institution of "separation of Church and state," whose conscious and deliberate purpose was to effect a complete divorce between the order of human law, which is the state, and the law of God—both the natural law and the law of the Gospel.[4] The law of separation was intended to constitute a monist society, surrounded by the impregnable wall of a juridical monism, and subject to a single power whose sovereignty was absolute, total, ultimate, and motivated in its exercise only by the old *raison d'etat* in its new form, the General Will in the sense of Rousseau. In the theory of separation there was one society, one law, and one power.[5]

Leo XIII's adversary was therefore at once a religious and political philosophy and also a kind of polity. It was a radically new idea about the whole purpose of human life; it was also a new concept of law (*novum ius*), a new kind of state (*genus id rei publicae*), minutely described in *Immortale Dei*. On the face of them "freedom of religion" and "separation of Church and state" were legal institutions; but in the Leonine analysis of them these laws were inextricably linked to the allegedly universal principles of sectarian Liberalism. He saw these laws as power-instruments consciously designed to effect a thoroughgoing cultural change in the Catholic nations, so called, by destroying their traditional religion.

In the face of this adversary Leo XIII had to validate three broad principles which had been systematically discarded. The first principle was that society, no less than the individual, is subject to the sovereignty of God; hence his development of the theme of public religion in a twofold sense, to be explained. The second principle was that the state—the order of human law, and government as its effective author—is part of the moral universe, subject to the law of God; hence his theme of the divine law as "the principle of the whole juridical order" (*principium universi iuris: Libertas*). The third principle was that society[6] is part of the present Christian economy, subject to the law of Christ; hence his central theme, the traditional thesis that there are two societies, two laws, and two authorities, with all the implications of this thesis.

Something will have to be said about all three of these principles. However, the purpose is to set forth Leo XIII's doctrine on the relation of government to the order of religion. Consequently, the exposition that follows does not pretend to be complete. The major effort will be to follow the contours, so to speak, of Leo XIII's doctrine and to observe how the logic of contradiction, always necessary in a polemic, operated to shape it, at the same time that its main lines remain always true to the tradition.

Public Religion

Here there are two questions. The first concerns the public profession of faith in God and public worship of God by organized societies of men; this is "public religion" in the strict and narrow sense. But there is a broader sense to the term. The faith and cult of a society are intimately linked to its culture and civilization. Hence there is the broader question of "the philosophy of the Gospel" (to use Leo XIII's phrase) as the inspiration of all human civilization and culture.

Public Faith and Worship

From the standpoint of Catholic doctrine the question of public religion in this strict and narrow sense presents no difficulties. The question is put simply in terms of ethical and theological principle; is society, as well as the individual, bound to profess faith in God and to worship Him; and if so, what should be its faith and its manner of worship? The answer to the question is given in similar terms.

The first premise of the answer is the rational truth that society, no less than the individual, owes its origin to God. God is the author of man's nature; and man's nature is essentially social. Consequently man in his social life is not less under the dominion of God than man in his individual life. From this premise it follows that man's primary social duty is obedience to the First Commandment of God. The mandate which heads the Decalogue binds the individual to the cult of the one true God, through faith, adoration, thanksgiving, and prayer. This mandate likewise binds society. Negatively, it forbids idolatry— specifically, in the text of Leo XIII, the idolatry inherent in the political religion of laicism with its cult of reason and of the political power. Positively, this law commands that the faith of society should be the true faith, the one faith which God in the present economy has certified to be the true faith.

Here the theological premise enters: in the present economy God has certified the Catholic faith to be the one true faith. Therefore this faith and this faith alone is by divine law to be the public religion of mankind—the faith of individual men and the faith of organized societies. And the social duty of worship is to be rendered in the form that is pleasing to God, that is, according to the rites and forms of Catholic worship.[7]

This first question and its answer present, I say, no theoretical difficulties. And in the practical order, under normal circumstances, the question tends to solve itself *ambulando*. A society that is, and knows itself to be, genuinely Catholic will spontaneously recognize and fulfill its duty of public worship in Catholic forms. A society that is religiously pluralist, but that knows itself to stand within the Judaeo-Christian tradition, will still recognize its duty of public worship, and will fulfill it in a manner suited to its pluralist texture. I say, under normal circumstances the question of public worship presents no great practical difficulties. However, Leo XIII was not dealing with normal circumstances. He faced the fact that a militant quasi-religious sect, the sectarian Liberals, had abolished all manifestations of Catholic public religious cult in the nations of historically Catholic culture, as a symbol of their determination to destroy the ancient culture itself and to substitute a "new order" in which society would be professedly atheist. Hence the question of public cult came sharply to the fore, as a social duty, and as a symbol of society's more comprehensive duty of obedience to the law of God.

Two specialities of this public duty of faith and worship must be noted. First, inasmuch as it is incumbent on organized human societies, on men in their civic capacity, this duty is not exactly the same duty that is incumbent on the faithful within the community of the Church, on men in their ecclesiastical capacity, so to speak. Men in this latter respect are bound, for instance, by the ecclesiastical law which further specifies the divine law and makes attendance at Mass obligatory on Sunday. In contrast, the duty of public worship which is incumbent on organized societies is not subject to this ecclesiastical specification. The body of the faithful go to Mass on Sunday formally as the faithful, not as the citizenry. The citizenry formally as such offers its due tribute of worship on what are called "state occasions," occasions on which organized society gathers, at least in the persons of its representatives, for the performance of public actions that are properly the actions of the temporal community and not the actions of the Church community. On such occasions, especially the more solemn ones, the social duty of making acts of faith, thanksgiving, petition, etc., becomes operative.

Secondly, it is supposed that compliance with this duty on the part of the citizens and their governmental representatives is spontaneous. That is, it is motivated simply by an understanding of the divine law; it is not enforced by human statutory law under pain of sanction. If it be a matter of liturgical services, the initiative comes from the Church, which alone possesses the right to organize the public liturgical worship of society. If it be a matter of proclaiming a day of thanksgiving, or a day of prayer in times of emergency, etc., the initiative will be taken by governmental officials. In neither case will there be question of the intervention of civil law, making such observances legally binding on the body politic. It is beyond the competence of civil government and beyond the rightful power of human law to coerce or constrain the citizen to make acts of religious faith or worship.[8] Indeed, there would be no justification in Catholic doctrine for anything like the Edwardian or Elizabethan Acts of Uniformity, by which attendance at church service on Sunday at the parish church was rendered compulsory, under pain of punishment.[9] In what concerns public acts of worship the proper function of government is to assist in providing the occasions on which the citizenry and public officials may freely fulfill the obligation imposed upon them by divine law. If government were to go farther, it would transgress the line of distinction between Church and state.

Christian Culture and Civilization

The question of public religion in the strict sense concerns the social observance of the First Commandment as it binds men and societies of men in the present Christian economy. However, Leo XIII's wider concern was the observance by organized society of all the laws of God, both natural and evangelical, that are pertinent to the political, social, economic, and cultural life of man.

In this sense I have elsewhere distinguished between the worship of God by society and the service of God by society.[10] Whereas the obligation of worship is occasional, the obligation of service is constant. It is also comprehensive; it bears upon all the institutions of society and upon all the organized forms of action which society may undertake. Leo XIII points to this comprehensive obligation when he speaks of "the most important duty," incumbent on societies as upon individuals, "to embrace in mind and in manner of life (*animo et moribus*) the religion" which God has revealed.

The encyclical in which this phrase occurs, *Immortale Dei,* is usually given the title, "On the Christian Constitution of Societies." The word "constitution" is not to be taken here in the modern, more strictly legal sense, as if Leo XIII were chiefly discussing the structure of formal written law, constitutional or statutory, that ought to prevail in a Christian society. The word has rather its broader and more ancient sense, visible in Aristotle, of "a common way of living." In this sense the word denotes the whole pattern, order, and style of life that obtains in a society in consequence of the beliefs and convictions that are commonly held and that express themselves in a total complex of institutions, customs, conventions, mores, social usages and attitudes, traditions, habits of thought and action.

Whether any or all of these things have the sanction of human law or not is a secondary question. Unless one is to fall into the rationalist and individualist fallacy of cultural voluntarism, which asserted that men could "make" or "alter" culture at their own arbitrary will, supported by force, one must maintain that human law does not "make" a Christian culture or civilization. The famous phrase of St. Ambrose, *"Lex non facit ecclesiam, sed fides Dei"* ("Faith in God, not the law, constitutes the church"), might here be adapted. However difficult it may be to define what is meant by culture, it is at least true to say that any culture is the product of an inner form, the development of an entelechy, a dynamism operating from within, which shapes the thinking, the behavior, the climate, and all the creative activity of a society and of its members. It is this inner form or dynamism—what he calls in *Immortale Dei* the "species et forma" of a Christian society—that Leo XIII is constantly seeking to define or describe.

The descriptions and definitions are given, not in terms of legal experience, but in terms of "the Christian philosophy," whose principles are as broad as they are imperious. They demand institutionalization in order that they may be effectively operative in the life of society; but they do not necessarily demand institutionalization in this or that precise historical form. Leo XIII indicates the all-encompassing breadth and the delicate temper of the Christian philosophy in a brief reference to earlier times, less troubled than his own: "There was once a time when the philosophy of the Gospel governed societies. In that age the virtue and influence of Christian wisdom had penetrated into the laws, the institutions, the customs of peoples, and into all their social relationships." The sentence does not enshrine a sheer piece of nostalgia for a vanished Golden Age. Still less is it a summons to return to the past and to its institutional forms, as if the Christian effort today were to seek the restoration of a feudal society, or of the medieval *regnum* and *imperium,* or the papal suzerainty over political rulers, etc. The sentence implicitly defines, if you will, an "ideal," the ideal of a Christian society. A society whose constitution—that is, whose common way of life, however it may be politically and legally institutionalized—is permeated and shaped by the virtue and influence of Christian wisdom, is the Christian ideal.

This ideal, precisely in order that it may be an ideal, is defined in broad terms. Moreover, the definition, though it is suggested by medieval society, does not suppose that the Christian ideal was actually realized in the medieval period; Leo XIII was certainly enough of a historian to recognize the defects and imperfections, the immaturities and indeed the evils that marred the medieval achievement. What he is interested in is the principle, first stated in *Inscrutabili* and endlessly repeated thereafter, that the doctrine of Christ, the wisdom of the Gospel, the Christian philosophy in its full articulation of natural and supernatural truths and laws, furnish the inner form and dynamism of a style of social life which will be fully human because it is Christian. Therefore these truths and laws ought to permeate the whole fabric of society and animate all its institutions. As the Christian faith ought to be confessed by the mind (*animo*), so it ought to be confessed in action (*moribus*).[11]

It is not possible or necessary here to develop further this dominant Leonine theme, that the wisdom of the Gospel ought to be the inspiration of human culture and civilization. My purpose was simply to note the fact that this is the dominant Leonine theme. It encloses, and subordinates to itself, all that he has to say about the secondary question, the relation of religion to government and to the order of law. Obviously, the Christian society needs a good structure of law. However, Leo XIII set only a relative and inferior value upon human law as a means toward a good social order.

One might further say that, in proportion as a society approaches the Christian ideal, law becomes less and less important. If Leo XIII seems to emphasize, at least at times, the value of governmental and legal action, the reason lay in the fact that the "Catholic nations" in his day had departed very far indeed from the Christian ideal, not indeed primarily in point of their legal structure (there were still many Concordats in legal effect) but rather in point of their profession of the Catholic faith *animo et moribus*. In any event, the cardinal and indispensable creative principle of the Christian ideal was stated by Leo XIII when he said that "the truth, once it is brought out into the full light of day, is by its nature wont to send its rays streaming far and wide, gradually permeating the minds of men," and then in turn permeating their common manner of life (*Immortale Dei*).

A Distinction of Questions

This is the place to note a simple distinction whose importance can hardly be overemphasized, since it is fundamental to Leo XIII's whole doctrine on Church and state. It is the distinction between the order of divine law, natural and revealed, and the order of human law; between ethical and theological principle and legal rules; or, if you will, between principles and their application. This distinction is simply an aspect of Leo XIII's fundamental principle in this matter, namely, the distinction between the Church and state, between the Christian community and the political community, between the spiritual authority of the Church and the secular authority of government, between the Christian law and the civil law.

The purpose of divine law, natural and revealed, is to make man good as man, to make men virtuous by obliging them to conform their whole lives, personal and social, to the intentions of nature and to the higher intentions of Christ. Divine law further requires that man should act "in the way that a good man acts" (I-II, q. 96, a. 3, ad 2), that is, out of an inner right intention. The sanction is eternal. In contrast, the specific purpose of human law is to make a society good as a society, to create an order of social rectitude that is the necessary condition of man's pursuit of his goodness as man. What human law formally and proximately envisages is not man as man but man as citizen. Even in so far as human law applies to society the precepts of natural justice, "it is sufficiently (*fere*) the function of the legislator to make the citizens obedient through the application of a common system of control (*communi disciplina adhibita*), coercing those who are wicked and prone to crime, with a view to deterring them from evil and getting them to strive after what is right, or at least with a view to making sure that they commit no offense or injury against society" (*Libertas*).

In other words, the function of human law is to assure those minimal conditions of actualized morality within society which are necessary for the coexistence and cooperation of the citizens "toward the common good of justice and peace" (I-II, q. 96, a. 3 c). Human law can compel men to do what natural law prescribes and to avoid what natural law forbids, since this is necessary if men are to live together peacefully. But it cannot oblige a man to do good and avoid evil out of a motive of virtue. This manner of virtuous action "does not fall under the precept of law, although it is the end to which the legislator intends to lead" (I-II, q. 96, a. 3, ad 2), since law is a discipline that is ultimately moral in its purpose as well as in its origins.

However, the moral purposes of human law are not coextensive with those of the eternal law; much less are they coextensive with the sanctifying purposes of the law of Christ. Again the reason is that law is also a social discipline, coercive in its action. Consequently, "human law falls short of the eternal law" (I-II, q. 96, a. 2, ad 3). Given the sinful condition of mankind, a gap inevitably separates *quod semper aequum et bonum*—the things that man ought to do because they are right and good in themselves—and *quod possibile et utile,* the things that man can be compelled by law to do because they are necessary for the *publica utilitas,* the public advantage of society.

It is not necessary here to develop further the differential character of divine law and human law, of true theological principles and good legal rules. It is sufficient to say that the distinction between moral and theological questions and questions of human law derives from the fact that the former raise only one issue—the issue of truth and right, whether natural or revealed; whereas the latter raise two distinct issues. Legal questions do indeed raise an issue of truth and right, the *quaestio iuris,* the relation of the proposed enactment to the order of moral and theological principle. But they also raise an issue of prudence, the *quaestio facti,*[12] the relation of the proposed enactment to the common temporal good of the society for which it is proposed. Legal questions therefore depend for their right solution, not only upon general principles of the moral or theological order, but also upon an intermediate set of norms, the norms of jurisprudence and political wisdom. The goodness of human law is judged by a moral and theological norm; it is also to be judged by a juristic norm, the exigencies of the common good in determinate circumstances. Both norms together govern the application of principles in given situations of fact.

The traditional doctrine has always exhibited these two complementary concepts of human law. There is the concept of human law as reflective of the universal order that ought to exist, in consequence of God's holy will; and there is the concept of law as directive of the historical order that actually exists, in consequence of man's sinful condition. Human legislation therefore raises problems in ethics and theology; it cannot bypass questions of truth and right. Human legislation also raises problems of prudence; it cannot be detached from questions of social fact—questions of concrete "possibility," as St. Thomas calls them, and similarly concrete questions of *publica utilitas*.

Moreover, the jurist is conscious of the limitations of his instrument; he is aware of the distinction between what men ought to do or avoid in virtue of divine law, and what men can or cannot, ought or ought not to, be compelled to do or avoid in virtue of human law, *disciplina cogens metu poenae*. Both the science and art of jurisprudence and also the statesman's craft rest on the differential character of law and morals, of legal experience and religious or moral experience, of political unity and religious unity. The jurist's work proceeds from the axiom that the principles of religion or morality cannot be transgressed, but neither can they be immediately translated into civilized human law. There is an intermediate step, the inspection of circumstances and the consideration of *publica utilitas*, the public advantage to be found, or not found, in transforming a moral or religious principle into a compulsory rule for general enforcement upon society. And there is a distinct set of norms which govern this transformation, this legalization of moral or religious principle; these norms mediate between the order of ethical and theological principle and the order of human law, whether constitutional or statutory.

This traditional doctrine furnishes, I say, the key to the doctrine of Leo XIII. It is true that he gave to the tradition a particular manner of statement, a distinctive configuration, a special *impostazione*, to use the indispensable Italian word. His polemic intentions were controlling. He had to join together what sectarian Liberalism had put asunder, divine law and human law. In consequence, his emphasis had to fall so heavily on the moral and theological norm of law that the nice balance between this norm and the juristic norm, which is characteristic of the tradition (as stated, for instance, by St. Thomas), is disturbed. Nevertheless, it goes without saying that the substance of the tradition remains intact; this will appear in what follows. Meanwhile, in connection with what has just been said about public religion one illustration of the distinction between questions of divine law and questions of human law may be mentioned here.

There is the question, whether the Catholic faith, the one true faith, ought by divine law to be the public religion of all human societies, embraced by them *animo et moribus;* with the theologically consequent question, whether any other religion may claim public existence within human society on equal title of divine right. And there is the question, whether the Catholic faith, the one true faith, ought by human law to be established as the official "religion of the state"; with the juridically consequent question, whether any other religion may claim public existence within this particular state on equal title of legal right. These two questions are distinct, with the distinction that obtains between divine law and human law. The first raises only the issue of revealed truth; the latter also raises the issue of the public advantage of a particular political community.

There is no text in Leo XIII which would warrant the identification of these two questions. On the contrary, their distinction is sufficiently marked. For instance, the leading text in *Immortale Dei* distinguishes clearly enough between the duty of public religion itself and the duty of caring for the public religion. The first duty is laid upon "civil society" as a whole; it is a matter of divine law by reason of the origin of civil society from God through nature. And the duty is discharged by appropriate public acts of the virtue of religion— acts of faith, worship, and thanksgiving —performed by citizens and public officials. The text further indicates that these public acts on "state occasions" are to be the expression of a vital Christianity that pervades the mind of the community and informs its whole manner of common life. The text then addresses itself to a distinct subject. The duty of caring for the public religion (*cura religionis*) is laid upon government (*principes*) by reason of the special responsibility of the public power to the common advantage (*communi utilitati*) of the citizenry. It is discharged by appropriate acts of legislation (*religionem . . . auctoritate nutuque legum tegere*). The appropriateness of these legislative acts must be judged in the light of all the traditional canons of good human law. These canons will determine the special question, whether the care of the public religion ought or not to include the legal institutions of establishment and intolerance.

It might also be noted that an act of legislation is not formally an act of the virtue of religion; it is not an act of faith, worship, thanksgiving, or petition. Its formal effect is not an increase of grace in citizens or public officials, but the creation of a juridical situation within the state. It is therefore clear that the question of the care of the public religion by government through the coercive agency of law is to be distinguished from the question of the public profession of religion by society in free acts of faith, worship, and service.

The same distinction of questions may be put in another way. By divine law the Church, as a perfect society in her own right, has an inherent right to public existence within the human community, ev-

erywhere and always. Moreover, the Church is the only religious society that can, under valid appeal to divine law, claim the right of public
existence; for she is the uniquely authorized religious society in which
the sacred order of man's salvation assumes social and public form in
the present Christian economy. All this is a matter of theological
principle; it is cardinal in Leo XIII's exposition of the Gelasian thesis.
There is then the further question, which concerns the Church's
mode of public existence. Should the public existence of the Church,
which is her right by divine law, also assume the modality of legal
existence, which would accrue to the Church by right of human law
within a particular political community; and further, should the exclusive nature of the Church's divine right to public existence assume
a legal modality in a human law which would deny public and legal
existence to all other religious associations? This is the same distinction of questions, theological and legal, now applied to the existence
of the Church as a society.

In his general doctrine Leo XIII is at some pains to distinguish
matters of ethical and theological principle from matters of public
law. For instance, he distinguishes between the theological principle
of *concordia* and the legal institution of a Concordat. Harmony of
action between Church and state (*ratio concors in agendis rebus:
Libertas*) is presented as an absolute value; the value of a Concordat is
presented as relative to circumstances: "Situations sometimes arise in
which another manner of harmony also has value for peace and freedom. . . ."

The principle of *concordia* rests simply on moral and theological
premises; it is a universal and transtemporal principle which requires
application everywhere and always. As a principle it is validated independently of any consideration of factual historical circumstances. In
contrast, a Concordat, as a legal technique for the actualization of the
principle of *concordia,* makes further appeal to a juristic norm; its
specific appeal is to the necessity or utility of this legal institution in
determinate circumstances, as a means to an end. The necessity of a
Concordat, like the necessity of any human law, is not unconditioned;
it is related to circumstances. In contrast the necessity of *concordia* is,
strictly speaking, unconditioned; it is born immediately of the coexistence of the two societies, as each comes into existence by divine law,
respectively natural and evangelical. Harmony between the two societies is an intrinsic demand of the Christian order itself in its very idea.
The formalization of the principle of harmony in legal and contractual form adds something to the principle itself. The addition must

therefore be justified, not solely by appeal to the intrinsic necessities of the Christian order in its idea, but also by appeal to the contingent necessities created by the facts of a particular historical situation.

What has been here briefly said about the distinction between general principles and their application in human law as fundamental to the doctrine of Leo XIII, will receive further confirmation in what follows. We may turn now to his second great theme.

The State and the Moral Order

Sectarian Liberalism said that the Sovereign People, "as it is singly under the rule of itself alone, so it lays imperatives upon itself, all by itself"; its own arbitrary will, as the expression of the supreme sovereignty of reason, is "the sole source of the whole order of law and right" (*omnium iurium: Libertas*). In its legislative action the Sovereign People does not need to take account of any objective canons of truth and justice; in the sectarian Liberal universe there were no such canons. Consequently, into the legal order, which is the state, all manner of commands, prohibitions, and permissions may enter at the will of the multitude; and they all enter on exactly the same title, in that all of them are equally expressions of the sovereign, lawless, popular will. What is true and what is false, what is good and what is evil, what is right and what is wrong—all enter the state *eodem iure,* and all find equal footing within the state. Everything is equally legal and therefore equally moral, which has the sanction of the popular will. Human law is good by one criterion alone: it is freely made by a power which submits its acts to no measure or law higher than its own will.

This was the thesis that Leo XIII contradicted. His counter-thesis was that the state, the order of human law, is subject to the law of God, which, antecedent to any human legislation, determines what is to be done and avoided. Human law must be related to the law of God as to the transcendent principle of its origin, content, and efficacy: "The force of human laws lies in this understanding of them: that they have their source in the eternal law, and may not give sanction to anything which is not contained in it as in the principle of the whole juridical order" (*Libertas*). It was this understanding of human law that formed the whole burden of Leo XIII's argument against the Revolution; necessarily so, since it was precisely the rejection of this understanding that furnished the chief content of the Revolution, and explained why it was a Revolution. It destroyed the classic and

Christian concept of human law which underlay the concept of the state as "the rule of law."

From this basic premise Leo XIII directed a sharp polemic against the sectarian Liberal thesis that asserted, in the Leonine translation of it, that "what is false exists on the same juridical footing as what is true" (*falsum eodem iure esse ac verum*: *Libertas*); in other words, that the distinction between truth and error, right and wrong, is irrelevant to the juridical order, whose sole function is to register the fact of a majority decision and to enforce all majority decisions *aequo iure*.

In contradiction, Leo XIII insists that the legal equation of truth with error and of right with wrong violates the principle of the whole order of law, which is precisely the distinction fixed by the moral law between truth and error, right and wrong. This distinction does not derive from the will of man, and it cannot be obliterated by the will of any multitude of men, and it is binding on the legislative action of the state as upon the individual actions of men. From this principle it follows that truth and error, right and wrong, do not gain entrance to the juridical order of society on the same title, nor do they hold place there *eodem iure*. Within the order of law, which is the state, the true and the good gain place on title of right; the evil and false can gain place only on title of toleration. For human law, like the human conscience itself, is forbidden to command what is wrong, to affirm what is false, or to favor what is evil.

This is the doctrine that is sometimes digested—one might perhaps better say, disguised—in the dictum, "Error has not the same rights as truth," or in the even less illuminating dictum, "Error has no rights." What these dicta attempt to state, rather badly, is nothing other than the principle, central to the Western and Christian civilizational tradition, that the order of human law is subject to a moral norm. Part of the essence of constitutionalism, which is itself the essence of the political and legal tradition of the West, is the doctrine that the state is a form of moral action; that it is bound on the law of God; that its legislation must reckon with the unalterable distinction fixed by divine law between truth and error, justice and injustice; that the human legislator is faithful to his function when he commands what is good and forbids what is evil; that he may never command what is evil; that the sanctification of evil is always wrong even when the legalization of evil is necessary. The whole doctrine is rational: "Falsum eodem iure esse ac verum, rationi repugnat" (*Libertas*).

This is the constitutional principle that Leo XIII opposed to the sectarian Liberal dogma that the state is beyond good and evil; that it is a law unto itself; that it may, on the principle that it is itself the Divine Majesty, "separate" its legal enactments from the order of divine law. The issue here was crucial; it touches the very nature of political society. In this governmental claim to omnipotence Leo XIII saw not only an appalling blasphemy against the majesty of God but also a great menace to the freedom of man: "In public affairs the power of government is separated from its true and natural principle, whence it draws all its effectiveness for the common good. The law which determines what is to be done or avoided [i.e., the moral law] is made a matter of the free decision of majority opinion. This is a path that slopes precipitously downward to the rule of tyranny" (*Libertas*). Indeed, if the power that fashions the order of human law is not bound to any objective canons of truth and justice, there is an end both to the rule of law and to the rights of man in the traditional sense. The state has become the amoral rule of force wielded by a statistical majority or by the party in power. "*Nihil praeter vim relinquitur,*" says *Libertas,* succinctly, ominously. Then no human freedom is safe.

In contrast, Leo XIII insists, only when "the king is under God and under the law" (Bracton's phrase, which aptly sums up Leo XIII's doctrine) is a free society possible: "So the way to tyranny is barred. Government may not gather everything to itself. The rights of individual citizens are safeguarded; so too are the rights of the family and of all the orders of society. There is assured to all a true freedom, which consists, as We have said, in the empowerment to live according to the laws of right reason" (*Libertas*).

When he has said this much, Leo XIII has fulfilled his polemic intention, which was to restore the state to its proper place as part of the moral order. But he has not yet said everything there is to be said about the order of human law. He has laid down only one norm for the legal order, the moral norm. Solely from the principle that the moral law is the necessary norm of all human legislation, only one conclusion is permissible—the single one which Leo XIII himself draws, that human law "may not give sanction to anything that is not contained in it [the eternal law] as in the principle of the whole juridical order." The conclusion is negative. It is a "thou shalt not" spoken to the state in the name of the sovereignty of God. Its effect is to constitute human law in its true character as a moral discipline, and thus to confront the legislator with an imperious *quaestio iuris:* is his contemplated action in accord with the eternal law? Confronted with this question the legislator knows that his power is limited.

But for the moment this is all he knows. The further question, what are the positive empowerments and duties of government and how far do they extend, still remains to be settled. For instance, from the doctrine that human law may not give sanction to what is false or evil it would be a long step to the proposition that human law ought to give sanction to everything that is true and good. And it is a still longer step to the proposition that what is erroneous and evil ought always to be suppressed by force of law. These steps are much too long for logic or good legal philosophy to take. Certainly Leo XIII does not thus speedily take them. His doctrine, as so far set forth, fulfills his polemic intention, which was to make clear that human law is not simply a rule of action but also a pronouncement on the value of action; that it ought to indicate what is good and what is evil; that good and evil are the conditions of legal obligation. The effect of this doctrine is, I say, to set definite limits to the power of the state, not to give full definition to its duties and empowerments.

There remain the further questions: what imperatives of divine law ought to be translated into legal rules for society? What further specification of principles inherent in the order of truth and justice ought to be effected by positive human legislation? What evils and errors should law undertake to exterminate? Questions such as these are not instantly answered by appeal singly to the moral norm of law, to the concept of law as a moral discipline. Certainly Leo XIII did not attempt thus summarily to answer them. In particular, his doctrine as thus far set forth—that human law has its sanction in the eternal law, and that it may not itself sanction what the eternal law refuses to sanction—does not by itself settle the second, concrete problem with which we started—the problem of the twin legal institutions of establishment of the truth and intolerance of error. In what concerns this problem only one conclusion may be drawn from that part of Leo XIII's doctrine which we have so far seen—the conclusion that law may not establish error and be intolerant of truth. This is precisely what sectarian Liberalism proposed to do, and did. In so doing, it violated the moral norm of law; and on this ground alone it merited summary condemnation.

The question, whether the law should establish the truth and be intolerant of error, admits of no such summary answer. It demands prior consideration of the two further characteristics of law. Law is a *communis disciplina*, a social discipline directed to the purpose of justice and peace in the community; it is therefore subject to a juristic norm—the general and particular exigencies of the common good, the needs and the advantages of the community. Law is also a *disciplina cogens,* a coercive discipline ultimately effective *per vim et metum,* through force and fear; it is therefore subject to a political norm, the norm of wisdom in the use of force. The particular laws of establishment and intolerance must find their justification in terms of these two norms. An appeal solely to the moral and theological norm of law is not enough.

The State and the Christian Economy

To the constitutional principle, rooted in reason, that the state is part of the moral universe and that the power of government is limited by the eternal law of God, Leo XIII organically joins the principle of Christian constitutionalism, derived from divine revelation, which asserts that society[13] is part of the Christian economy and that the power of government is further limited by the law of Christ. In developing this theme his polemic intention is directed against the social and juridical monism which lay behind the formula, "separation of Church and state."

The formula is misleading in one respect. As a society the Church was not separated from the state but incorporated into it, made part of its legal structure, in a new way. The juridical effect of the law was to establish the Church, by law, as one of several voluntary associations of a religious character, all of them legally equal as associations, all of them entirely enclosed within the monist state and surrounded by its supreme law. All of them owe their corporate existence and their freedom of action to the state; all of them are subject to the superior sovereignty of the state. This was "union of Church and state" of a new kind. The juridical essence of the whole arrangement lay in the assertion that, "if the Church possesses any rights or any freedom of lawful action, she is said to possess these rights and freedoms by gracious concession of governmental officials" (*Immortale Dei*).

This violent "union" of Church and state into one society, effected by the politicization of the Church, was the premise for the real "separation," the separation of the two laws. The order of human law was divorced from the order of divine[14] law in principle—that is, on the sectarian Liberal principle of juridical monism. Civil law is the highest and only law; the Sovereign People is the supreme and single legislator. Therefore religious truth and morality, and ecclesiastical legislation, are to be positively excluded from all influence on the order of public law, even in those matters to which the laws of the Church had traditionally been regarded as relevant—the affairs canonically known as *mixti iuris*.[15]

Leo XIII consistently defined sectarian Liberal separation in terms of this conclusion and its premise: " . . . in public affairs it is a matter of obligation (*fas est*) to abandon the commandments of God and to have no regard for them when it is a question of making civil laws. From this premise there follows the disastrous conclusion that the affairs of state and Church must be separated" (*Libertas*). The premise was the theory of society as monist, under the undivided power of an omnicompetent religio-political power; the conclusion was the theory of law as monist and as endowed with an unlimited reach into all the affairs of society, including religious affairs. (Elsewhere I have called attention to the regalist character of the whole theory.)[16] The separation of the two laws followed on the "union" of the two societies. The essence of separation of Church and state lay in this complexus of a social and a juridical monism—in the theory that there is one society, one law, and one power.

Against this theory Leo XIII invokes the solemn principle:

> The Son of God, Creator and Redeemer of human nature, is King and Lord of the earth, and He possesses supreme authority over men, individually and in their lawful associations. . . . Therefore the law of Christ ought to have full vigor (*valere*) in human social relationships, in such wise as to be the leading guide not only of private life but also of public life (*Tametsi futura*, 1900).

The same encyclical defines the law of Christ:

> By the law of Christ We mean not only the natural precepts of morality and the commandments received from God in the Old Testament to which Jesus Christ gave new perfection, definition, interpretation, and sanction; We also mean all the rest of His doctrine and all the institutions expressly established by Him. The first of all these institutions is the Church; indeed all the institutions which have Christ as their author are contained within the Church in all their rich abundance. . . . Wherefore the law of Christ is to be sought and found in the Church. . . .

From this premise Leo XIII condemns both the violent "separation" of the two laws and the no less violent "union" of the two societies proposed by sectarian Liberalism. The larger subject, to which more extensive development is given in the Leonine corpus, concerns the harmony of the two laws; but here I shall deal with it only briefly. The theological principle is clear: the law of Christ, as declared by the Church, is the necessary norm for human legislation in all those matters in which the spiritual authority of the Church is competent. Three such matters receive lengthy treatment: domestic society (the marriage contract and matters of domestic morality), the organization of education (the respective roles of Church, family, and state),[17] and the Social Question (the whole socio-economic institutionalization of society, as a moral as well as a technical problem). To these three a fourth may be added, public morality in its most general sense.

There is no need here to go into these matters in detail. I would, however, emphasize the leading characteristic of Leo XIII's doctrine: he constantly presents the law of Christ as a principle that limits the scope of human law and government. His argument is always for constitutionalism, for limited government, against the *principatus sine modo, sine lege*, of the sectarian Liberals. His quarrel with the theory that separated the two laws was precisely on the ground that this separation left government unlimited in its power. With the law of Christ and His Church rejected as a limiting norm of political rule and legal enactment, there are no longer any sacrednesses left in society; everything is liable to profanation by the rough hand of government. A juridical monism which leaves government totalist in its scope is a form of tyranny, whether power is in the hands of a man, a party, or a majority.

Leo XIII is no less sharp in his condemnation of the social premise and principle on which the separation of the two laws rested. I mean the theory that society is monist in its structure; that no institutions exist by native right intermediate between the individual and the state; that no institution may exist apart from the state, much less above it; that all free associations within the state have their existence and their rights solely on title or governmental concession; that the Church is simply one of these free associations, subordinate in its existence and action to the political power, as are all the rest.

If one is to understand why Leo XIII condemned "separation of Church and state" in principle, it cannot be too strongly emphasized that this legal institution, which violently effected a juridical "union" of Church and state through a subordination of the Church to the state, was consciously intended to be the vehicle of a theological judgment on the nature of the Church. In sectarian Liberal theory government, as the political projection of the autonomy of reason, was fully entitled to be the supreme judge of religious truth. Theological judgments lay within its competence because it was omnicompetent. Like reason itself, government was "the highest principle and source and judge of truth" (*Libertas*).

Consequently, against this aspect of separationist theory—the juridical "union" of Church and state by the law which ruled that the Church is a voluntary religious association chartered by the state—Leo XIII emphasized two principles essential to the law of Christ. The first is that the Church exists as a society in her own right, a divine right; that the Church is a spiritual and supernatural community *sui generis*; that the Church is governed by an independent authority. From this premise Leo XIII consistently draws, as his first conclusion, what he calls "the principle of principles," that is, the freedom of the Church.

The principle includes the freedom of the Church as a spiritual authority, its independence in the exercise of its divinely given legislative, judicial, administrative, and disciplinary authority. The principle also includes the freedom of the Church as a spiritual community; this freedom is the prerogative of each of its members, of the Christian family, and of all the institutions within the Church, as, for instance, the religious orders and congregations. Moreover, the spiritual freedom of the Church as a community importantly includes a civil freedom, an empowerment in the face of civil society—the freedom "to follow the will of God and do His bidding within society, and not to have obstacles set in the way" (*Libertas*). This is, in Leo XIII's favorite phrase, the freedom to be "at once a Christian and a citizen," a man subject to a dual allegiance, but undivided in the inner unity and integrity of his conscience by any conflict between the two authorities, ecclesiastical and civil, to which he owes obedience.

The second principle which Leo XIII opposes to separationist theory is the exclusive right of the Church to be the judge of religious truth and moral practice. To make judgments on religious truth and morality is to point out to men the way to eternal salvation; but "man's guide to heaven is the Church, not the state; this is the office committed to the Church by God, that she should exercise discernment and decision (*videat ipsa et statuat*) in the things that have to do with religion" (*Immortale Dei*). In this office the state has no share at all; for "the order of civil affairs, for all its value and seriousness, does not in any sense go beyond the confines of this earthly life" (*Cum multa*). The state is neither a theologian nor a pastor of souls. It would be "an injury to faith," says *Sapientiae christianae*, to deny that "the governance of souls has been committed to the Church alone, in such wise that the political power has no share at all in it." Here again Leo XIII is arguing for the principle of Christian constitutionalism against the omnicompetence of the sectarian Liberal state.

Having thus denied to government all right to make theological judgments, he proceeds to contradict the actual theological judgments which the sectarian Liberal state made and enforced upon society by the twin institutions of "freedom of religion" and "separation of Church and state." For the sake of emphasis I repeat that in Leo XIII's analysis the legal aspect of these institutions was indivisible from their explicit premises—the false religious philosophy that conceived conscience to be *exlex,* and the false ecclesiology that conceived the Church to be one among many voluntary associations of believers. The legal institutions were condemned in principle because their principles were theologically false. The condemnation goes straight to these theological falsities. The argument does not move on the plane of human law but on the plane of theological truth. It touches the plane of human law only in virtue of the principle, already set forth, that bad dogmas cannot make good law, or conversely, that laws cannot be good which positively sanction what is false.

The laws of the sectarian Liberal State embodied the theological judgment that "there is no difference between disparate and contrary forms of religion" (*Immortale Dei*), for the reason that all religions are simply manifestations, equally valid intrinsically, of a freedom of conscience that is equal in all men. In contradiction, *Immortale Dei* condemns the opinion that all religions are "equally acceptable, equally good, equally pleasing to God"; and *Libertas* elaborates the condemnation of its premise, the philosophy of the "free conscience" that is a law unto itself.

Second, the separatist laws embodied a consequent theological judgment that "society should adopt exactly the same attitude toward various religions and grant the same rights to each of them without distinction" (*Libertas*). Seen in its proper polemic perspective, the condemnation of this pregnant proposition comprises several interrelated assertions. (1) It is just as wrong for society to regard all religions *pari modo* as it is for the individual so to regard them; for society as well as the individual is bound, with the help of divine grace, to the acceptance of the faith which God has revealed to be the true faith, whose truth has been divinely certified by evident signs of credibility. A heterogeneity of religions within society is an evil; "the profession of one religion is necessary in society" (*Libertas*), with a necessity imposed by divine law. (2) It is an arrogant presumption on the part of government to say that it "grants" rights to this one true religion, embodied in the Catholic Church. The rights of the Church as a spiritual authority and as a religious community derive immediately from the law of Christ. It is for the state simply to recognize the existence of these rights and to observe the limits that they set upon its own authority. (3) The law of Christ, which is the only valid title on which any religion may base its right to existence, has not endowed all religions indiscriminately with the same rights and freedoms; all religions do not exist *aequo iure* and do not possess *eadem iura*. (4) Therefore a law based on the theological judgment that all religions inherently possess the same divine rights is as wrong as the judgment itself. Government has no competence to make this theological judgment; the judgment itself is false; therefore the legislation in which it issues is intrinsically vitiated. This kind of law is inadmissible, in principle, by the Church.

Taking its stand upon the law of Christ, "the Church judges that various kinds of divine worship are not entitled to existence by the same law as the true religion" (*divini cultus varia genera eodem iure esse, quo veram religionem, Ecclesia judicat non licere: Libertas*). The judgment of the Church is theological; it falls adversely upon an opposed theological judgment and by consequence upon the law which positively sanctions the falsity. In its exclusive office as the judge of religious truth and moral practice the Church "does not communicate the binding force of law to anything except what is true and good" (*nihil impertiens iuris nisi iis quae vera quaeque honesta sint: Libertas*). This, in another mode of expression, is the same principle which has already been set forth—the principle that human law may not give positive approval to what is contrary to the order of truth and justice.

Finally, the separatist laws embodied the ecclesiological opinion that the Catholic Church "is entirely similar to all the other associations contained within the state" (*Immortale Dei*), and therefore "the Church of God is to be subjected to the rule and control of government, just like any other voluntary association of citizens" (*Libertas*). Leo XIII contradicts with the assertion that the Church of God is an independent and autonomous society and authority in her own right. And from this premise it follows that it is a violation of the nature of the Church and of the law of Christ for government to establish the Church by law as one among many voluntary religious associations within the state. A law which thus defines the juridical status of the Church is an iniquitous law for the familiar two reasons: first, government has no power to define the nature of the Church, and second, this particular definition is false.

I would remark here that this whole argument still leaves unsettled the more particular problem with which we began—the problem of the twin legal institutions of establishment and intolerance. The argument is entirely theological. Its premise is the theological doctrine of the two societies, two laws, and two authorities. From this theological premise judgment is passed both on sectarian Liberal theory and also upon the legal institutions in which it issued. The judgment is theological, and negative. But one may not make this negative theological judgment the premise of immediate affirmative legal conclusions. For instance, it is not permissible to argue thus: because the twin separatist laws are illegitimate, contrary to the law of Christ, therefore it follows immediately that the twin legal institutions of establishment and intolerance are necessary, demanded by the law of Christ. This manner of argument cannot be found in Leo XIII. Moreover, the conclusion does not follow from the premise, if one has in mind the traditional distinction between matters of divine law and matters of human law.

It is one thing to make the judgment that a particular law is bad; this may be done immediately upon inspection of its relation to the moral and theological norm of law; the answer to the *quaestio iuris* is instantly controlling, by itself. It is quite another thing to make the judgment that a particular law is good; in order to do this one must also consider its relation to the juristic norm, *publica utilitas,* and to the political norm, wisdom in the use of force. The goodness of a law depends also upon the answer to the *quaestio facti:* is this law necessary or useful for the common good in the given circumstances? The morality of a law is not an immediate guarantee of its necessity or utility. Still less is the badness of one law an immediate proof of the goodness of its contrary. The argument stated above seems to labor under a methodological defect. There will be occasion to point out in what follows that an immediate passage from the order of legal necessity to the order of theological truth is invalid. By the same token the inverse passage is likewise invalid—that is, from the order of theological truth to the order of legal necessity. Correct method here is controlled by Leo XIII's fundamental principle—the distinction between Church and state as it appears in the distinction between questions of divine law and questions of human law.

Governmental Care of Religion

In its own doctrinaire way sectarian Liberalism most assuredly "took care" of religion—with something of a vengeance. Leo XIII condemned this manner of care, as a violation of the essential structure of the Christian economy, which is constituted on the bedrock doctrine of the two societies, two laws, and two authorities. But there was another aspect of the controversy which is visible in this sentence: "When the sovereignty of God over man and over human society has been rejected, it follows consistently that there is to be no public religion in public life; there further follows a most complete carelessness (*maxima incuria*) about everything pertaining to religion" (*Libertas*). Leo XIII condemned this complete carelessness. The question now is the positive one: in what concerns the care of religion by the public agencies of law and government, what does Leo XIII require in terms of the full body of Catholic principles, theological, political, and legal? Within the larger answer to this general question we should find the answer to the particular question of establishment and intolerance.

Leo XIII rejects the principle of sectarian Liberalism that religion is a thing "alien and of no interest" to society and therefore to government. The text in *Immortale Dei* which affirms the contrary principle, that the care of religion is a duty of society and of government, lists the following concrete duties. "Rulers" are to hold sacred the name of God. Among their chief offices are those of extending favor to religion (*gratia complecti*), upholding it by their good will (*benevolentia tueri*), protecting it by the authority and force of law (*auctoritate nutuque legum tegere*). Finally, they are not to establish any institutions or make any administrative decisions (*instituere aut decernere*) which would be contrary to the welfare of religion.

The text indicates that the care of religion by government includes both positive and negative duties; but both kinds of duty are expressed with great generality. What is affirmed is simply the principle itself; its manner and extent of application are not determined. Moreover, the personal note in the text illustrates the way in which the long shadow of "the good Christian prince" still touches these late nineteenth-century pages; there seems to be a reminiscence of the days when the good of religion depended upon the personal "favor" and "good will" of the prince, rather than upon the cold text of law—or even, one may risk adding, upon the warm faith of the people.

More directly, Leo XIII's special problematic appears: as he conceived the problem, religion had fallen upon evil days on account of the hostility and ill will of governments which had been captured or influenced by the "sects"—by the Masons and their socialist, communist, and anarchist allies.[18] The problem of religion in society had become to an enormous extent the problem of the will of the government, whether it was benevolent or malevolent. The situation was unhealthy from almost any point of view. Ideally speaking, the fortunes of religion should never become so entangled with the policies of government; but such entanglements are inevitable when politics becomes the field of ideological battles.

Leo XIII derives the social duty of faith and worship from the origin of society in the natural law. However, the governmental duty of caring for the public religion is derived from the purpose of government: "Those who rule over others rule only for one purpose, that they may further what is of advantage to society" (*Immortale Dei*). But true religion, so runs the further argument, is a thing of highest advantage to society; therefore the care of it counts among the purposes of government. Leo XIII's pages are full of descriptions of the advantages which true religion brings to society. However, what matters here is the basic principle. Human society is not an ultimate end in itself; it is called upon to serve the ultimate ends of the human person, whose destiny is eternal. This duty of service founds the duty of a public care of religion:

> One and all, we men are destined by our birth and adoption to a good that is supreme and definitive, to be reached in heaven after this frail and fleeting life is ended. All our purposes must be centered on this ultimate purpose. Since the full and perfect happiness of men depends upon its achievement, this achievement is for every individual man so important that nothing more important can be conceived. Consequently, civil society, which is intended by nature for the common advantage, must in its service of the public prosperity have full consideration for the good of its citizens, to the end that it may never put any obstacle to the attainment of this most high and un-

changeable good that they freely seek; indeed, to the end
that it may offer the most favorable possible conditions for
the attainment of this good. The first of these conditions is
created by seeing to it that religion, which unites men to
God, is preserved in its inviolate sacredness (*Immortale
Dei*).

Here the care of religion is described as a general responsibility of
"civil society"; it devolves upon all the orders of society, not merely
upon the political order as represented by government. Again it is
stated that the responsibility is both positive and negative; and again
too the description is quite general. However, the central principle is
firmly laid down. Human society must be an advantage, not an obsta-
cle, to man in his pursuit of his ultimate purposes. Consequently, the
care of religion is high among the functions of those who must care
for the public advantage.

Furthermore, it is suggested that the care of religion is indirect
rather than direct.[19] What government directly serves is the public
advantage, not the Church as such. Governmental care of religion
does not terminate directly at religion itself—at the substance of religious faith or religious unity. These are sacrednesses which are to be
preserved inviolate—even, and indeed especially, from government.
Political action terminates at a political end, which is exactly described in the text; this end is the creation of *opportunitates* and *facilitates*—a favorable environment within the body politic—which may
indirectly assist men in the pursuit of their eternal purposes. Since
these purposes transcend the whole order of temporal life, the assistance rendered by government to men in their pursuit can only be
indirect.

One further text may be cited, to focus more exactly the Leonine
concept of the origin of governmental duties to religion:

It is the intention of nature that we should not merely be,
but that we should also be moral. Hence man makes this
demand upon the tranquility of public order which is the
proximate purpose of the organized community—the demand that it should allow him to be a moral being, and
what is more, that it should furnish him with sufficient
assistance toward the perfection of his moral nature, a
perfection that consists in knowledge and in the practice
of virtue. . . . Consequently, in establishing institutions
and laws attention must be paid to man's moral and reli-

gious nature and its perfection must be kept in view
(*Sapientiae christianae*).

The compass of this one general "demand" is indeed wide; it furnishes the basis for all the particular obligations incumbent on society to have regard for religious truth and moral principle in the whole manner of its social, political, and legal organization. The point is that this demand comes from the bottom up, so to speak—that is, it comes from the people, in terms of a natural and Christian right. This is the customary and characteristic Leonine perspective, in distinction from the frequent canonical perspective, which tends to regard the duties of the state toward religion as being imposed from the top down—imposed, that is, by the action of the authority of the Church directly upon government. Again in this text the negative and positive aspects appear: man is not to be hindered in his religious and moral life, and he is positively to be assisted.

So far all is clear, because so far all is quite general. The difficulty begins with the question, what are the precise empowerments and limitations of government, acting through the instrumentality of law, in the public care of religion? Here we touch what is always the central problem of theoretical as well as practical politics: granted that such-and-such a value is integral to the common good, what are the scope and limitations of government in its furtherance? What should the law undertake, or not undertake, to do? How far does its power extend and at what frontiers does it stop? This question is always difficult; it is particularly difficult when the social value in question is the delicate value of religion.

The difficulty is amply illustrated by history, not least by the history of the Christian ages. In those days popes and emperors shared the same one purpose—to establish right Christian order based on the true religion. But the record shows how sharply they often broke with one another on the question, in what respect does the care of religion fall to emperor, king, or prince; in what sense does it fall to pope, bishop, or priest? Where is the line to be drawn between the respective jurisdictions of *imperium* and *sacerdotium?*[20] The passage of time, and all the transformations that time has effected, [has] not lessened the difficulty but augmented it.

The question then is, what principles does Leo XIII lay down for this question, the empowerments and limitations of government in the care of the public religion? In a sense he lays down only one principle—the distinction between Church and state and their neces-

sary harmony, or in the more pertinent concepts, the distinction between the two laws, divine and human, and their necessary harmony.
However, since this principle is complex, it may help toward clarity to
distinguish four principles, all of them simply aspects of the great
general principle.

The Purpose of Government

The text from *Sapientiae christianae,* quoted above, after speaking
of the human person's "demand" that the order of society should be
moral and Christian, goes on: "But right order is here to be observed:
nothing is to be commanded or forbidden except in the light of the
respective purposes of the civil society and of the religious society."
The appeal is to the distinct purposes of Church and state, as the
controlling principle in determining the respective roles of government and religion in the moralization and Christianization of society.
For the moment it is a question of the political principle here asserted, that the function of government is always and only a political
function directed to political ends—juridical order, political unity,
social peace, right conditions of freedom, the general welfare. The
function of government remains political, no matter what aspect of
the public advantage may be envisaged by governmental action—religious, economic, cultural, etc. This principle is suggested clearly
enough in *Immortale Dei* and *Libertas*. But it is still clearer in *Rerum
novarum* (1891); and it is both legitimate and necessary to apply the
doctrine of this later encyclical to our present subject. Principles that
control the action of government control all manner of governmental
action, regardless of the field in which it is deployed.

Rerum novarum, adhering to the Western Christian political tradition, makes it clear that government, strictly speaking, creates nothing; that its function is to order, not to create.[21] Perhaps more
exactly, its function is to create the conditions of order under which
original vitalities and forces, present in society, may have full scope to
create the values by which society lives. Perhaps still more exactly, the
only value which government *per se* is called upon to create is the
value of order. But the value of order resides primarily in the fact
that it furnishes *opportunitates, facilitates* (the Leonine words, cited
above) for the exercise of the freedoms which are the rightful prerogative of other social magnitudes and forces. These freedoms, rightly
ordered, are the true creative sources of all manner of social values.

It is therefore altogether in the line of Leo XIII's thought to say that the primary and indispensable care which government owes to religion is a care for the freedom of the Church. Religion, even as a social value, is not created by government but by the Church. The role of government is to see to it, by appropriate measures both positive and negative, that the Church is free to go about her creative mission; and likewise to see to it that such conditions of order obtain in society as will facilitate the fulfillment of the Church's high spiritual task. In the task itself, *cura animarum,* government has no share at all. But within limits it can make possible or impossible, easier or more difficult, the Church's exclusive task of caring for the needs of souls.

This care for the freedom of the Church means two things, in accord with what has been said above about the two senses of the formula. It means the assurance that the ministers of the Church as a spiritual authority will have the full freedom for their apostolic ministry in all its forms. It means also the assurance that the members of the Church as a spiritual community will have possession of their native freedom to live as Christians and citizens, to do the will of God within society without having obstacles put in their way. This latter freedom, as *Rerum novarum* makes particularly clear, creates a demand on government and on other social orders that they should provide proper conditions of social welfare and economic prosperity. Leo XIII struck a new note in his insistence on the economic and social conditions of spiritual freedom; the creation of these conditions is itself part of the care of religion.

Under ideal conditions within society, in the absence of serious disorders, this care for the freedom of the Church in the two senses mentioned would be, it seems, the only duty of government. The principle of Leo XIII here merits analogous application:

> Without a doubt the intervention and action of these (public) powers are not indispensably necessary, when conditions in labor and industry reveal nothing which offends against morality, justice, human dignity, the domestic life of the worker. But when any of these values is menaced or compromised, the public powers intervening in proper fashion and in just measure, are to do a work of social salvation; for it falls to their charge to protect and safeguard the true interests of the citizens under their obedience.

Analogously, the action of government in the interests of religion is not indispensably necessary when conditions in society reveal nothing that might injure or menace religious values, in so far as these are integral to the general welfare. In what concerns the care of religion, as in all other governmental functions, the criterion for legal or administrative action is its necessity for the common good. Leo XIII clearly states the principle: "If therefore any injury has been done or threatens to be done to the interests of the community—the kind of injury which cannot otherwise be repaired or prevented—it is necessary for public authority to intervene" (*Rerum novarum*). Evidently, the injury or threat must be so substantive, clear, and present as to constitute a social evil or the danger of a social evil. Government and law do not concern themselves with sin in general or with every manner of sin, every instance of private wrongdoing.[22] An evil must assume substantial social proportions before government may take cognizance of it. There must be question, in the phrase of *Libertas*, of *pernicies rei publicae*, damage to the body politic; for government may not command or forbid anything except in the light of its own proper purposes, purposes that are always public—the pursuit of the general welfare or the persecution, if the term may be allowed, of what damages the public welfare.

Finally, as governmental action is prompted by necessity of circumstances, so it is confined to the minimal achievement that is necessary in the circumstances. Again Leo XIII states the principle clearly: "In all these cases [of social disorders] the force and authority of law ought obviously to be employed, within certain limits. These limits are determined by the same principle which demands the aid of law—the principle, namely, that the law ought not to undertake more, nor ought it to go farther, than the remedy of evils or the removal of dangers requires" (*Rerum novarum*). This is a statement of what I have called the political norm of law—wisdom in the use of force, which dictates that the use of force be minimal.

From all this it follows that governmental care of religion, like all governmental functions, will vary in its extent and limits, in accordance with the norm of necessity. Tillmann exactly expresses the substance of Leo XIII's thought:

> The care and protection of religion and morality, the furtherance of popular education, and the promotion of science and art are the most noble office of the state. The Catholic view of things does indeed firmly acknowledge

the independence of the whole area of human culture; nevertheless, since this view sees the function of the state as the furtherance of the common welfare, it also recognizes that the state has to a considerable degree a right of co-determination (*Mitbestimmungsrecht*) in all questions of spiritual and moral culture (marriage, the family, the school, lower and higher education). In the order of concrete actuality it is of course most difficult to set limits to the intervention of the state. In any event, what must be recognized is that the special character of this whole area demands a large measure of freedom and independence, without which it cannot flourish. "The state should always, and especially in cases in which the discharge of great cultural functions falls to its account, hold itself prudently back; it should simply lay foundations, and bring into existence contexts and forms, which will make it possible for the free human personality and for various cultural communities fully to exploit their own religious, spiritual, and moral energies."[23]

It may be alleged that Leo XIII is not always faithful to this political concept of government. It may be said that in *Immortale Dei* and *Libertas*, for instance, he maintains a more paternal concept which permits and requires that government should exercise a more extensive police action in the areas of religion and culture than would be permitted or required by the political concept of government exhibited in *Rerum novarum*. If there is a difficulty here, it is more apparent than real. If his doctrine is closely analyzed, and if attention is paid to its polemic context, it will be seen that it is always in substance consistent with itself. It cannot be successfully maintained, for instance, that in *Rerum novarum* he holds the principle, "As much freedom as possible, as much government as necessary" (as he certainly does); whereas in *Libertas* he holds the principle, "As much government as possible, as much freedom as necessary" (as some seem to think he does).

There is indeed a certain difference between the two doctrines, but it does not touch the substance of principle. What makes the difference is the polemic context of *Libertas*—the sectarian Liberal aggression against the historic Catholic nations. The crucial fact here is not that the nations were Catholic, but that the masses within their borders were ignorant. What swings Leo XIII to a paternal concept of government is the fact of the *imperita multitudo,* the ignorant masses. His argument is simple. The ignorant masses are incapable of defending themselves, their culture, their faith, their identity as peoples, against the Revolutionary aggressor. Therefore it is necessary that government should defend them. It is necessary that government should take them under its parental tutelage, act towards them as *parens patriae,* use in their behalf its *patria potestas.* The defense of the patrimony of truth and morality that had formed the substance of their national tradition falls of necessity to government. Not only are the masses incapable of defending themselves; the Church itself cannot adequately defend them without the powerful assistance of government. The action of government is necessary in the circumstances to the action of the Church itself.

Therefore the criterion of governmental action in the care of religion is still the criterion of necessity. The measure of this governmental action, even when it goes to the lengths of quasi-paternal care, is still proportioned to the necessities of the situation, as created by contingent fact. In Leo XIII's mind and text it is not a question of what is ideal in principle, but of what is necessary in fact. No one will proclaim it as ideal that the masses should be ignorant, religiously illiterate and culturally backward, in such wise as to render necessary an extensive paternal program of governmental care of religion.

Not only is the canon of necessity still the criterion of governmental action; the evil which government is called upon to combat is represented as a social evil of substantial proportions. It is to be noted that Leo XIII does not authorize coercive action against the "sects" simply because of their errors but because of their activism. The "sects" do not fall under the cognizance of government because their doctrine was heretical but because their action was conspiratorial. The organized sects had, as it were, furnished false philosophy with feet, chiefly in the form of the legal institutions of "freedom of religion" and "separation of Church and state." It is this philosophy on feet that ought to be dealt with, "lest it creep abroad unto the ruin of the commonwealth" (*ad perniciem rei publicae: Libertas*). The conspiracy was against that true freedom and lawful order which are the very foundations of the state. And the judgment that the institutionalized doctrines of the sects constitute a social evil, present and grave, is not a pure theoretical position; it is the verdict of social experience: "It is already sufficiently known what sort of situation has been brought about within society (by the sectarian Liberal institutions); it is a situation which men of wisdom and integrity rightly deplore" (*Immortale Dei*).

It ought therefore to be sufficiently clear that Leo XIII always consistently adhered to his political principle—that the action of government is singly toward the purposes of government, and that the motive and measure of its action are furnished by the necessities of the common good. The principle is invariable; its demands in different situations will vary according to the necessities of the situation. To his consistency Leo XIII joined realism, the pragmatic realism of the prudent jurist. There are times, he says in effect, when governmental care of religion may be a simple exercise of the police power, minimal in its scope. There are other times when it may be an exercise of *patria potestas,* which may indeed go to considerable lengths, but which remains actually minimal when looked at in the light of the needs of the situation.

The Purpose of the Church

"But here right order is to be observed: nothing is to be commanded or forbidden except in the light of the respective purposes of the civil society and the religious society." This central Christian constitutional principle also establishes the purpose of the Church as a limiting principle of governmental care of religion. The sacred order as such is exclusively in the care of the Church.

First of all, it may be well to mention—what is sometimes forgotten—that the new sharpness which Leo XIII gave to the distinction of Church and state had, as an important consequence, a clarification of the principle that in its care of religion the political power is not acting as the vicegerent, the functionary, the instrument of the Church. It is acting out of duty indeed, but it is also acting in its own autonomous right. It is not a case of *gladius sub gladio;* government is not wielding the material sword *pro ecclesia,* but *pro republica;* it is not acting *ad nutum et patientiam sacerdotis,* but *ad nutum et patientiam populi* (to use, and furnish antitheses to, the famous phrases of *Unam sanctam*). Schmidlin puts the matter well: "Thus Leo was the first Pope who relinquished in every form all residue of medieval ecclesiastical supremacy; he positively proclaimed the full qualifications and the relative autonomy or sovereignty of the politico-social power."[24] Leo XIII put an end to all curialism or hierocratism—or whatever one chooses to call the right-wing medieval theory.

By the same token he put an end to regalism in all the forms it has assumed from Constantine to the last of the Bourbons and Hapsburgs. Governmental care of religion is not a care of "ecclesiastical affairs"; the Church cares for her own affairs. A fortiori it is not a share, however diminished, in the *regimen animorum;* the governance of souls is exclusively the function of the Church. From this it further follows that governmental care of religion does not mean care for the purity of faith in the members of the Church; this too is exclusively the function of the Church. Nor does it mean care for the spiritual unity of the Church, her unity of faith and discipline; the Church alone is responsible for her own unity and she has within herself all the means necessary to its conservation. Finally, along the same line, the duty of caring for religion does not authorize government to introduce a "crime of opinion" into its statute books. The theory of *crimen opinionis*—the theory that error may be repressed by government simply because it is error—has no footing in Catholic doctrine. Just because a philosophy is false it does not become, in its adherents, legally justiciable.

It is not permissible to distort in this sense Leo XIII's polemic against "the modern liberties." In the exercise of his supreme teaching office he condemned rationalist individualism as a spurious philosophy. But this condemnation does not make this philosophy, as a system of ideas, the object of legal intolerance. What Leo XIII protested against was the legal institutionalization of *opinionum mendacia,* fallacious opinions, in such wise that they became a social force— really a form of organized action, as all law is a form of action. His argument does not run thus: "These opinions are fallacious; therefore they ought not be permitted within the State." No such rapid conclusion is permissible in the light of his political principle, as already set forth. His argument is more subtle, and entirely true to his own principle. It is not, he says in effect, to the public advantage that the philosophy of rationalist individualism should be embodied in legal institutions ("the modern liberties" in the sectarian Liberal sense); that it should thus receive the authorization and backing of government; and that it should thus become an engine of war against traditional Christian faith and culture. To launch or sustain this legal institutionalization of error would be socially disastrous. Therefore it is wrong for government to embark on this program. We are very far here from *crimen opinionis.*

The care of religion therefore does not establish government as a Spiritual Father, a Schoolmaster, a Judge of Good Ideas, or an Inquisitor into Bad Ideas. One thing more is of some importance. The distinction of Church and state forbids government, in the name of a care for religion, to make religion a political end, or to make religious unity a means to the end of political or national unity. Religion is not part of the common good in the sense that it molds a nation into a unity and thus subordinates itself to the inferior unity that it molds. This is not Leo XIII's concept of the matter. He holds a loftier view.

He holds that religion is part of the temporal common good only in the sense that the order of civil life, although a proximate end in itself, must facilitate the passage of man to a higher life, which is that of the blessed in heaven; for this reason the common life must be impregnated with the values of religion; and therefore a responsible care for the common good must include a care for religion in the common life. Concern for national unity is no part of his perspectives. On the contrary, he depicts governmental care of religion as simply a witness to the fact that the purposes of society and government are not the highest purposes of man. They are only temporal and terrestrial purposes; therefore in their pursuit care must be taken not to hinder, but positively to further, the eternal purposes of man's immortal spirit. In this sense governmental care of religion ought to be disinterested; it should not look for political rewards, whether in the form of political unity or still less in the form of an allegiance of religion to the government that cares for it.

It may be maintained with some show of evidence from history that there is always a bit of danger in delivering to government the care of anything that is precious to man as man. It is especially dangerous to deliver the sacred things of the spirit into the keeping of the processes of power. As a principle, the duty of governmental care of religion is true; in practice, this duty has been made the pretext for actions and policies most damaging to religion. Perhaps the greatest danger in modern times is one that, curiously enough, Leo XIII never alludes to—the alliance of religion with nationalism, the idolatrous creed of modern government, into whose ambiguous service government is prepared to press even the sacred order of religion.

In any event, the distinction between Church and state is the essential principle that must confine governmental care of religion within its proper bounds, as these are set both by the nature of religion, which is transcendent to the temporal order, and also by the nature of the state, whose purposes never transcend the temporal order. All the abuses and ambiguities that history has seen have had their origin in some violation of this cardinal principle.

The Principle of Preference

The third principle which Leo XIII adduces in this matter is the principle of "favor and protection" for the true religion. This is simply an aspect of his fundamental moral principle that the objective order of truth and justice is the norm for all human action. As we have seen, he urged this principle against the subjectivist and relativist rationalism which maintained that "all ideas are free and equal." In contradiction, Leo XIII insists that truth inherently claims preference over error; good over evil; justice over injustice. In the face of these objective values neutralism or indifference are theoretically immoral attitudes. They are also practically impossible attitudes, since in practice they are equivalent to negation: "To make the judgment that there is no difference between disparate and opposed forms of religion has for its obvious result a refusal to believe in or practice any religion. And this is really atheism under another name" (*Immortale Dei*). Because the sectarian Liberal legal institution of "freedom of religion" pronounced and enforced upon society this false theological judgment, it was condemned.

A well-known text in *Longinqua oceani* illustrates the relation which the rule of preference for truth over error has to the order of human law, to the state. The text refers to an *error tollendus:*

> . . . there is an error which must be done away with. No one is to think that it follows from this [from the debt which the Church owes to the American constitutional situation] that America furnishes the example of the ideal (*optimi*) status of the Church; or that it would be universally permissible or advantageous for the sacred and civil orders to be disjoined and set apart from one another after the American fashion. The fact that among you Catholicism is in a state of security (incolumis) and that it increasingly prospers and grows is altogether due to the inner riches which by divine endowment form the strength of the Church. If no one stands in the way of them, if no obstacle is put to them, they come pouring forth; nevertheless they would produce more plentiful results if, in addition to freedom, they enjoyed the favor of the laws and the patronage of the public power.

In the last sentence the Pope is not undertaking to predict, as it were, by hindsight what the history of the Church in America would have been, had it been other than it has been. Nor is he suggesting that the future would be more blessed, if America were to alter the constitutional situation to which the blessings of the past have been largely due. Nor is he in any sense implying that there is in the American constitutional situation, as it exists in America, an *error tollendus,* an error to be done away with. On the contrary, in the immediately preceding context he has said that the Church in America "owes a debt of gratitude to the justice of the laws under which America lives and to the whole character of a good constitutional commonwealth" (*sua debetur gratia aequitati legum, quibus America vivit, moribusque bene constitutae rei publicae*). Certainly there is no error in laws that are just and in a constitution that is good.

What Leo XIII has in mind is a theoretical error bearing on a point of principle. The error was on the part of those who wished to take the American constitutional situation, in which the Church does not enjoy the favor of the laws and the patronage of the public power, as the premise for a generalization to a universal principle. It should be said here that these men were not American Catholics;[25] they were Europeans, who were either doctrinaire theorists, or simply desperate men, striving to break out of the impasse created by the confusion of religion and politics that had for so long been characteristic of the Latin countries. In either case it is highly unlikely that they understood the United States any better than Montesquieu understood England. These men, I say, wished to take the legal experience of the Church in America as the premise upon which to erect a definition of an ideal of legal experience that would be everywhere valid, everywhere permissible, everywhere advantageous. There was really a double error in this generalization.

First, there was the error of thinking that any form of legal experience can be universalized. This is the error of the doctrinaire, the man with the univocal mind, who does not understand the nature of law or—what is closely related—the nature of politics. Systems of law cannot be divorced from their *Sitz im Leben,* packed up and labeled, and made articles for export. A constitutional system, like a form of political regime (with which it is always closely allied), is good because it fits the necessities of the society for which it was devised; because it is reasonably in accord with what Ehrlich called "the living law" of the people; because, in a word, it is for the public advantage of this particular public. But "peoples" are not univocal entities, interchangeable at will. Nor are their political and legal systems sheer works of art, fashioned *more geometrico;* they are products of history, patterned by all manner of "prejudices," in the sense of Burke.[26] There is therefore no type of legal experience which could be generalized to the point of saying that it would be ideal for all peoples, everywhere and always. This is the first error at which Leo XIII struck. Some men were saying that the American constitutional system would be good for all peoples because it was good for the American people. This was political and legal nonsense.

But there was a more dangerous kind of nonsense latent in the Continental generalization from the American experience. The men who made the generalization lifted their assertions out of the field of history into the field of theory, out of the contingent order of law and politics into the absolute order of ethics and theology. The premise of their argument was that it is good, in certain historical circumstances and in point of political and legal principle, that the *res catholica* does not have the favor of the laws and the patronage of the public power. From this premise they concluded that it is true, in full theoretical generality and in point of ethical and theological principle, that the *res catholica* should not have the favor of the laws and the patronage of the public power. The *error tollendus* was not in the premise but in the conclusion. More exactly, the error was in the consequence of the argument—in the precipitous passage from the concrete order of law and politics to the abstract order of ethics and theology.

First, this manner of argument offended against the distinction upon which I have already perhaps sufficiently insisted, as pivotal in the doctrine of Leo XIII—the distinction between the order of divine law and the order of human law. Leo XIII willingly admitted that American constitutional law is good law. What he will not admit is that the goodness of American legal experience can be made the basis for theoretical conclusions. What is good law is not therefore true dogma. What is defensible on grounds of the public advantage, which raises a *quaestio facti,* is not therefore demonstrable on grounds of ultimate truth, which raises only a *quaestio iuris.* The Continental argument was inconsequential, invalid, as an argument. It ignored the differential character of law and ethics, of legal experience and theological principle. It confused *quod utile et possible* with *quod semper aequum et bonum.* It erred in arguing from the pragmatic order of legal goodness to the speculative order of universal truth.

Secondly, this error of method was dangerous to another principle. Here as always it is the *quaestio iuris* that is Leo XIII's dominant concern. Here as always he speaks as theologian and moralist, not as jurist and statesman. And the *quaestio iuris* he has constantly in mind is this: are all ideas and religions and moralities free and equal; or is there an objective truth—a single true religion and a universally valid morality; and since the latter, does not this religious and moral truth have an inherent claim to preference over error; and since it does, is not this inherent right of truth a norm also for the legal order which is the state? The hasty Continental generalization from the American experience risked colliding with the endlessly repeated Leonine answer to this *quaestio iuris*.

American constitutional law provides freedom for the truth but not favor; it protects the freedom of the truth but not the truth itself. This law, said Leo XIII, is equitable in the circumstances; it properly forms part of the American *res publica bene constituta*. Nay more, said the Continental theorists in effect, the American Constitution is a perfect reflection of the inner constitution of the moral universe and of the Christian economy. In this generalized statement the *error tollendus* appears. One of the principles of the moral universe and of the Christian economy is the principle that the truth has an inherent right not only to freedom for itself but also to preference over error; that the affirmation of the truth is to be protected not only because it is free but because it is true; and finally, that these inherent rights of truth are a norm for the legal order of society, which is bound on the inner order of the moral universe and of the Christian economy. This was the principle whose denial was implicit in the hasty generalization of the Continental theorists. To put the matter very briefly, in elevating American law to the norm of universal truth, they denied that the universal truth is the norm of all human law.

The lesson in method which Leo XIII reads in *Longinqua oceani* has a further implication. If it be true, on the principle of the distinction between divine and human law, that good laws do not necessarily make true dogma, it is no less true on the same principle that true dogmas do not necessarily make good law. The line of distinction between the two laws may not be transgressed from either direction. One may not make a dialectical passage from the order of good human law to the order of true divine law without prior consultation of the single norm of divine law—the certified truth itself, whether rational or revealed. By the same token one may not make the inverse passage without prior consultation of the special norm of human law—the public advantage. This brings us to the next topic.

The Principle of Tolerance

Leo XIII's polemic preoccupations are perhaps most visibly revealed in his doctrine on the attitude of government and law toward the problem set by the social fact of religious division and moral incoherence in the community. One is immediately impressed by the brevity of his treatment. A small paragraph in *Immortale Dei,* a somewhat longer one in *Libertas,* and very little elsewhere in the corpus—surely this is not much space to devote to the problem that had been central in post-Reformation politics, indeed that is permanently central in world politics. Nevertheless, Leo XIII's treatment was adequate for his purposes as these were fixed by his special problematic—the sectarian Liberal aggression against the historic integrity of the so-called Catholic nation. Moreover, despite his brevity, he touches all the essential principles.

First, he touches ever so lightly the fact that error and evil, religious division and moral discord, are permanent aspects of our sinful human condition—a condition that is the object of a divine permissive will: "God allows evils to exist in the world" (*Libertas*).[27] He concludes to the principle that "it is right for the rulers of society to imitate the ruler of the world." As the Scholastic axiom has it, tolerance is concerned only with evils (*tolerari non dicuntur nisi mala*). However, tolerance itself is not an evil. It is "right"; it is an imitation of God; it is an act of virtue—the virtue that distinguishes the jurist and statesman, political prudence. It is evil to will that evil should be done; it is unwise to will that evil should never be done; but to will to permit evil—that is good. Thus in St. Thomas' phrases Leo XIII sums up the matter. Thirdly, he asserts the principle that at once makes necessary the virtue of tolerance and also sets the limiting norm for its exercise, namely, the exigencies of "the common good," the public welfare, in given circumstances.

What is more important, he makes his whole doctrine hinge on his cardinal principle—the distinction between Church and state, between the order of ethics and theology and the order of law and politics, between the dogmatic judgments of the Church and the legal decisions of government.

The judgments of the Church on matters of doctrine are transtemporal, independent of circumstances. No *quaestio facti* enters into their making; and they are unalterable. They may collide with social fact—with indifference, skepticism, disbelief, opposition; but they make no concessions to fact. The Church does not indeed ignore the facts of history, since she must live in history. Moreover, there is a legitimate sense in which she is disposed to adapt herself to changing historical contexts. This adaptation is "a valid idea, if it be understood to mean a certain reasonableness of attitude which can be squared with the demands of truth and justice. That is to say, under the provision of some good the Church shows herself accommodating (*indulgentem*); she allows for circumstances to the extent that the sanctity of her duty permits" (*Libertas*). But there is a limit:

> The case is otherwise with practices and doctrines which changing morals and fallacious opinions have ushered in, contrary to the dictates of religion. There is no holiday from religion, truth, and justice. And since God has commanded that these greatly holy things should be under safeguard by the Church, it is altogether foreign to her nature to expect her to dissemble—to put up with what is false and unjust or to connive at what is harmful to religion.

Here Leo XIII was squarely in his problematic, caught in the tragic impasse of his age. In these words he might well be summing up the pontificate of Pius IX. It was not possible for the Church to be "accommodating" in the face of the "practices and doctrines" of sectarian Liberalism, or to "allow for" the Revolution and the Risorgimento as if these movements were simply instances of legitimate historical change. For the Church to accept a "freedom of religion" and a "separation of Church and state" predicated on the dogmas of *conscientia exlex* and *principatus infinite potens* would not be to "allow for circumstances." It would be to betray the truth and abdicate a sacred duty. Leo XIII sustains Pius IX's prophetic protest—a rude protest, in the way that prophets are rude—against sectarian Liberal society, a protest whose justice and historical significance are only now beginning to be appreciated by scholars.

However, Leo XIII does not enforce upon organized society and its government the same single norm of judgment and action by which the Church must abide: "The Church does not impart the binding force of law except to what is true and good; nevertheless, she is not unwilling that the public power should tolerate things that are at variance with truth and justice" (*Libertas*). The distinction is sharply drawn. The state is not the Church; it is not Christ's Body Mystical but only the terrestrial body politic. Its actions, unlike those of the Church, are not governed by the single norm of what is true and just. Its actions are indeed subject to this norm; hence the state "may not and ought not to approve evil or to will it for its own sake" (*Libertas*). However, this is not the sole norm of the legal order; there are also "the precepts of political prudence" (*Libertas*). These precepts are truly mandatory on the action of the state, and at times they take precedence over what the abstract dictates of right and wrong might demand; they require that evil and error should be tolerated in the interests of the state's highest purpose, which is to secure, by prudent use of the instrumentality of coercive law, the public welfare of the whole body politic. Therefore the legal decisions of the state are governed by two norms, not by one.

This is the traditional doctrine. Nevertheless, it must be admitted that Leo XIII gives it a special *impostazione*. The juristic and political norms of law seem to enter almost as an afterthought, if the word is not too strong. Certainly the impression is created that appeal to them is permitted only grudgingly. The text does not breathe magnanimity. All this is understandable in the circumstances. Leo XIII's overwhelming concern had to be with the moral and theological norms of law; this was the point at which sectarian Liberalism had broken with the tradition.

There was another factor. In the face of this particular adversary, it could not but seem academic, not to say dangerous, to attempt to represent the nice balance which the tradition strikes between the moral and juristic norms of law. Part of Leo XIII's essential argument was that the sectarian Liberal laws could not possibly be for the common good—least of all within the historic Catholic nations. The dogmas of the lawless conscience and the monist totalist state could only issue in the common destruction. The "modern liberties" as predicated on these dogmas could only be the Augustinian *libertas perditionis*. To justify them in the name of the juristic norm of law would be nonsense. *Genus id rei publicae* that is described in its premises, ethos, and effects by *Immortale Dei* could be accepted by a reasonable man only under the pressure of dire necessity, lest some worse tyranny befall:

> If a form of government anywhere exists, or can be imagined to exist, which aggressively and tyrannically persecutes Christianity, and if one matches it against the particular type of polity which we have been describing, the latter may appear the more endurable of the two. Nevertheless, the principles on which it rests are in them-

selves, as we have said, of such a nature that no one ought
to approve of them (*Immortale Dei*).

Who indeed will approve of the principle that government is the Divine Majesty; that its law is the single and absolutely sovereign law;
that the order which this law creates is the Universe; and that within
this man-made Universe there is no place for God?

Leo XIII's polemic context explains another specialty in his construction of the tradition, namely the terms in which he states the
juristic norm of law. He speaks of the "common good," the "public
welfare," "greater evils" and "lesser evils." This is customary language. What is special is the fact that he never alludes to the concrete political good and evil which St. Thomas ranks highest in the
scale of political goods and evils and which therefore is essentially
constituent of the juristic norm: "Now the welfare and security of a
multitude formed into a society lies in the preservation of its unity,
which is called peace. If this is lost, the value of social life itself is lost.
Indeed by reason of its inner discords the multitude becomes a burden to itself. Therefore the chief concern of the ruler of a multitude
is to insure the unity of peace" (*De regimine principum*, I, 17). For St.
Thomas the greatest political evil was dissension, schism, rupture of
the public peace. Peace, the work of justice, is the highest political
end.

However, it is altogether understandable that Leo XIII did not
adduce the exigencies of social unity and public peace as the concrete
norm for governmental use or non-use of its police power in the field
of religion and morals. The fact was that sectarian Liberalism had
rent the unity and peace of the so-called Catholic nations; the further
fact was that this unity and peace would not be restored to these
nations by any concessions to sectarian Liberalism, even if such concessions had been doctrinally permissible. The "two Frances" and the
"two Spains" and the "two Italies" stood over against each other,
irreconcilable as the Revolution was irreconcilable with the Tradition.
Unity and peace—so said both sides in the conflict—would come
only by the triumph of one over the other.

In Leo XIII's own case the impasse was illustrated, curiously
enough, by the toughness of the stand he took against the Italy of the
Risorgimento, while he was disposed to be considerably more gentle
toward the France of the Revolution. In either case, within the ideological and political realities of the time, and even apart from theological considerations, the "unity which is called peace" could not be

an operative concept. Both parties to the struggle demanded unity and peace—but each on its own terms. Leo was no more intransigent than Lemmi. The ideological struggle had been projected into politics, beyond recall. Politics itself had become a controversy over the ultimate ends of man; and when politicians quarrel over such ultimate ends, instead of simply agreeing on the proximate ends of politics and then quarreling over the best means of reaching them, politics and society are in a state of decadence. Then you have "wars of religion." Then if the issue is to be decisively settled, the likelihood is that the settlement will come as it has in fact come in Spain (at least temporarily), by the triumph of the Tradition over the Revolution—a triumph won by force of arms under the leadership of a militant party, and sustained by force of law under the government of a dictator.

In Leo XIII's circumstances it would have been idle to suppose that a common meeting ground for the contending parties would be furnished by the concept of that unity which is peace—a unity of the political order, which is simply an instrumental unity, based on the rational shared consent of the whole community, both governors and governed, to cooperate toward the proper and proximate ends of the political community, even in the absence of agreement about the ultimate purposes of man and about the way that God has marked out for their achievement. Neither side in the conflict could envisage such a political unity; both wanted a religious unity. The sectarian Liberals wanted to establish political unity on the basis of their political religion, "a new religion, in which divine worship will be accorded to human reason, under contempt for the sovereignty of the immortal God."[28]

The contrary position was most visible in Spain, the typical "Catholic nation," where political unity apart from Catholic religious unity was grotesque in itself and impossible in practice.

Moreover, both sides recognized that their desired politico-religious unity could only be established by force of law. This is the key point. The great prize in the ideological struggle was control of government, with all that this control meant in the way of legal power to establish the desired institutions and ideas and to repress the repugnant ones, especially in the matters of public worship, marriage, and education. The operative premise was that government is to represent and enforce a truth proclaimed to be transcendental. The only question therefore was, what truth shall government represent—the truth of the Tradition or the "truth" of the Revolution? No government could represent both, either in theory or in fact. Not in theory, because the two were mutually exclusive. Not in fact, because in fact there were two Spains, Frances, and Italies, and the sectarian Liberals would no more admit that Italy, for instance, was still a Catholic nation than Leo XIII would admit that Italy was no longer a Catholic nation.

So, I say, "the unity which is called peace" could not be made an operative concept in the circumstances. No less inoperative were two other traditional doctrines of Western society.

The first of these is the political doctrine of representation, according to which government is not some sort of supra-societal representative of naked transcendental truth, charged with the task of making the people over, by force of law, into the image of a preexistent ideal of truth and virtue. On the contrary, government is the existential representative of the people, charged with a function of ministry rather than rule; or more exactly, charged with the duty of making its rule a ministry to the people, to the public advantage—a concept that is never an abstraction or an ideal, when considered as the political end of government. The former kind of representationalism was characteristic of sectarian Liberalism; the latter is Western and Christian. Secondly, there is the legal doctrine of consent, as thus expressed by the Carlyles:

> There is really no doubt that the normal political judgment, whether practical or theoretical, of the Middle Ages down to the end of the sixteenth century was that the positive law was the expression of the will and consent of the whole community, including the king; and that the conception of writers like Bodin and Barclay that the king was the legislator represented an alien and intrusive principle.[29]

Certainly Leo XIII was no partisan of Bodin or Barclay. The doctrines of representation and consent are implicit, for instance, in his complaint against the sectarian Liberal laws on the ground that they were introduced "without any consideration of the people, even though they profess the Catholic faith" (*Libertas*). These doctrines are also implicit in his doctrine on tolerance, which requires government to take account of what is actually "there" in society, even though in terms of sheer divine law certain things have no authorization to be there. On the other hand, Leo XIII was in no position to make effective appeal to these two traditional ideas. In his polemic context—the

defense of the Catholic nation against the sectarian Liberal state—
the whole question of representation and consent had to be pretty
much left out. Or rather, these doctrines were used, implicitly, in a
special way. Leo XIII's factual supposition was that the Catholic nations were still Catholic; therefore they could not be existentially represented by a sectarian Liberal government. Again, the sectarian
Liberal laws on religion were inherently vitiated by their premises;
hence there could be no question of a Catholic people consenting to
them. This was what had to be made clear; and this was about all.

There is a final aspect of the question of tolerance. In the text of
Leo XIII tolerance appears as simply a matter of government with-
holding its arm, not actually striking at error and evil. The principle
of tolerance is indeed presented as a principle that limits government. But it seems to impose limits only on the action of government
in given circumstances, not on the powers of government. Such is the
appearance. However, is this the whole of the matter? If the premises
of the principle are more closely examined, does it not follow that this
principle in given circumstances also imposes limits on the very powers of government? Does it not disarm government, instead of simply
bidding it withhold its arm? Does it not deprive government of weap-
ons, and not simply forbid their use? In the perspective of these questions the problem of tolerance is seen in a different light. It is one
thing to say that government has a right to repress certain errors and
evils, but is inhibited in the exercise of its right by given circumstances. It is quite another thing to say that in given circumstances
government simply has no right to repress certain errors and evils.
There is a difference between saying, "I can but I won't," and saying,
"I won't because I can't." With these questions asked, this point
made, we are finally prepared to tackle the secondary problem with
which we started—legal establishment and legal tolerance.

Legal Establishment and Legal Intolerance

Concordatary literature amply testifies to the legitimacy of these
two correlative institutions. What needs clarification is the foundation, in authority and in argument, upon which their legitimacy rests.
There seems to be some difference of opinion. Briefly, one view holds
quite simply that these legal institutions are necessary in virtue of
divine law whenever and wherever they are possible in the light of
religio-social fact. The other view holds more complicatedly that they

are legitimate in terms both of divine law and also in terms of the canons of human legislation when they are necessary or useful for the common good of both Church and society.

Anatomy of an Anonymous View

The former view in its more extreme expositions has given rise to widespread belief that when Catholics possess the requisite political power they are obliged in principle to use the coercive force of government to repress other religious beliefs, more or less severely; whereas when they lack political power they suspend their principle, recur to expediency, and defend a general civil right to the free exercise of religion. In other words, Catholics are intolerant when it is possible to be intolerant; they are tolerant only when it is necessary to be tolerant. Intolerance is the ideal, justified by principle; tolerance is an evil, justified as a lesser evil by factual circumstances. If this popular belief is true Catholic doctrine, it is indeed good that it is popular. But if it is not true, its popularity is a scandal.

In presenting the first view I wish to make it clear that I am not attributing it to any particular author.[30] The fact is that I shall deliberately sharpen its propositions, somewhat after the fashion in which Leo XIII sharpened the propositions of sectarian Liberalism. He did this in order to lay bare the inherent and official intentions of the movement in their pure doctrinal state, before they became obscured by the compromises that were necessary for political success on the historical scene. In the same way it is necessary to get at the official and inherent intentions of the Church in their pure doctrinal state before they descend into the arena of history.

In its sharpened form the view under consideration makes the following simple argument for legal intolerance. The leading principle is that error has no rights, certainly not the same rights as truth. Therefore it follows that error ought to be suppressed whenever and wherever it is possible to suppress it. It further follows that government has an inherent duty and a consequent right to repress error whenever and wherever possible. A parallel argument is made for the institution which creates the legal situation within the state, and also the alliance with government, that are the juridical premises of intolerance. The principle is that the Catholic faith has an exclusive divine right to be the public religion of men and societies. Therefore it follows that Catholicism ought to be established as the official "religion of the state," with all the juridical consequences that follow upon this legal status, whenever and wherever possible. It further follows that government has an inherent duty and consequent right thus to legislate, whenever and wherever possible.

Therefore this theory is disjunctive. Legal establishment and legal intolerance are called the "thesis"; they are matters of principle and they are the ideal. The absence of these institutions is called the "hypothesis"; it is a situation in which principle is suspended because it is inapplicable by reason of religio-social circumstances. It is therefore a situation that is evil, in itself and in principle.

The argument that justifies the hypothesis starts from a fact—the fact of religious pluralism within a given society. From this fact it follows, as a further matter of fact, that a governmental attempt at legal establishment and legal intolerance would result in disturbance of the public peace. Therefore the legal situation of the hypothesis, remaining evil in principle, appears as a lesser evil, in point of fact, than the evil of social dissension that would ensue upon an attempt to introduce the legal situation of the thesis. Therefore the situation of hypothesis is to be tolerated. The reason for toleration is necessity. Toleration is to last as long as the necessity for it lasts. Toleration is to end as soon as intolerance becomes possible.

Thus presented in its most naked form, this theory reveals three major characteristics.

First it assumes that the duty and right of assuring the exclusive rights of truth and of denying all rights to error within society, by governmental application of coercive restraints, is the ultimate political principle that must control the action of government. This duty and right are likewise the ultimate juridical principle that must preside over the construction of the legal order. The disjunction holds: *per se* government ought to repress error, because error has no rights; *per accidens* government may be excused from its duty, because error is sometimes irrepressible without damage to the public peace. In other words, the thesis is ultimately based on one duty of government—its duty to the truth. The hypothesis is based on another duty of government—its duty to the public peace. The implication seems to be that the latter duty is of a lower order than the former, as the hypothesis is of a lower order than the thesis.

Second, this theory asserts that the legal criterion for the induction of the thesis—legal establishment and intolerance—is "possibility"; whereas the legal criterion for recurrence to the hypothesis is "necessity." Therefore the jurist who works with this theory has only one question to answer: when and where it is possible for government to establish Catholicism and "exterminate" heresy? The conditions of possibility are variously defined. Some require simply an absolute majority of Catholics within a given region-state. Others require a totally Catholic population in the moral sense—in the sense that the percentage of dissenters is trifling. Others require a totally Catholic population in an absolute sense. In any case, the standard of judgment is quantitative.[31]

The quality of the Catholic population does not enter into the argument. That is, little if any attention is paid to the prevailing level of religious knowledge and practice, to the general educational and cultural level, to the level of political self-awareness—in a word, to the question whether laws are being framed for Catholic masses or genuine Catholic people, for an ignorant and apathetic Catholic multitude or for a Catholic body politic that is reasonably literate—religiously, politically, culturally. Moreover, in so far as this theory may appeal to the common good, the appeal takes the form of an abstract assumption—the assumption that whenever and wherever the population is Catholic the public advantage is inevitably served by legal establishment and legal intolerance. Catholic unity—so runs the argument—is the highest social good; therefore it follows that this method of preserving Catholic unity, by governmental coercion of dissenters, is both necessary and good, when it is possible.

Finally, the dominant characteristic of this theory is the manner in which it formulates the Catholic idea in the matter of the governmental care of religion. An enlarged content is ascribed to the ideal. It is not sufficient to say that the Catholic ideal is a society whose members profess their faith *animo et moribus;* whose manifold institutions are all permeated with the Christian spirit; whose public life includes duly occasional acts of public worship; whose government is obedient to all the traditional principles of rational and Christian constitutionalism; whose legal order exhibits a harmony between the divine law, natural and revealed, and the civil statutes in the crucial affairs that are *mixti iuris*—domestic society, education, socio-economic organization, and public morality. Even if all these elements were present, the situation would still not be ideal; for the ideal must include a special element of legal experience, the experience embodied in the twin institutions of establishment and intolerance. Unless Catholicism is established by law as the official religion of the state, unless all other religions are "exterminated" by law from public existence, the ideal has not been reached.

Establishment and intolerance are not ideals in a relative sense—

in the sense that they serve the public utility in given circumstances of social and religious fact. They are ideals in an absolute sense. They are invested with an absoluteness of value that matches the absoluteness of the principle to which they make appeal—the principle of the exclusive rights of truth over error. Government is not to be intolerant to a greater or less degree because this particular measure of intolerance is a human imperative in accord with the full body of norms and rules that regulate human law. Government is to be intolerant because intolerance is a divine imperative which makes intolerant laws a religious ideal. Establishment and intolerance are not to be defended, at times and in given circumstances, because they are good law. They are always to be defended, in principle, because they are true dogma. They are not applications of principle; they are principles in themselves. The government that is not intolerant is not a Catholic government, ideally speaking. The state in which the legal premise of intolerance does not exist is not a Catholic state, ideally speaking.

If therefore, using this theory as the criterion, you would find the ideal Catholic state, do not look at contemporary Brazil, Ireland, Portugal, Bavaria, or the Rhineland provinces; or at the Austria of 1855, or at the Poland of 1925. In none of these Catholic countries are the abstract requirements of the Catholic ideal fulfilled. Look instead at the Kingdom of the Two Sicilies under Ferdinand I, at the Republic of Ecuador under Gabriel Garcia Moreno, at Italy under Mussolini, at Spain under Isabella II and under Generalissimo Franco. Only in these countries will you find the ultimate distinguishing work of the Catholic ideal—the legal establishment of Catholicism as the sole official religion of the state, and the legal exclusion of all other cults from public existence.[32] Only in these countries, according to the theory under consideration, will you find the inherent and official intentions of the Church fulfilled to perfection. It is true that you may not find in these countries a Catholic people that intelligently and actively professes its public faith *animo et moribus*. You may even find a degree of religious dissension that erupts into assassination, as in the case of Moreno, or into a bloody civil war, as in the case of Spain. You certainly will fail to find the fulfillment of the Western Christian ideal of political life and government, which is certainly not dictatorship. No matter. You do find establishment and intolerance, and therefore you find the ideal Catholic state.

I repeat, I am here sharpening the argument. That there is an ideal of Christian Society professing itself as such, to which men in community are universally obliged, in virtue of a whole body of rational and revealed truth, is a proposition that I do not question.[33] I am not questioning it, much less denying it.

The issue here being raised—indeed here being forced—concerns only the content of this transtemporal ideal. If it were simply a question of defending establishment and intolerance *in situ,* there could be no argument; for the Church has approved these institutions *in situ.* The argument begins when they are defended *in abstracto,* as inherently necessary to the ideal, which is fashioned antecedent to any consideration of historical *situs.* Then the question rises, does the Church so defend them? If, to speak concretely, it were simply a question of composing an apologia for contemporary Spain in terms of the full body of Catholic theological, ethical, jurisprudential, and political principles, again there would be no argument; for it is altogether legitimate to compose such an apologia. The argument begins when the apology for Spain is lifted into a loftier universe of discourse—the discourse of the universal Church; when it is elevated to a higher level of abstraction; when, in a word, an apologia for the Spain that exists is transformed into a definition of the Christian society that ought to be—a definition that pretends to be doctrinal, to appeal only to principle, to formulate the ideal, the norm, and the goal of all organized Christian political and legal effort.[34] Then the question rises, is this passage from concrete apologia to abstract definition warranted by the requisite authority and argument?

Speaking more generally, if it were merely a matter of arguing that the twin institutions of establishment and intolerance were, or are, necessary and useful for the public advantage in the special religious, sociological, cultural, and political circumstances of the historic Catholic nation (the Ecuador of 1862, for instance), the argument would meet no challenge; for this is the manner of argument that Leo XIII would make—a complex, rounded argument that involves a *quaestio facti.* The difficulty begins when these institutions are extracted from their historical and sociological locus of implantation, and projected as metahistorical ideals; when in consequence it is asserted that their imposition is necessary whenever and wherever it is possible. Then the question rises, is this Leo XIII? Is this the tradition?

The Traditional View: Pius XII

The authority of Leo XIII cannot, I think, be claimed by the position outlined above in the naked form necessary to reveal its inner intentions (again I explicitly disavow any intention of attributing the position to any Catholic author, living or dead). Moreover, the argument made for this view does not follow the far more complicated and flexible contours of Leo XIII's argument. This point ought to be clear, if my lengthy exposition of his argument has been both clear and correct. However, the whole matter has been considerably clarified by the latest statement of the tradition, made by Pius XII on December 6, 1953, in a notable discourse to an audience of Italian Catholic jurists.[35] The major question in the discourse was legal toleration of error and evil; but the principles outlined by the Pope are not without relevance to the question of legal establishment.

The problem explicitly raised by the Pope concerned "the practical living together of Catholic and non-Catholic communities" within an international society somehow juridically organized. Consequently, the question explicitly discussed was that of a "well-defined statute that would be valid for the entire territory of the individual sovereign states which are members of such a community of nations," a statute that would regulate the relations between government and the order of religion and morality. However, the Pope discusses these two related questions in terms of the traditional principles of the universal Church. It cannot therefore be successfully maintained that the principles of solution which he lays down are valid and applicable only and exclusively to the problem of toleration in the international community; that they are consequently irrelevant to the problem as it arises within individual nation-states or region-states. The doctrinal intentions of Pius XII were not thus restricted. His appeal is to universal principles, universally valid; valid therefore wherever and whenever the problem of toleration arises—anywhere on the face of the earth where there is government and where there are error and evil. This is in fact the initial outstanding significance of the discourse—that Pius XII confronts the problem in the full universality of its position; and in the face of it, thus confronted, he makes his statement of the tradition. His statement is in perfect continuity with the statement made by Leo XIII; obviously, both Popes were stating the tradition. However, Pius XII's statement marks a certain progress within the tradition.

The progress was occasioned and made necessary by the march of mankind's political history. This has always been the case when it is a matter of the Church's tradition with regard to the Church-State relationship. With no change in doctrine, but under development of doctrine, the Church must keep herself "related" to the facts of man's political life—whether they mark the decay of the *imperium* and the rise of the *regnum* and *civitas;* or whether, as is the case today, they mark the passing of the sovereign nation-state in the ancient modern sense (the adjectives are juxtaposed deliberately; the sovereignty of the modern state has become ancient to the point of anachronism), and the struggling emergence of a juridically organized international community.[36] These political changes do not indeed change the doctrine of the Church; but they do "open" the problem—or reopen it, if you like—and in this sense they open or reopen the way to progress within the tradition.

Pius XII reveals his characteristic sense of the complexity of the problem. It ranks, he says, among the problems, "sufficiently difficult and complicated, which cannot be resolved with a simple yes or no." For instance, one may not brusquely ask: "Has a Catholic state the right to repress heresy? Answer—yes or no." The categories in which the question is asked, and in which the answer is demanded, are much too simple for the problem.

Leo XIII could indeed keep his problem relatively simple; for it was at bottom a simple problem—the issue of sectarian Liberalism within the historic Catholic nation. And since the doctrine and the intentions of the movement were quite simply wicked, Leo XIII could oppose to them a resoundingly simple No. Pius XII does not confront any such highly determinate adversary, within so tightly restricted a context, in an atmosphere so surcharged with polemic. His standpoint is that of the universal Church as it exists in the world of the nations as they presently fumble toward some manner of common family life. He confronts the international community, composed of peoples who are "divided into those who are Christian, those who are non-Christian, those who are religiously indifferent, or deliberately laicized, or even frankly atheistic." Consequently he confronts the condition of humanity itself, its tragic condition of error and ignorance, religious division and moral incoherence. The breadth of this view makes the problem exceedingly complex; but it also banishes all manner of particular polemic pressures and permits what was not permitted to Leo XIII—an altogether serene and balanced presentation of traditional principles. What is at stake is the common good of the universal Church, as well as the good of the Church within particular national contexts. Correlatively, what is at stake is the good of the common human life of the peoples of the world, as well as the good of individual peoples. The ground chosen is the highest possible.

At the outset of his thought Pius XII fastens firmly onto a historical fact—what may rightly be called *the* twentieth-century fact—the hesitant emergence of a juridical community of nations. It is not simply a brute fact, from which nothing follows. It represents a political progress, indeed a moral progress, that corresponds to the intentions of nature. There is here "an ascent from the lower to the higher, that is to say, from a plurality of sovereign states to the highest unity," a unity that is within the designs of the Creator Himself. Consequently this kind of fact permits conclusions of a properly theoretical order. It leads to a "fundamental theoretical principle" that is decisive for political and legal action. The principle is thus phrased:

> Within the limits of what is possible and licit, to promote that which assists unity or makes it more efficacious; to rule out that which would disturb unity; at times to put up with things that cannot be cleared away at the moment— things for the sake of whose removal the community of peoples must not be allowed to suffer shipwreck; for the reason that a higher good is expected from this community.

The breadth of Pius XII's problem enables him to rise to doctrinal perspectives in all their purity, and therefore to set at the center of his doctrine the principle which Leo XIII, as I have said, could not have made operative—the principle of "that unity which is called peace," the unity and peace which are man's highest temporal good.[37]

This is the tradition as stated by St. Thomas: "Therefore the chief concern of the ruler of a multitude is to insure the unity of peace." Moreover, with the restoration of this principle to its proper centrality as the guide of political and legal action, Pius XII's doctrine on human law shifts from the emphasis which Leo XIII found polemically necessary, to the emphasis which is proper to the tradition itself when its statement is undisturbed. Leo XIII's emphasis fell upon the moral origins of human law; Pius XII's emphasis falls upon the political purposes of human law. That law ought to be reflective of the transcendental order of truth and justice as it exists in the mind of God; that law must be directive of the temporal community as it actually exists on earth—both these concepts are integral to the tradition, in Leo XIII as in Pius XII. But a choice of emphasis is possible; and Pius XII's is the more traditional choice, the choice dictated by the intrinsic necessities of doctrine rather than by the extrinsic necessities of polemic.

In what concerns the general structure of his doctrine Pius XII exactly follows Leo XIII and the tradition. The structure is set by the distinction between Church and state; between the order of divine law and the order of human law; between the order of conscience as it confronts the demands of truth and right, and the order of government as it confronts the demands of the public advantage; between the order of theological judgment and the order of legal decision. These orders are to be kept distinct but not separated; they are to be related but not confused.

For the Church one norm of judgment is alone decisive: "the objective truth and the obligation of conscience toward what is objectively true and good." Therefore the Church is committed to "the unconditioned denial of everything that is religiously false and morally evil. In this regard there never has been and there is not now any vacillation on the part of the Church, or any compromises, either in theory or in fact." The echo of Leo XIII is clear. Still clearer is this almost verbal echo: "That which does not correspond to the truth and to the norm of morality has not, objectively, any right either to exist or to be propagated or to act." The quality of inner rightfulness is communicated to human action and utterance by their correspondence to objective norms of truth and justice. The basic questions of right and wrong, truth and error, are not left to arbitrary human answering. These questions have been answered by the law of God, natural and revealed. Man's part is to discover the answers, not to invent them. The ideas of "truth" and "right" are sacred; men may not tamper with their content or use them to cover their own wayward thoughts and wanton passions. This is pure Leo XIII, pure tradition.

No less traditional is Pius XII's teaching that, whereas the theological and moral judgments of the Church are controlled only by one norm, the legal decisions of the state are controlled by two. But here there is a difference between the two supreme teachers, in the sense that Pius XII adjusts more nicely the balance between the two norms of human law.

No less strongly than Leo XIII he insists that human law is subject to a moral norm: "Before all else it is important clearly to affirm that no human authority, no state, no community of states, whatever their religious character, can give a positive mandate or a positive authorization to teach or to do what would be contrary to religious truth or moral goodness." This is the doctrine of *Libertas,* that human law "may not give sanction to anything that is not contained in [the eter-

nal law] as in the principle of the whole juridical order." Pius XII
simply reaffirms the first principle of political morality, the central
principle of Western constitutionalism, which limits the power of the
state by subjecting it to the imperatives of the moral order.

However, within the context of his new and broader problematic
Pius XII's attention is chiefly directed, as Leo XIII's was not, to the
question of the positive empowerments and limitations of government, as these are defined in the light of the juristic norm which he
has already laid down—the safeguard and promotion of the unity
which is peace. His special question concerns the use of the coercive
power of law against error and evil. Granted that government may
not positively direct men to do or teach what is false and wrong, when
and under what conditions may it or may it not forcibly inhibit men
from such action or teaching? This is properly the jurist's question,
and it is not an abstract question.

Pius XII states it with all clarity and concreteness: "Can it be that
in determinate circumstances He [God] does not give to men any
mandate, does not impose upon them any duty, does not even give
them any right to restrain and repress what is erroneous and false?"
This is a much more searching question than Leo XIII ever put. It
goes directly and with all serenity to the heart of this difficult matter
of the duties and rights of human government in this divided, sinful
world. The answer is given with no less directness and serenity: "A
glance at reality gives an affirmative answer." Yes, there are circumstances in which human authority has neither mandate nor duty nor
right to use its coercive power against error and evil.

The "reality" which returns this affirmative answer is the reality of
the world as it is—a world which is wholly under the omnipotent and
wise governance of God, and yet a world in which "error and sin exist
in ample measure; God rebukes them but He lets them exist." This is
Leo XIII's argument, the traditional argument. But Pius XII draws
out much more clearly than Leo XIII the conclusions that are implicit in it. There are two chief conclusions. The first bears upon a
point of moral principle; the second, upon a point of political principle.

The first conclusion is this: "Therefore the affirmation [that] religious and moral aberrations ought always to be inhibited, when inhibition is possible, because tolerance of them is in itself immoral,
cannot be valid in its unconditioned absoluteness." In order to reveal
its fallacy and to appreciate the concluding phrase, "in its unconditioned absoluteness," the affirmation here invalidated ought to be

broken down into three propositions: (1) Toleration of evil is itself evil; (2) therefore it can only be justified as a lesser evil; (3) therefore it is immoral to tolerate evil when it is possible to suppress it (for in these circumstances the argument "from the lesser evil" does not hold).

None of these propositions are valid in their unconditioned absoluteness. Toleration of evil may be wisdom and virtue, as it is with God. It may not be simply a lesser evil but a means to a higher good, again as it is with God. The norm for coercive action against evil is not the "possibility" of such action. It is therefore false to assert, as a matter of absolute and unconditioned principle, that religious and moral aberrations ought always to be suppressed when it is possible to suppress them. God Himself does not adopt this norm of action. Neither does the Church: "With regard to . . . tolerance in determinate circumstances—tolerance even in cases in which it would be possible to proceed to repression—the Church has been led to act, and has acted, in accord with that [kind of] tolerance," throughout her history, "always for higher and more compelling motives." Pius XII clearly rejects the criterion of "possibility," proposed in the anonymous theory outlined above, as the norm for intolerant legal action. Whatever may have been the policy and practice of Catholic governments, so called, the doctrine and action of the universal Church stand against the idea that the Catholic thing is to be intolerant when possible, tolerant only when necessary.

Pius XII's second conclusion is this: "The duty of repressing moral and religious aberrations cannot therefore be an ultimate norm of action. It ought to be subordinated to higher and more general norms which in certain circumstances permit, and indeed even make it perhaps seem to be the better course, that error should not be inhibited, in order to promote a greater good." Here Pius XII correctly adjusts the balance between the moral and juristic norms of law.

Indeed the moral norm may never be violated by positive legal enforcement of what is evil. But when it is a question of deciding whether precepts of truth and right are to be transformed into compulsory rules of social behavior, and when it is a question of deciding whether error and evil are to be inhibited or not inhibited, it is the juristic norm that obtains the primacy. To say that the duty of repressing moral and religious aberrations is the ultimate norm of legal action is to misunderstand the purpose of government and the idea of law. It is, as it were, to turn things upside down. There are higher and more general norms which control the discharge of this duty. Indeed these norms in certain circumstances even cancel the duty itself and therefore deprive government of all right to legislate against religious or moral error. There are circumstances in which God, from whom all well-ordered authority ultimately flows, "does not give man any mandate, does not impose in any duty, does not even give him the right" to adopt intolerant legislation. In these circumstances government does not merely find its arm shortened; it is disarmed. It is not merely forbidden the exercise of jurisdiction; it is deprived of jurisdiction.

Here Pius XII goes a step beyond Leo XIII in clarity of doctrine. The reason for the progress is the consistent application of the traditional principle that the chief duty of the ruler, than which he has no higher duty, is to insure the unity which is called peace. The demands of social unity and peace, as they become concrete in determinate circumstances, are the highest and most general norm for the legislative action of government in what concerns the order of religion. By firmly asserting the primacy of this juristic norm Pius XII sets things right side up, so to speak. It is the traditional doctrine. It does indeed filter through the text of Leo XIII, but in an image of itself that is somewhat distorted by the prism of his polemic, which required such a heavy accent on the moral form of law. By reason of the great breadth and complete serenity of his perspectives Pius XII is able to let the accent fall where it more properly belongs.

This then is the nicely balanced structure of Pius XII's doctrine on the norms of human law as they bear upon the problem of tolerance and intolerance. This structure accounts for several noteworthy aspects of his doctrine.

Most striking is the emphasis on "circumstances," on the *quaestio facti*. Moreover, this question is presented with no shrinking from its breadth and complications. The jurist is given two sets of facts to consider.

First, there is the question of the religio-social facts of the situation that confronts him. And this situation itself is described as being twofold. There is the special situation within a particular national or regional community; and there is the wider situation within the international community. The jurist is first obliged to consider the facts of this twofold situation. He is then obliged to consider a second factual question: what will be the actual effect of the alternative courses of action—in the case, legal tolerance or intolerance—within this total situation? Here again both aspects of the situation command attention, and in due order. In his concern for the unity and peace of his own community this jurist may not blot out from his view the "fundamental theoretical principle" which is today supremely controlling—the unity and peace of the international community. Indeed, this latter is the "higher good," which he must consciously seek. His complex task is thus described:

> In his decision he will let himself be guided by the damaging consequences which would result from tolerance [within his own state], as compared with those [other damaging consequences] which would be spared the community of states by the acceptance of the formula of tolerance; therefore [he will let himself be guided] by the good which, according to a wise prognosis, will flow to the international community as such, and indirectly to the state which is a member of it.

In consequence of this broad position of the *quaestio facti,* and in consequence too of the broad conception of the common good to which it leads, the Catholic jurist (or state) is forbidden all nationalistic narrowness, all isolation of national concerns from the higher concerns of the international community and the universal Church. The Catholic jurist (or state) is called upon to view the problem of tolerance vs. intolerance in the same perspectives in which the universal Church views it: "In individual cases the attitude of the Church is determined by the consideration of what will safeguard the *bonum commune*—on the one hand, the common good of the Church and of society within individual societies, and on the other hand, the *bonum commune* of the universal Church, of the reign of God over all the world," and the common good of the international community, wherein the reign of God is also to be established.

This broad definition of the common good, as the controlling juristic norm for the problem of toleration, is not to be found explicitly in Leo XIII; his problematic confined him explicitly to the nation-state. The broader definition marks a progress within the tradition. The facts of present-day political life, wherein the intentions of nature are revealed,[38] have given new meaning to the traditional *quaestio facti.* In response, the traditional doctrine discloses its latent virtualities; it develops to meet the new demands.

A second accent falls on the autonomy of the jurist or the state in this matter of legal decision in so far as it involves the *quaestio facti:* "The Catholic statesman himself, before all else, will have to decide whether this condition is verified in the concrete case." The competent authority on the question of fact is a lay authority. On his own view of the facts the layman will have to give a prudent answer to the question, which is the permissible legal course, the prudent political course, the better course all round—tolerance or intolerance? He will have to decide whether "the non-inhibition [of error and evil] can be justified in the interests of a higher and broader good." In affirming the autonomy of the lay authority of the state in matters of legal decision Pius XII is again fully in the tradition of Leo XIII, whose clarification of the traditional doctrine of the "two societies" had made this principle newly clear. Pius XII only applies the principle a bit more firmly to the matter of legal decisions that affect the relation of religion to the order of human law, that is, to the state.

The autonomy of the individual state is, of course, only relative. That is, it is subject to two limitations—one political, the other religious.

The political limitation derives from the fact that the international community exists (at least inchoatively) and that its common good is the higher good. In consequence, a limitation is imposed on the sovereignty of the individual state in its legal decisions. Pius XII indicates this limitation in his formulation of the probable international statute:

> Within the confines of its own territory and for its own citizens each state will regulate religious and moral affairs by a law of its own. Nevertheless, in the whole territory of the community of states there will be permitted to the citizens of every member-state the exercise of their own ethical and religious beliefs and practices, in so far as these do not contravene the penal statutes of the state in which they reside.

The suggestion here seems to be that the writ of the international community should also run within the territories of all member-states. This tolerant writ, necessary and rightful within the determinate circumstances of the international community, would establish the "norm that the free exercise of a religious or moral belief and practice which has value in one of the member-states should not be inhibited by means of laws and coercive measures of state within the whole territory of the community." This norm of the international community would be likewise a norm within the individual states, in consequence of the obligatory concern that individual states must have for the higher good of the broader community.

The second limitation, to be recognized by the Catholic jurist, is religious: "In what regards the religious and moral field he will also ask the judgment of the Church." Pius XII explicitly reserves this judgment to none other than the highest authority: "In such decisive questions which affect international life he alone is competent in the ultimate instance, to whom Christ has entrusted the guidance of the whole Church, the Roman Pontiff." Moreover, while reserving final judgment to the Holy See in the person of the Roman Pontiff, the Pope is at pains to make clear that he has nothing up his papal sleeve, as it were. It is not as if the Catholic jurist were to make his prudent judgment in the light of the given set of principles and norms, and then ask the judgment of the Church, only to find that the Church would alter his judgment in the light of some other hitherto unproduced principle. On the contrary: "For weighing pros and cons in the consideration of the *quaestio facti* there are no norms valid for the Church other than the norms which We have indicated as valid for the Catholic jurist and statesman, even in what concerns the ultimate and supreme judgment of the case."

In other words, the autonomy of the jurist or statesman is limited by the authority of the Church only in the sense that it is limited by the norms which Pius XII has just laid down in all their fullness. What the Church wants—all that the Church wants—is that these norms should be honestly applied by the jurist. The Pope does not reserve to himself the right to make the final legal decision for the jurist, or to substitute his own judgment for the jurist's judgment. The legal decision is squarely in the hands of the jurist.

But the Pope does reserve exclusively to himself the judgment as to what set of principles and norms the jurist is to use in coming to his legal decision. The jurist is not left to his own devices; nor is he to be guided by what are only received opinions;[39] nor is he to feel called upon to be more Catholic than the universal Church. Pius XII clearly tells the jurist three things, in effect: (1) that in matters of legal decision affecting the relation of religion to the order of law he, the jurist, is the competent lay authority; (2) that in reaching his decision he is to follow the traditional norms of the Church; (3) that he himself, the Roman Pontiff, has just stated these norms—all the norms there are; there are no others.

Explicit too in the whole Allocution is the assertion that its strongly structured doctrine presents the norms of the Church in their only correct and traditional *impostazione*. Here therefore a conclusion is permissible.

In the anonymous theory sketched above legal intolerance was stated to be the "thesis"; legal tolerance, the "hypothesis." Will this manner of categorization stand in the light of Pius XII's doctrine? I should think not. The Allocution makes it clear that tolerance and intolerance are alternative modes of legal action, each of which must find its justification in terms of identically the same set of principles and norms. You would therefore more correctly say that both tolerance and intolerance are "hypotheses," subsumed under the one complex but unitary thesis. Each of the alternative hypotheses is an application of this unitary thesis to divergent circumstances. Both of them are legal decisions; neither of them is dogma. Both of them therefore must appeal for their validity to the same criterion. Each of them is valid if it represents a prudent answer to the papal *quaestio facti,* an answer given in the light of the moral and juristic norms of law, under due regard for the primacy of the latter norm. Intolerance may be good law; but so too may tolerance. Neither may claim to be ideal law in an absolute sense, but only in a relative sense; that is, each of them may claim to be ideal for the circumstances for which it was designed.

As legal decisions both tolerance and intolerance stand outside the category of "thesis"; for the thesis contains only general principles and universally valid norms. Within the ambit of the thesis you do not find legal intolerance performed as an ideal of legal experience, waiting only for circumstances in which the realization of this ideal may become possible. Within the thesis you do indeed find the principle of religious unity. You find, as an ideal, the Christian society which unitedly confesses its faith *animo et moribus.* This is the theological ideal; it is solely a question of religious principle. But the thesis itself does not automatically include the legal institution of intolerance as an ideal, even for the territory of a particular society which may exhibit religious unity. Before this institution can be validated a question of fact has to be resolved. The thesis itself does not answer such questions of fact; it simply presents the principles to be applied in answering them.

Pius XII's Allocution states the Catholic thesis; it does not canonize legal intolerance as an ideal. On the contrary, it suggests that you will find legal intolerance exactly where you will also find legal tolerance—at the end of a complex argument leading to a practical and prudential judgment. You will find both institutions outside the category of principle, inside the category of applications of principle. Therefore the Catholic doctrine is not disjunctive in the sense of the anonymous theory outlined above. It is disjunctive—indeed multijunctive—only in the sense that the same set of norms may require diverse application in divergent sets of circumstances.

A Unitary Doctrine

It would be pointless to argue the relative merits of the diverse applications—for instance, to argue the question, whether the constitutional law which governs 28 million Catholic Spaniards is "better law" than the constitutional law which governs 32 million Catholic Americans. The argument would be pointless because the situations are incommensurable. It would be like the famous drunken argument on the question, which is greater—St. Patrick or the Fourth of July? The more decisive thing is to know the right manner of argument for or against either of these legal decisions, for or against any legal decision affecting the relation of human law—that is, the state—to the order of religion.

This right manner of argument has been outlined by Pius XII. It is now possible for Catholic lay jurists—or, if you will, Catholic communities or Catholic peoples—anywhere in the world to begin with exactly the same set of principles and norms, and to argue the case for or against their regional or national legal decisions in terms of these same invariable principles and norms. They may reach different conclusions. For instance, the Spanish Catholic lay jurist may conclude to Article 6 of the *Fuero de los españoles;* the American Catholic lay jurist may conclude to the First Amendment to the Constitution of the U.S. But what matters is the identity of the norms of judgment. The point is that the American and the Spaniard would both be arguing from a unitary premise, complex in its content, which would be mutually shared as the doctrine of the universal Church. They would both be using a single complex standard and measure of judgment on the legitimacy, necessity, and utility of legal decisions for the public advantage. And at the end of their arguments each would be entitled to pronounce on his own legal decision substantially the same verdict: "This is good law—necessary and useful for the public advantage. This is not ideal law in any absolute sense. This is only man-made law; it is not God-given dogma."

The consolidation of Catholic doctrine in this unitary form would be a contribution to the comity of nations as well as to the unity of Catholic peoples throughout the world. The consolidation would be completed if Catholic doctrine on legal establishment, as the juridical premise of intolerance, were to be given the same configuration that has already been given to the Catholic doctrine on intolerance.

Pius XII did not explicitly touch the question of establishment in its classic modern legal sense.[40] Speaking of Concordats, he says: "It is possible that in the Concordat the Church and the state may proclaim their common religious conviction." But this is not establishment in the sense, say, of the 1851 Concordat with Spain. As made by governmental officials, the proclamation that a particular national society shares the faith of the universal Church has only the value of its own truth: is this official utterance truly representative of the actual public faith of the people in whose name it is made? This manner of official utterance is indeed a witness to a twofold truth—to the social truth that the faith of the people is the Catholic faith, and to the religious truth that the Catholic faith of the people is the true faith. But this is only witness, not law. It has no juridical consequences in the form of legal intolerance of other religions. It does not create, in Pius XII's formula, a "constitutional situation." It does not of itself dictate the "extermination" from public existence of confessional groups who would say that the religious and social witness given by government did not represent their convictions. Consequently this is not the classic canonico-legal concept of establishment with which I am here concerned.

Pius XII also condemns separationism: "The Church cannot approve the complete separation of the two powers as a matter of principle, or as a thesis." Here again he is in the tradition of Leo XIII, defending the same principle, rejecting the contrary principle. But the context is significant. It has to do with Concordats, which are, he says, "an expression of cooperation between Church and state." The "two powers" are the spiritual authority of the universal Church, represented by the Holy See, and the political authority within a given regional or national society. Pius XII here preserves the perspectives of the entire Allocution, which are those of the universal Church as it confronts the individual states that are actual or potential members of an international community.

Therefore the "separation" here explicitly condemned is a separation between the Holy See and the multiple sovereign powers within the international community. Non-cooperation with the Holy See is condemned when it is proposed as a principle or thesis; when it is asserted therefore that the supreme authority of the universal Church is irrelevant, in principle, to the common life of the international community and its member-states; when it is asserted that the

Holy See has, in principle, neither the right nor the duty to take measures, in concert with authorities of state, to safeguard the religious interests of Catholic communities everywhere; when it is asserted that authorities of state have in principle, neither the duty nor the right to lend their cooperation to such measures. The basic principle at stake, with Pius XII as with Leo XIII, is cooperation between Church and state; it is the Leonine principle of *concordia*.

But the context of its new assertion is not precisely Leonine. Pius XII is not explicitly concerned, as Leo XIII chiefly was, with collaboration between the religious authorities and the political powers within the nation-state. Indeed his concern is that these intramural collaborative measures should always be subject to the higher judgment of the Holy See to which, in its incumbent, he has explicitly reserved the final competence in matters affecting international life—and today all forms of intramural cooperation do affect international life.

Moreover, in a carefully phrased passage Pius XII makes it clear that not all the legal provisions of a Concordat, though they may be necessary or useful within a particular national context, receive with equal force the approval of the universal Church. When the Holy See consents to a Concordat, it sincerely consents to the whole Concordat. "But with the mutual acknowledgment of both of the contracting parties its intimate meaning admits of degrees. It can signify an express approval. But it can also mean a simple tolerance, in accord with the two principles which are the norm for the living-together of the Church and of her faithful with the powers and with men of another belief."

To put the same thing in other words, cooperation between Church and state admits of degrees, according to circumstances. Certain forms of it are essential—primarily, as the text goes on, the assurance of the freedom of the Church. Other forms of it—legal protection, financial subsidy, etc.—may be justified, or perhaps only tolerated, in the light of special circumstances. But there is no warrant for generalizing these latter forms of cooperation into an ideal. The expertise of the trained jurist comes into play. But in the final instance, if any generalizations are to be made, they may be made only by the ultimately competent authority, the Roman Pontiff himself.

Pius XII asserts the principle of cooperation in its highest terms— in terms of the supreme duty and right of the Holy See to insure that the essential purpose of the Church is fulfilled in all forms of cooper-

ation between Church and state, intranational and international. He
clearly states this purpose in stating the purpose of the instruments
that are contractual acts of the Holy See: "Concordats therefore
ought to assure to the Church a stable condition of right and of fact
within the state with which they are concluded, and to guarantee to
the Church full independence in the fulfillment of her divine mission." There is here the Leonine accent on the freedom of the
Church in the full meaning of that traditional formula. The assurance
of that freedom, by whatever measures are appropriate in the circumstances, is the essential cooperation that the political powers owe to
the Church as a community and as an authority.

Does this whole doctrine lead to the conclusion, adopted by the
anonymous theory outlined above, that legal establishment in the
classic modern sense, with its juridical corollary of intolerance, is
the ideal in an absolute sense—a matter of principle that requires
realization whenever and wherever possible? Does Pius XII's specially
accented condemnation of "complete separation of the two powers"
impose this conclusion? To say that it does would certainly be to go
beyond the text itself. What is more, this conclusion would seem to be
out of harmony with the text. The more harmonious interpretation
would construct a theory of establishment in the classic legal sense on
lines parallel with the lines of Pius XII's doctrine on intolerance.

Legal establishment in this narrow sense, like intolerance, is a matter of human law. It is therefore to be judged "in accord with the two
principles which are the norm for the living-together of the Church
and her faithful with the political powers and with men of another
belief." Legal establishment in this sense, like intolerance, is not
"thesis," not an absolute unconditioned ideal. Its imposition is not
justified by the criterion of "possibility." The judgment on its validity
is not instant, *rechts von oben;* it must wait upon a prudent answer to
the *quaestio facti.*

And the *quaestio facti,* in Pius XII's position of it, is not put thus:
"Is there or is there not in this territory a Catholic majority—a Catholic unity, relatively or morally or absolutely speaking?" Rather the
question of fact is put thus: "Is this legal institution necessary or
useful for the common good—both of Church and state within a
particular society, and also of the universal Church and the international community? What does a wise prognosis reveal with regard to
its probable effects, good and bad, within a particular society, as com-
pared with its effects upon the unity and peace which is the higher
good, the unity and peace of the international community?"

This view of legal establishment in the narrow sense is a prolongation, rather than an interpretation, of Pius XII's text. But the prolongation is, I submit, harmonious with the doctrine of the text. If therefore the full Catholic doctrine on establishment and intolerance were consolidated in this form, the constitution of a unitary Catholic position, permitting a variety of applications, would be complete.

Notes

1. EDITOR NOTE: The galley pages, with editorial changes by Murray, for this article are to be found in Lauinger Library, Special Collections, Murray Archives, file number 7-536.

2. Leo XIII uses the formula, "religion of the state," only once; it appears in a letter to the Cardinal Vicar of Rome (August 23, 1900) on Protestant propaganda in Rome, which is directed against "that religion which has been declared the religion of the state" (*Acta Leonis XIII*, Bonne Presse edition [Bayard: Paris. s.d.], 6, 144). The formula has canonical standing in a dozen or more Concordats from the days of Pius VII to 1929. The strict legal meaning which I adopt here, and shall return to later, is the meaning attributed to the formula by Pius XI in a comment on the Lateran pacts. It is to be understood, he says, "that according to the Statutes and Treaties the Catholic religion and it alone is the religion of the state, with the logical and juridical consequences of such a situation of constitutional law, especially in respect of propaganda" (Letter to Cardinal Gasparri, May 30, 1919; Lo Grasso, *Ecclesia et status: De mutuis officiis et iuribus fontes selecti* [Romae, apud aedes Universitatis Gregorianae, 1939], pp. 326–27). The essence of the matter is that establishment is an act of legislation on the part of government, which decrees that there is only one official public religion; whence it follows that the force of law is to be used to exclude all other confessions from public existence and activity. This is establishment in the proper legal sense; it is inherently related to intolerance as premise to conclusion. There are other milder, diminished concepts, from which no intolerant consequences flow, at least not in fact. But I shall be concerned only with the strict classic legal concept. It seems to be a modern concept. Whether it has medieval antecedents is a dubious question. Generally speaking, in earlier medieval practice and in later medieval theory it was rather the Church which established the state, i.e., the political power and the public law—whatever there was in the way of public law. The notion of the political power establishing the Church seems to be related to modern concepts of legal sovereignty, as they appeared on the European Continent.

3. EDITOR NOTE: This notion of the "outlaw conscience" permeated Murray's analysis of the problems that Leo XIII faced. For Murray's first treatment of conscience and law, see 1945b, "Freedom of Religion, I: The Ethical Problem," pp. 244ff. For its first appearance in the Leonine series, see 1952a, "The Church and Totalitarian Democracy," pp. 553–55. See also pp. 158–59 of the second essay of this collection, "The Problem of Religious Freedom."

4. I consistently use the term "state" to designate the order of human law and of governmental acts—administrative, judicial, police—whereby the living action which is public order is established and sustained. The term "society" has a wider meaning. EDITOR NOTE: For Murray's four-part division of social entities, see 1951b, "The Problem of the 'Religion of the State,' " Note 6, pp. 330–32.

5. EDITOR NOTE: Murray had earlier developed this monist reading of the Third Republic in 1953b, "Leo XIII on Church and State: The General Structure of the Controversy," and 1953c, "Leo XIII: Separation of Church and State." Monism came in two varieties, regalism and hierocratism, depending on whether the state or the church attempted to reduce the social order to a monism. By 1948 Murray had positioned John of Paris as an opponent of both forms of monism (1949b, "Contemporary Orientations of Catholic") and by 1954 had reinterpreted all of church/state history as temptations to monism (1954d, "On the Structure of the Church-State Problem").

6. EDITOR NOTE: Here and at two other places in the galleys Murray edited out the word "state" and substituted the word "society." In all three instances, Murray's deepening sense that the principal target of the church's temporal concern is society as a moral reality, not the state, called for the substitution. Here, in the first and third principles, Murray has taken a problem that Leo described in terms of church and state and redefined the interaction to be between church and society, what Murray described as a "nicety" that Leo did not always observe.

7. The duty of social worship binds human societies no matter what may be the form of their political regime—monarchic, democratic, dictatorial, etc. It would be false to say that this duty is not binding on a society organized of democratic bases.

8. I am not concerned here with civil enforcement of a "Sunday rest." This is a matter that touches on the public order. Even here, strictly speaking, government does not enforce a religious duty. It simply creates the conditions of public order wherein the performance of the religious duty is facilitated.

9. I also assume that there would be no warrant in Catholic doctrine for

the famous Elizabethan "Bloody Question"; cf. Christopher Devlin, "The Failure of the English Inquisition," *Month,* Feb., 1955, pp. 101–9.

10. EDITOR NOTE: See 1951b, "The Problem of 'The Religion of the State,'" pp. 342–43, note 13.

11. Whether the Christian ideal also includes, as elements of the ideal in an absolute sense, the legal experience enshrined in the institutions of legal establishment and legal intolerance is a question later to be discussed. Other elements of the ideal will also appear later, notably the constitutional ideal of a society structured in accord with the distinction between Church and state and their necessary harmony of action.

12. EDITOR NOTE: *Quaestiones juris* and *quaestiones facti* are Pius XII's terms, which Murray adopts. At face value they resemble Murray's notions of theory and practical judgment, respectively. In this scenario, Pius XII develops a theory, *quaestio juris* (a set of principles); the laity apply them. Murray will equate *quaestiones facti* and lay practical judgment later on (pp. 108–12). Here, under the label of *quaestiones facti,* Murray also appears to give the interpretation of the overall moral content of historical civil orders to the pontiff. But the overall moral content of the Anglo-American public philosophical tradition is precisely the moral content that is under contention. Murray claimed that it developed independently of the church, under the inspiration of non-Catholics, much less nonclerics. Here Murray is appealing to papal authority to back up his reading of the best of Western political development. The inadequacies of his earlier practical reasoning/theoretical reasoning distinction show through when applied to cultural contents that attain development in historical societies.

13. EDITOR NOTE: Another substitution of "society" for the galley term "state." See note 6 above.

14. EDITOR NOTE: Murray substituted this term "divine" for the term "Christian" in the galleys, suggesting that this separation was contrary to natural law theism as it was opposed to Catholic law.

15. EDITOR NOTE: Murray will later give a general description of these *res mixti* (matters over which civil society and the church share jurisdiction). Earlier he had listed the following:

> . . . the husband-wife relationship, the parent-child relationship (including education), the political obligation, the human dignity of the worker, the equality of men as all equally in the image of God, the moral values inherent in economic life, the works of charity and justice which are the native expression of the human and Christian spirit, the patrimony of ideas which are the foundation of human society—the ideas of law, freedom, justice,

property, moral obligation, civic obedience, legitimate rule, etc., etc. There is also the thing, sacred in its destination, whereby the Church occupies ground in this world, namely, her legitimate property. (1953c, p. 209)

These lists, of course, are rather comprehensive. They constitute the *res sacra* of human existence over which the natural order and the revealed order exercise authority. This *res mixti* exists because (1) the natural order has in its own right a spiritual or sacral dimension (the orientations toward the divine that are built into human nature) and (2) the person's eternal salvation (within the order of redemption) is in part dependent on behavior in that natural order.

16. EDITOR NOTE: "Regalistic" refers to the civil power's attempt to destroy the dualistic structure of society by subjugating the religious order to itself. It is a type of "monism"; the other type, coming from the church side, Murray calls "hierocratic." See note 5.

17. EDITOR NOTE: Murray maintained that the public education system in the United States was not solely a creature of the state or government. Rather, it was a forum over which the three institutions mentioned here shared jurisdiction. For his argument see 1949d, "Law or Prepossessions," chapter 6, "Is It Justice? The School Question Today," *WHTT;* 1962b, "Federal Aid to Church Related Schools."

18. EDITOR NOTE: See 1952a, "The Church and Totalitarian Democracy," for a lengthier description of the conspiracy that Leo XIII thought he faced.

19. EDITOR NOTE: Murray's development of the direct/indirect distinction grew out of the question of the means that are proper to civil society and to the church (see 1948i, "St. Robert Bellarmine on the Indirect Power," and 1949b, "Contemporary Orientations of Catholic Thought."

20. EDITOR NOTE: Murray had tried to draw such a line in response to Pius XII's call for all people of good will to participate in post-World War II reconstruction. See 1943b, "Current Theology: Intercredal Co-operation: Its Theory and Its Organization"; 1944c, "Toward a Theology for the Layman: The Pedagogical Problem," and 1944d, "Toward a Theology for the Layman: The Problem of Its Finality."

21. EDITOR NOTE: See 1953d, "Leo XIII: Two Concepts of Government." There Murray isolated a social order that Leo XIII recognized as possessing its own autonomy vis-à-vis the political order. He then moved on in 1954b, "Leo XIII: Two Concepts of Government: Government and the Order of Culture" to find why Leo XIII allowed as much freedom as possible in the economic order, but not in those of culture, communications, education, and religion.

22. EDITOR NOTE: A year after this was written, Murray developed an argument on the use of civil coercion in the support of public morality, focused on the censorship issue. That article (1956f, "Questions of Striking a Right Balance: Literature and Censorship") then became Chapter 7 of *WHTT*, "Should There Be a Law," pp. 155–74. The use of that argument against Catholics involved in a censorship campaign led to 1956a, "The Bad Arguments Intelligent Men Make." For Murray's 1960 comments on the limits of civil law, see chapter 12, "The Doctrine Is Dead: The Problem of the Moral Vacuum," *WHTT*, pp. 275–94.

23. Fritz Tillmann, *Handbuch der katholischen Sittenlehre*, Vol. 4, Part 2: *Die Verwirklichung der Nachfolge Christi: Die Pflichten gegen sich selbst und gegen den Nächsten*, pp. 441–42.

24. Joseph Schmidlin, *Papstgeschichte der neuesten Zeit*, Vol. 2: *Pius IX and Leo XIII (1846–1903)*, p. 356.

25. I do not think I have myself ever made this generalization consciously and advertently; if I have ever given the impression of making it, I wish here to correct the impression. Certainly I do not erect the American fact of a religiously pluralist society into a principle, as if somehow society ought to be religiously pluralist. Nor do I erect the American constitutional law which deals with this fact into an ideal in some absolute sense. I have indeed maintained, and do maintain, that the First Amendment, within the American religious, political, and social situation, can be defended in principle—as will later appear, in terms of the two principles which Pius XII lays down as normative. But this is not to make a dogma out of American law, to transform a law that is good *in situ* into a principle that would be valid *universim*. Nor do I argue that full religious liberty ought to obtain within particular societies simply because they are democratically organized. Political forms do not alter theological or ethical principles, or invalidate the norms of human law that derive from traditional legal philosophy. Finally, I do not hold that the freedom of the Church ceases to be in principle a privileged freedom, simply because a democratic form of government obtains. Nor do I say that a general guarantee of freedom of religion is the absolutely sufficient and ideal way to guarantee the freedom of the Church. I do not hold that the case for American constitutional law—"no establishment" and "no intolerance"—can be legitimately made simply on the grounds that the U.S. is a democracy in the Anglo-American tradition. Anymore than I hold that the case for Spanish constitutional law—establishment and intolerance—can be made simply on the ground that a manner of religious unity obtains in Spain and makes possible these institutions. No such simplism of argument is valid. This question will recur when we deal with Pius XII's two principles that are normative in this matter.

26. Law, says Fr. Gilby in dependence on St. Thomas, is an "act of art about contingent material" (*Between Community and Society* [London: Longmans, 1953], p. 286). The contingency of the material is decisive for the art.

27. EDITOR NOTE: This (almost proof-text) appeal to Leo XIII and the scriptural source behind it is new to Murray. He will appeal directly to the relevant scriptural texts in the documents written during his silencing (1958b, "Church and State: The Structure of the Argument," and 1959d, "Unica Status Religio," as well as in "The Problem of Religious Freedom").

28. EDITOR NOTE: Cf. "Leo XIII on Church and State: The General Structure of the Controversy," *Theological Studies* 14 (1953): 5–6.

29. R. W. and A. J. Carlyle, *A History of Medieval Political Theory in the West*, Vol. 6: *Political Theory from 1300 to 1600*, p. 511.

30. EDITOR NOTE: On March 2, 1953, Alfredo Cardinal Ottaviani delivered what was thought to be a repudiation of Murray's church/state position; see Ottaviani, "Church and State: Some Present Problems in Light of the Teaching of Pope Pius XII," *The American Ecclesiastical Review* 128 (May 1943): 321–34. On December 6, 1953, Pius XII delivered an address that Murray at least considered a repudiation of Ottaviani; see Pius XII, "Ci riesce: A Discourse to the National Convention of Italian Catholic Jurists. Official Vatican Press Office English Translation," *American Ecclesiastical Review* 130 (February 1954): 129–38. On March 25, 1954, Murray delivered an address at Catholic University of America that dealt with both talks. Much of the following is contained in the notes of that last talk. For a discussion of these events, see Donald E. Pelotte, *John Courtney Murray: Theologian in Conflict* (New York: Paulist Press, 1976), pp. 37–54.

31. EDITOR NOTE: For Murray's earlier discussion of the Catholic majority argument, along with his beginning understanding of a Catholic people, see 1951b, "The Problem of 'The Religion of the State,' " pp. 349–52.

32. These are the only four countries in which by concordatary law a constitutional situation was created within which the Catholic religion was established as the single (*sola, unica*) "religion of the state," with the express added proviso that all other cults are excluded ("*con exclusion de cualquier otro culto,*" as the 1851 Concordat with Isabella II puts it). In other Concordats the formula, "*religio rei publicae,*" or some equivalent, appears: with Guatemala (1852), Costa Rica (1852), Honduras (1861), Nicaragua (1861), San Salvador (1862), Venezuela (1862), Colombia (1887), Serbia (1914); but the complementary formula, "*exclusis aliis,*" or its equivalents, does not appear. The texts may be found in A. Mercati, *Raccolta di concordati in materie eclesiastiche tra la Santa Sede e la autorità civili* (Roma, 1919). The full text of the 1862 Concordat with Ecuador is given in English in S. Z. Ehler and J. B. Morrall,

Church and State through the Centuries (London: Burns and Oates, 1954), pp. 273–80. In more recent Concordats, beginning with Pius XI, the initial provisions customarily deal, in one or other way, only with the freedom of the Church. It would be true to say that in latter years the "union" of Church and state chiefly envisaged in Concordats is a matter of juridical and diplomatic relations between governments and the Holy See.

33. EDITOR NOTE: The first part of this sentence, as it appeared in the galleys, read: "That there is an ideal of the Catholic confessional state, professing itself as such, to which organized political society is universally obliged . . . " Here is another example of Murray's deepening control over the society/state distinction.

34. All Catholics assert that the religious unity of the peoples of the world is the object of the will of God and the prayer of Christ: "*Ut omnes unum sint.*" This ideal is qualified only by the mystery of the divine predestining decree. There are the profound words of our Lord Himself: "Do you think I have come to bring peace on earth? No, believe me, I have come to bring dissension" (Lk. 12:51). Unity is the ideal; dissension is the actual condition of mankind—a condition that is not simply brute fact but theological fact, inasmuch as it is related to the mystery of predestination. The question that is not mysterious but merely troublesome concerns the actual religious unity of the historic "Catholic nation," as it has existed since the Revolution or even before. P. Guerrero, S.J., has thrown some light on this question in a discussion of Spanish fundamental law, which supposes, he says, the Catholic unity of Spain. His argument, briefly, is that you do not find in Spain a plurality of religions; what you find is a plurality of attitudes toward Catholicism, ranging from extreme fervor to extreme hostility. He distinguishes four kinds of "Catholics": "There are the good Catholics, more or less fervent. There are the sincere Catholics, who do not, however, practice, by reason of dissipation, carelessness, or enslavement to the passions. There are those who have been baptized as infants and have received the mark of some one or other contact with the Church; but who thenceforth have continually lived without the least spiritual culture, in absolute religious ignorance, to the point where all concern for the transcendental has more or less died in them, even though they have never conceived sentiments or ideas positively hostile to religion, or at least have not fundamentally assimilated such sentiments. Finally, there are those who at bottom (*en el fondo*) believe, because at one time in the past they had explicitly believed, and as a matter of fact have not consciously denied their faith; but by reason of their alienation from the Church, whose influence is lost on them for various reasons, and by reason of their subjection to factors of anti-Catholic influence which have inspired in them both adverse prejudices of a cultural or social kind and also diverse political and

economic interests, they not only do not practice but even make war on the Church in general and especially on the clergy." This fourth class of anti-Catholic "Catholics," the author says, made the Civil War. The third and fourth classes are "those who most need the tutelage of a regime which would help to create the conditions of ideological health, Catholic culture, and social justice in which they might fully develop the seeds of faith and Catholic life which they bear in the depths of their souls because these seeds were once sown there and have never been eradicated" (*Razon y fe* 148 [1953], nn. 666–67, pp. 8[9]). This is an honest argument; it is even reminiscent of the realism of Leo XIII. But what has it got to do with "ideals" in the absolute sense? Governmental tutelage that is "needed" may be justified by the need. Is it therefore to be erected into a universally valid theological ideal? It may be that in Spain government will be a power of salvation unto those who do not believe—except *en el fondo*. Time will tell. But is this a theological principle? P. Guerrero elsewhere abandons the plane of apologia, on which the above argument moves and has its validity, and soars to the heights of the theological ideal. We Spaniards, he says, "do not assert that our regime is a practical and viable ideal for all peoples; we only say that it is a theological ideal for everybody, inasmuch as God wills all nations to be Catholic and to be governed *en católico*" (*ibid.*, 149 [1954], n. 675, p. 330). "Only" this, indeed. And who has established it as God's will and as a theological ideal that a Catholic community should be divided into the above four classes, in such wise as to make necessary an extensive governmental tutelage of ignorant and hostile Catholics? And who has proved that this manner of tutelage, because it is necessary in concrete circumstances, is therefore itself a theological ideal? This is what I mean by the passage from the plane of apologia to the plane of theoretical construction, pure principle, from the contingent necessities of history to the inherent demands of principle.

35. EDITOR NOTE: The text of Murray's galleys offered a footnote number here and on page 104 (note 37). However, as the original editor of those galleys penciled in the margins, the galley note page lacked a content for both numbers. For Pius XII's talk to the jurists, see note 30, above.

36. EDITOR NOTE: Murray's first venture into problems of the international common good was spurred by Pius XII's call to "all men of good will" to participate in postWorld War II reconstruction. From that starting point, he then had to address the question of lay autonomy and spirituality (as suggested in note 20) and then the present issue of civil religious freedom. For the reconstruction problem, see 1944a, "The Juridical Organization of the International Community," and 1944b, "The Pattern for Peace and the Papal Peace Program."

37. EDITOR NOTE: The galleys offered a note but no content here. See note 35.

38. EDITOR NOTE: "Intention of nature" is Murray's terminology for a principle that he considers derived from natural law or human nature, now understood to be capable of development through time, that is, to be contingent, not absolute. Most of Murray's explanation of the developments of natural law occur in his discussions of American constitutionalism (see, for example, chapters 1, 2, and 9 of *WHTT*). For an early treatment of Anglo-American political philosophy as the arena in which these intentions were developed, see 1951b, "The Problem of 'The Religion of the State,' " pp. 335–36.

39. EDITOR NOTE: Murray's term "received opinion," used here and elsewhere in these articles, seems to be what is called a theological note. Theological notes define the degree of theological certainty that attaches to particular theological claims. For Murray to claim that, say, Ottaviani's doctrine on establishment is merely a received opinion is to admit that a majority of theologians hold it to be in line with more essential aspects of Catholic faith. But it is only that, an opinion of theologians, not a matter of faith. For a listing of the various theological notes and a discussion of the degrees of certainty that attach to each, see Dionne, 1987, "Theological Notes," pp. 23–25; "Notes, Theological," *The Catholic Encyclopedia;* and "Theological Notes," *Encyclopedia of Theology,* ed. Karl Rahner (New York: Seabury Press, 1975), pp. 1678–85.

40. EDITOR NOTE: From this point on, Murray attempts to dismantle the claim that at least establishment of Catholicism as the religion of the state remains a Catholic "ideal." Again, the canonists in Murray's view ran two distinct arguments, one that concluded to establishment and another that concluded to intolerance. I discuss the fate of these two arguments in section IV of the general introduction.

2

The Problem of Religious Freedom[1]

By Murray's count, the Secretariat for Christian Unity worked through five different texts on its way to the document that the Council approved as *Dignitatis Humanae Personae*.[2] The first two, the "first" and "second" texts, were written during the first session of the Council (October to December 1962) and were the result of attempted compromises between August Cardinal Bea's Secretariat for Christian Unity and Cardinal Ottaviani's Conciliar Theological Commission. Murray was not present at this first session and had no role in shaping these first two drafts. Both texts attempted to justify religious freedom on the basis of the rights of conscience.

During and immediately after the third session (September to November 1964) two subsequent drafts (the *textus emendatus* and the *textus re-emendatus*) were written with Murray as their "first scribe." The central argument in both texts was that of his "The Problem of Religious Freedom."

A fifth text (the *textus recognitus*) was written while Murray was out of circulation because of a collapsed lung. The fifth text was presented to the Council on October 25, 1965, during the fourth session (September to December 1965). After the incorporation of several proposed amendments, a final text was approved and promulgated on December 7, 1965, as a conciliar declaration. The main argument of the fifth and final texts was grounded on the human right to search after the truth and to embrace the truth once found. Murray's principal line of argument entered the text, as we will see in the last article in this collection, as an addendum.

Murray composed our present article, "The Problem of Religious Freedom," before and during the third session, while he was also drafting the *textus emendatus*. The second section is a broad historical analy-

sis of the changing state of the religious liberty question, from the
Roman Empire to John XXIII. The first section abruptly presents the
canonist position and Murray's own argument "objectively" (so Murray claimed). In the third section, Murray tried to sketch the full range
of issues that separated him from the canonists.

Introduction

In a recent address to a seminar of the United Nations on freedom
of information Paul VI said:

> As you know, the Church also is busy with a somewhat
> different problem but one that is not without affinity with
> the present object of your research. It is the problem of
> religious freedom. The importance and amplitude of the
> question are so great that it has claimed the attention of
> the Ecumenical Council. It is legitimate to expect the
> promulgation of a text on the subject that will be of great
> import not only for the Church but also for all those—
> countless in number—who feel that an authoritative dec-
> laration on the subject is a matter of concern to them.[3]

This essay may serve to illuminate the formidable difficulties that the
problem itself presents. They arise from two general sources.

First, there is the variety of religio-social situations throughout the
world, and the differences among political traditions and regimes,
and the divergences in the historical experiences of the nations.

For instance, religious freedom has been an integral part of the
Catholic experience in the United States; the institution is considered
to have made a contribution to the vitality of the Church. Elsewhere,
perhaps chiefly in Spain, the institution is alien; the very notion connotes a hated *Liberalismo,* pernicious both to the Church and to a
cherished national religious unity.

Again, there is the more difficult problem of Christian communities in lands of non-Christian tradition and culture—Islamic, Hindu,
Buddhist. A declaration on religious freedom might be understood to
signify the will of Christians to constitute a "state within a state," and
to withdraw from solidarity with the existent national community.
The result might possibly be governmental legislation against conver-
sion to Christianity, as well as severe restrictions on missionary activity. Opposition on Christian grounds to governmental policies is an

accepted phenomenon in those countries in which government pretends to do no more than administer the affairs of society; it is considered a legitimate exercise of religious freedom. The case may be different in those countries in which government is undertaking the task of constructing the social order, in the name of an ideology of which government is the representative. In these circumstances, opposition, based on an appeal to religious freedom, might be considered disloyalty to the state.

Furthermore, there is the still more difficult problem of the Church in countries under Communist domination. Some conciliar Fathers are in favor of a strong condemnation of Communism, both as an ideology and as a regime, precisely in the name of religious freedom. Others are inclined to doubt the value or prudence of such a condemnation. Still others consider that it would do more harm than good. If the Council were to declare, explicitly or implicitly, that the atheist is not free to profess his ideology and to make it the basis of a socialist-materialist society, the retort might well be: "The freedom that you solemnly deny to us, we shall deny to you with equal solemnity and considerably more effect." There is also the more general problem of the atheist himself, and the secularist too. If the Council were simply to say to him that he is the enemy of the common good and therefore cannot be granted freedom, it would reveal itself as insensitive to the religious problem of today, of which the atheist and the secularist form so large a part.

Finally, there is the problem of making a declaration on religious freedom that will appeal to the common consciousness of all men of good will and furnish the basis of a badly needed dialogue between the Church and the world on this acute and universal problem. The scope of the Council calls for a pastoral act, which will at once clarify the doctrine of the Church and also demonstrate her concern for human freedom in this perilous age of ours.

The second source of difficulty is the contemporary state of Catholic doctrine on religious freedom. The fact is that serious differences of opinion presently exist within the Church. The fact was clearly demonstrated by the variant reactions to the three draft texts submitted in succession by the Secretariat for the Promotion of Christian Unity. Nevertheless, there is general agreement on the necessity of reaching a consensus and on the means of doing so, namely, the freedom of the conciliar dialogue, and the willingness of the Fathers to rise above any sort of apologetic complex and to approach the problem in the spirit of genuine theological inquiry.

The purpose of the present essay is not to present any personal views of the author. The essay undertakes, first, to state with all possible objectivity the two existent views on religious freedom (in order to avoid prejudicial characterization, they will be called simply the First View and the Second View), and second, to institute a dialogue between them, presenting the objections that each has to the other. In this way it may be possible to formulate clearly and without confusion the real issues.

At the outset, it may be useful to state the central question that is in dispute between the two Views. It concerns the care of religion by government. The technical term or phrase "care of religion" (*cura religionis*) is a post-Reformation coinage. But the problem goes back to the days when the Church first emerged into public existence within the ancient Roman Empire. It is a political problem, because it concerns the competence of government with regard to religion in society. It is a juridical problem, because it concerns the functions and limits of the coercive power of civil law in the same regard. It is a theological problem, because it touches doctrines of faith, chiefly in ecclesiology. It is an ethical problem, because it raises the issue of conscience and of human and civil rights. Hereinafter it will be called the "constitutional question." The practical reason is that nowadays an answer to the question of public care of religion is customarily provided, in one sense or another, in the constitutional law of organized political communities.

The Two Views

The First View

The problematic of religious freedom is abstract and simple. It is constructed by two related questions—the moral question of the rights of conscience, and the constitutional question.

With regard to the moral question, three cases are distinguished. First, there is the conscience that is not only subjectively formed in accord with higher norms (*conscientia recta*), but also formed by norms that are objectively true (*conscientia vera*). This conscience, which is the Catholic conscience, possesses the fulness of religious freedom, because religious freedom is rooted in objective truth. It is a positive concept. It is the social faculty of professing and practicing what is true and good, as the true and the good are objectively proposed by the eternal law of God (both natural and positive), subjectively manifested by a rightly and truly formed conscience, and authentically declared by the Church. Religious freedom in this sense is the requirement of the dignity of the human person. As a rational and moral being, man is constituted in his proper dignity by his adhesion to what is true and good. This is the religious freedom that the Church has always vindicated in the face of persecution of the truth.

Second, there is the case of the outlaw conscience (*conscientia ex-lex*). It recognizes no norms higher than its own subjective imperatives. Therefore it possesses neither rectitude nor truth. Therefore it has no rights; it can make no claim to religious freedom. Again the reason is that religious freedom is rooted in religious truth.

Third, there is the case of the sincere but erroneous conscience. It is formed in accord with higher norms that approve themselves to it, but these norms are not objectively true, at least not with the fulness of truth (*conscientia recta sed non vera*). Its rights are defined in terms of a distinction between internal personal freedom and external social freedom.

The erroneous conscience is endowed with internal personal freedom. It has the right not to be forced to abandon its religious convictions and practices and not to be coerced into acceptance of the true religious faith, against its own subjectively sincere mandate. It also has a right to reverence and respect on the part of others, and others have the duty of paying it reverence and respect. The respect, however, is not owed to the erroneous conscience as erroneous, since no respect is due to error, but to the man in error who is still endowed with that measure of human dignity which is synonymous with internal personal freedom. The duty here is therefore of the order of charity; its proper name is tolerance.

Furthermore, internal personal freedom is extended to include the religious freedom of the family—the right of parents to care for the religious upbringing of their children and to provide religious teachers for them. Finally, some affirm that internal personal freedom includes the right to public worship; others, however, deny this right, for the reason that a public act of worship is already an act of public propaganda.

The erroneous conscience has no right to external social freedom. That is, it has no right to public expression or manifestation of its beliefs in worship, witness, or teaching. In particular, it has no right publicly to propagate or disseminate its belief. The reason is that error has no public rights; only the truth has public rights, scil., rights to be exercised within society. Therefore the case of the erroneous conscience raises no issue of right in the strict sense, no issue of religious freedom in the proper sense. It raises only the issue of tolerance or intolerance. The erroneous conscience can claim no immunity from the repression of its external social manifestations by the public powers. This immunity, however, may be granted as an act of tolerance.

The constitutional question is solved by appeal to the same principle that governed the solution of the moral question, namely, that only the truth has rights, whereas error has no rights, within the public sector of society. This is the supreme juridical principle which controls the order of constitutional law and the action of the state. Whence it follows immediately that the public powers may never positively authorize the public existence of religious error. The legal attitude towards error can only be one of tolerance. On the other hand, the public powers have no right to violate the internal freedom of the personal conscience, or the freedom of the family, by compelling the profession or practice of any religion or ideology.

For the rest, the constitutional question is solved in terms of a distinction between thesis and hypothesis. The thesis states the ideal—the care of religion that constitutional law ought to provide, per se and in principle. The hypothesis states the concessions that may have to be made to circumstances—the care of religion that constitutional law may provide, per accidens and in view of circumstances.

The thesis asserts two general propositions. First, the state is bound not only on the natural law but also on the positive divine law whereby the Church was established. Therefore the state has the duty, per se and in principle, to recognize by constitutional law that the Church is a perfect society *sui iuris* and that it is the only religious society which has a right *iure divino* to public existence and action. Since Catholicism is, by divine law, the one true religion, it ought to be, by constitutional law, the one religion of the state. Whence it follows that no other religion may have, per se and in principle, a legal right to public existence and action within society. A religion that has no right to exist *iure divino,* can have no right to exist *iure humano.* Therefore, per se and in principle, all false religions ought to be "exterminated," that is, put beyond the bounds of public life and social action.

Hence the thesis affirms the legal institution of intolerance as the logical and juridical consequence of the legal institution of "establishment" (*unica status religio*). Together, these two institutions exhibit the ideal instance of constitutional law, the ideal solution to the constitutional question of public care of religion. The solution is internally consistent. The supreme juridical principle—the exclusive rights of truth—is transposed into the legal institution of the one state-religion. The obverse of the principle—the rightlessness of error—is transposed into the legal institution of intolerance. The special argument for this latter institution proceeds in two stages.

First, religious error *may* legitimately be repressed by law or by the police action of the state. Since error has no rights, no injury is done by this repression. The internal personal religious freedom of the erroneous conscience creates for it no external social freedom. Therefore the man of erroneous conscience cannot be considered reasonably unwilling to submit to the repressive action of the legitimate authority, the state. It is per se and in principle irrational to oppose the repression of what has no right to existence. Second, error *ought* to be repressed by the state. There are four reasons. First, error and evil are per se contrary to the rational and moral nature of man. Second, they are per se contrary to the common good of society, which is constituted by what is true and good. Third, they are per se injurious to the rights of others, especially their right to be protected from error and evil and to be left undisturbed in the profession of truth and in the practice of the good. Fourth, error and evil are per se a scandal, an occasion of moral wrongdoing and of defection from the truth.

This, in brief, is a statement of the thesis, the ideal, the solution to be given, per se in principle, to the constitutional question as a *quaestio iuris*. There remains the *quaestio facti*, the question of applying the ideal in practice. This question gives rise to the hypothesis. The distinction between thesis and hypothesis corresponds to the difference between national societies in respect of the religious composition of the citizenry.

Certain nations are Catholic, that is, the majority of the citizens are Catholic; or, as some prefer to say, the nation has historically reached the social consciousness of Catholic truth; or, as others prefer to say, the tradition of the nation has been a tradition of national Catholic religious unity. In these circumstances the thesis applies, per se and in principle. Other societies, however, are not Catholic; the religio-social situation is pluralistic; Catholics are only a minority; Catholicism has not permeated the national consciousness. In these circumstances the hypothesis applies, per accidens, as a matter of fact.

That is, the Church forgoes her right to legal establishment as the one religion of the state, with its juridical consequence, legal intolerance. The Church, however, gives no positive approval to the resultant constitutional situation. Per se the situation is an evil, but it may be regarded as a lesser evil than the evils which would result from application of the thesis. Therefore it may be tolerated, per accidens and in practice.

The supreme juridical principle of the exclusive rights of truth, and its pendant distinction between thesis and hypothesis, establish a rule of jurisprudence with regard to intolerance and tolerance. This rule prescribes intolerance whenever possible; it permits tolerance whenever necessary. (The degrees of legal intolerance will vary; the essential thing is that false religions should be denied public existence, action, and utterance. So too the degrees of tolerance may vary.) The political criterion, whereby the issue of the possibility of intolerance or the necessity of tolerance is to be decided, is the public peace. Within conditions of Catholic unity, where dissidents are a small minority, legal intolerance becomes possible without disruption of the public peace. It is, in fact, a means toward the public peace. In contrast, legal tolerance becomes necessary within conditions of religious pluralism, where Catholics are a minority. It is in turn a means toward the public peace. The religious criterion is the good of the Church. Within conditions of national Catholic unity the good of the Church is served by intolerance; elsewhere, by tolerance.

The First View puts forward its answer to the moral question, and its consequent answer to the constitutional question, as true, certain, and immutable, not only in respect of the constituent principles themselves but also in respect of their systematization (*impostazione*). The basic systematic concept is the exclusive rights of truth. The whole system, especially the disjunction between thesis and hypothesis, derives from this concept.

Moreover, this First View is declared to be the doctrine of the Church, supported by magisterial authority. The document of primary and definitive importance is alleged to be the Allocution of Pius XII, *Ci riesce*. There are two reasons. First, Pius XII affirms the basic systematic concept of the First View: "That which does not correspond to the truth and the norm of morality has, objectively, no right either to existence or to propaganda or to action."[4] Second, Pius XII proposes a doctrine of tolerance, not of religious freedom: "Not to inhibit it [error] by means of public laws and coercive methods can nevertheless be justified in the interests of a higher and greater good."[5]

Moreover, this doctrine is in continuity with Leo XIII. Thus, on the moral question: "Right is a moral faculty. Hence We have said— what needs to be repeated—that it is absurd to think that this moral faculty is granted by nature, impartially and without distinction, to truth and untruth, to decency and indecency."[6] Thus also, on the constitutional question and the issue of tolerance:

> Nevertheless, it is with a maternal judgment that the Church measures the heavy weight of human weakness; and she does not fail to note the direction being taken by events and opinion in this our age. For this reason, although she grants no rightfulness except to what is true and good, she is not unwilling that the public power should put up with certain things that are at odds with truth and justice, when it is a question of avoiding a greater evil or of gaining or saving a greater good.[7]

Other texts of the same tenor are adduced from Leo XIII. In addition, there is the catena of texts, beginning with Gregory XVI, in which the "modern liberties," especially freedom of religion, are condemned. Finally, *Pacem in terris* is considered to be simply a pastoral document, expressing the concern of the Church for the dignity of man. This concern is shared by the First View, in its defense of the right to internal personal religious freedom. For the rest, John XXIII leaves intact the doctrine of the duties and rights of the state in the order of religion, as presented by the First View. This doctrine is traditional and unalterable.

The supreme juridical principle of the exclusive rights of truth embodies an understanding of the medieval axiom: "Extra ecclesiam nullum ius." The thesis reproduces the sense of the medieval doctrine of the two swords, according to which the temporal sword is available "at the will and command of the priest" (*ad nutum et iussum sacerdotis*) for the protection of the religious unity of Christendom (*christianitas*) and for the extermination of heresy. The hypothesis states the sense of the medieval doctrine with regard to tolerance of Jews and pagans, their rites and beliefs.

Moreover, the First View stands in continuity with the doctrine of theologians during the post-Reformation religious conflicts. At that time, both Catholic and Protestant theologians taught the distinction between personal freedom of conscience and public manifestations of religious belief. In the latter regard, the state of the question was the same as it is today, namely, religious freedom in the civil order is the prerogative of the truth; error is to be treated with civil intolerance or tolerance, as the case might be. Moreover, in those days as also today, a sociological distinction was made. There were kingdoms and principalities within which unity of faith still prevailed, on the whole; the Reform had only begun to make inroads; its adherents were a small group, not well organized, not possessed of significant social or political power. Within these conditions of fact, the prince could exterminate the Reform, by measures of greater or less severity, without serious danger to the public peace. Hence the prince was obliged to proceed with the policy of extermination. In contrast, there were states within which the Reform was already well established and organized; it already claimed a sizable number of adherents, even among the nobility; it was therefore possessed of social and political power. Within these conditions of fact, the extermination of the Reform was no longer possible without danger of civil strife. Therefore tolerance became necessary and the prince was permitted to grant it, as the lesser evil. Per se and in principle, the prince's duty to care for religion constituted him the custodian of religious unity; per accidens and in practice, the prince was permitted to tolerate a plurality of religions within his jurisdiction.

On the other hand, the First View rejects certain conceptions of public care of religion that were prevalent in former eras. It recognizes that the modern Catholic nation is not the medieval Christian commonwealth; hence it denies that the religious prerogative of the emperor is to be transferred without alteration to the public powers in the Catholic state today. It denies that public care of religion may be prolonged into a *ius in sacra* or a *ius circa sacra*. It also denies the *ius reformandi* of the prince and its pendant, the *beneficium emigrationis*. It denies that the prince, by reason of his political sovereignty, is a competent judge of religious truth and *custos utriusque tabulae*. It rejects the notion that the prince, although he has no right to compel or impose religious faith, has nonetheless the duty and right to compel his subjects to hear the true word of God and to enforce outward conformity with the official faith. It admits therefore, in principle, that certain kinds of external constraint are incompatible with personal freedom of conscience.

In these respects, and in others, the First View represents progress within the tradition, a clearer and less confused understanding of traditional principles—in particular, the distinction between the religious order and the political order, and the limitations of political sovereignty in the order of religion. However, the First View maintains that progress within the tradition ended with Leo XIII and the systematization of his doctrine by subsequent canonists. Catholic doctrine has reached its final and definitive mode of conception and statement. It has defined forever the ideal instance of constitutional law with regard to public care of religion. Many changes have indeed taken place in the world since Leo XIII; in particular, there is a wide demand for religious freedom as a personal right and as a legal institution. These changes, however, represent decadence, not progress. Their sole historical effect has been to create more evils that the Church must tolerate; hence the scope of tolerance must be broadened. For the rest, the ideal remains, transhistorical, unquestionable.

The Second View

The problematic of religious freedom is concrete and historical. Its construction begins with a scrutiny of the "signs of the times." Two are decisive. The first is the growth of man's personal consciousness; the second is the growth of man's political consciousness. They were noted, in their relation, by John XXIII:

> The aspirations of the minds of men, about which We have been speaking, also give clear witness to the fact that in these our days men are becoming more and more conscious of their dignity. For this reason they feel the impulse to participate in the processes of government and also to demand that their own inviolable rights be guaranteed by the order of public law. What is more, they likewise demand that the civil powers should be established in accord with the norms of a public constitution and that they should fulfil their functions within limits defined by it.[8]

The political consciousness, which is the correlate of the personal consciousness, is further described:

> Moreover, the dignity of the human person requires that a man should act on his own judgment and with freedom. Wherefore in community life there is good reason why it should be chiefly on his own deliberate initiative that a man should exercise his rights, fulfil his duties, and co-operate with others in the endless variety of necessary social tasks. What matters is that a man should make his own decisions and act on his own judgment, out of a sense of

duty. He is not to act as one compelled by external coercion or instigation. In view of all this, it is clear that a society of men which is maintained solely by force must be considered inhuman. The reason is that in such a society men would be denied their freedom, whereas, on the contrary, they ought to be inspired, by all suitable means, to find for themselves the motive for progress in life and for the quest of perfection.[9]

Man's sense of personal freedom is allied with a demand for political and social freedom, that is, freedom from social or legal restraint and constraint, except in so far as these are necessary, and freedom for responsible personal decision and action in society. Freedom, not force, is the dynamism of personal and social progress.

The common consciousness of men today considers the demand for personal, social, and political freedom to be an exigency that rises from the depths of the human person. It is the expression of a sense of right approved by reason. It is therefore a demand of natural law in the present moment of history. This demand for freedom is made especially in regard to the goods of the human spirit—the search for truth, the free expression and dissemination of opinion, the cultivation of the arts and sciences, free access to information about public events, adequate opportunities for the development of personal talents and for progress in knowledge and culture.[10] In a particular way, freedom is felt to be man's right in the order of his most profound concern, which is the order of religion.[11]

Therefore the Second View holds that, in consequence of the new perspective created by the growth of the personal and political consciousness, the state of the ancient question concerning public care of religion has been altered. Today the question is not to be argued in medieval or post-Reformation or nineteenth-century terms, scil., the exclusive rights of truth and legal tolerance or intolerance, as the case may be, of religious dissidence. The terms of the argument today are, quite simply, religious freedom. The question is to know, first, what religious freedom means in the common consciousness today, and second, why religious freedom, in the sense of the common consciousness, is to receive the authoritative approval of the Church.

The Second View addresses itself to the question in its new historical and doctrinal state. However, two schools of thought seem to exist with regard to the method of setting forth the Second View, which they nonetheless hold in common.

One school regards religious freedom as formally a theological-moral concept, which has juridical consequences, scil., within the order of constitutional law.[12] The other school regards religious freedom as formally a juridical or constitutional concept, which has foundations in theology, ethics, political philosophy, and jurisprudence. The first school begins with a single insight—the exigence of the free human person for religious freedom. Only in the second instance does it raise what we have called the constitutional question. Consequently, within this structure of argument the political-juridical argument for religious freedom is secondary and subordinate to the theological-ethical argument. In contrast, the second school begins with a complex insight—the free human person under a government of limited powers. The constitutional question is raised at the outset; it is equally as primary as the theological-moral question. Consequently, the political-juridical argument for religious freedom is coordinate with the theological-moral argument. In other words, both religious freedom, as a legal institution, and constitutional government, as a form of polity, emerge with equal immediacy as exigencies of the personal consciousness in its inseparable correlation with the political consciousness.

The differences between the two ways of stating the Second View are not irreducible. In any event, three difficulties are alleged against the first structure of argument.

First, the notion of religious freedom as a human right seems to appear as a piece of theological-ethical theory, arrived at by a process of abstract argument, in a vacuum of historical, political, and juridical experience. The methodology here is vulnerable, in that it seems to divorce the issue of the rights of the human person from its necessary social-historical context. In contrast, in the second school of thought religious freedom presents itself concretely, as both a human and a civil right, embodied in a legal institution, which forms a harmonious part of a larger constitutional order of freedom. This order, in turn, appeals for its validity to traditional principles of politics, legal philosophy, and jurisprudence, as these principles are vitally adapted to the realities of historical experience today. In this fashion, religious freedom as a human right is validated in the concrete, by a convergence of theological, ethical, political, and jurisprudential argument. This methodology commends itself as more in accord with the historical consciousness that ought to preside over all argument about human rights.

Second, the first school of thought runs the risk of "overtheologiz-

ing" the notion of religious freedom as a human right and as a consequent norm for the juridical order of society. The result might be to
propose the legal institution of religious freedom as the "ideal instance" of constitutional law with regard to public care of religion.
This ideal would then stand in conflict with the constitutional ideal
proposed by the First View. In consequence, a false argument would
be set afoot. Traditional philosophies of politics, law, and jurisprudence do not recognize any such thing as an ideal instance of constitutional law. By reason of the very nature of law, the issue of the ideal
never arises. The function of law, as the Jurist said, is to be useful to
men. Necessity or usefulness for the common good—these are norms
of law. Legal institutions can never fall into the category of the ideal.
This risk of an idealization of religious freedom is avoided by the
second school of thought, in which the relativities of history receive
due attention.

Third, the first school of thought runs the risk of setting afoot a
futile argument about the rights of the erroneous conscience. This
argument may well be inextricable. In any event, it is irrelevant to the
constitutional question. The simple reason is that the public powers
are not competent to judge whether conscience be erroneous or not.
The good faith or bad faith, the truth or falsity of conscience are not
matters for adjudication by the civil magistrate, upon whom public
care of religion devolves. This unnecessary argument is avoided from
the outset by the second school of thought, given its complex starting
point, the personal and the political consciousness.

An orderly exposition of the Second View can best be made by
making the classic distinction between the question of definition or
concept (*quid sit*) and the question of judgment (*an sit, curita sit*).
Moreover, in the methodology here being followed, the conceptual
question is twofold: what is religious freedom, and what is its correlate, constitutional government.

The Conceptual Question

The question, what is religious freedom, is not to be answered a
priori or in the abstract. The fact is that religious freedom is an aspect
of contemporary historical experience. As a legal institution, it exists
in the world today in the juridical order of many states. It is not
simply a question of understanding what religious freedom meant in
the Third French Republic under the Law of Separation of December 9, 1905; nor of understanding what it meant under the Estatuto

Real of 1834 in the reign of Isabella II. For the theologian, the instant conceptual question is to understand what religious freedom means today, in so far as it presents itself as an exigence of the personal and political consciousness of contemporary men. From this point of view, the following description can be assembled.

First, religious freedom is obviously not the Pauline *elutheria,* the freedom wherewith Christ has made us free (Gal 5:1). This is a freedom of the theological order, an empowerment that man receives by grace. In contrast, religious freedom is an affair of the social and civil order; it is an immunity that attaches to the human person within society, and it has its guarantee in civil law. Obviously too, religious freedom has nothing to do with the statute of the member of the Church in the face of the authority of the Church, as if the Christian could somehow be free from obedience to the Church, which is absurd. Still less has it anything to do with the statute of the creature in the face of his Creator, as if man could somehow be free from the dominion of God, which is even more absurd.

Second, the adequate subject of religious freedom in its proper juridical sense as a human and civil right, guaranteed by constitutional law, is the body politic as such, the People Temporal—collectively, individually, and in their corporate associations. This follows from the very nature of constitutional law. The people are constituted a people *consensu iuris* (in the classic phrase), by their consent to a common law which touches all and is to be approved by all (in another classic phrase). Hence the people as such are the adequate subject of all the immunities and empowerments which the common law provides.

Third, the juridical notion of religious freedom is complex in its content. Within the concept it has become customary to make a general division between "freedom of conscience" and "the free exercise of religion" (this technical vocabulary goes back to the sixteenth century, and it is too late to change it now).

In its juridical sense, freedom of conscience is the human and civil right of the human person to immunity from all external coercion in his search for God, in the investigation of religious truth, in the acceptance or rejection of religious faith, in the living of his interior religious or nonreligious life. In a word, it is the freedom of personal religious decision. This freedom is essentially social. A man's religious decisions, however personal, are made in the social context of man's existence. In making them, a man has the right to be free from coercion by any human forces or powers within the social milieu. Society and all its institutions are obliged to respect this right and to refrain from coercion. By coercion, here and hereafter, is meant all manner of compulsion, constraint, and restraint, whether legal or extralegal. It includes such things as social discrimination, economic disadvantage, and civil disabilities imposed on grounds of religion. Today it importantly includes coercive forms of psychological pressure, such as massive propaganda, brainwashing techniques, etc.

The free exercise of religion is itself a complex concept. First, it is commonly understood to include a twofold immunity: a man may not be coercively constrained to act against his conscience, nor may a man be coercively restrained or impeded from acting according to his conscience. (The question of the limitation of this right will be dealt with later.) Furthermore, three aspects of the free exercise of religion are commonly distinguished.

Ecclesial or Corporate Religious Freedom

This is the right of religious communities within society to corporate internal autonomy. It is their immunity from the intervention of the public powers or of any social agency in the declaration of their own statute of corporate existence, in the determination of their own doctrine and polity, in their internal discipline and self-government, in the appointment of officials and in the definition of their functions, in the training and employment of ministers, in their communication with other communities and with recognized religious authorities in other lands. This freedom also includes the immunity of religious communities from employment by the public powers as *instrumentum regni*. In a word, this freedom is the corporate counterpart of personal freedom of conscience.

Here too is the appropriate place to locate the religious freedom of the family, the rights of parents with regard to the religious education of their children, and the rights of the religious school in relation both to churches and to families.

Freedom of Religious Association

This includes, first, the right to immunity from coercion in affiliating, or in ending affiliation, with organized religious bodies; and second, the same immunity in the formation of associations for religious and charitable purposes.

Freedom of Religious Expression

This is the right, both of individuals and of religious bodies, to immunity from coercion in what concerns the public worship of God, public religious observances and practice, the public proclamation of religious faith, and the public declaration of the implications of religion and morality for the temporal affairs of the community and for the action of the public powers.

The common legal and civic consciousness today recognizes that freedom of conscience and its corporate equivalent, ecclesial freedom, are freedoms *sui generis*. The first concerns man's personal relation with God, which is by definition an affair of personal freedom in a unique sense. The second concerns man's relation to God as lived in community, in accord with the social nature both of religion and of man himself. Hence the right to internal ecclesial autonomy is likewise *sui generis*. Finally, freedom of religious association, inasmuch as it includes immunity from coercion in the choice of one's religious affiliation, possesses the same quality of uniqueness as freedom of conscience and ecclesial freedom, to both of which it is directly related.

On the other hand, the personal or corporate free exercise of religion, as a human and civil right, is evidently cognate with other more general human and civil rights—with the freedom of corporate bodies and institutions within society, based on the principle of subsidiary function; with the general freedom of association for peaceful human purposes, based on the social nature of man; with the general freedom of speech and of the press, based on the nature of political society. The exercise of these more general human and civil rights, whether personal or corporate, takes place in the public domain, and therefore it becomes amenable to regulation by the public powers, in accord with recognized and reasonable criteria. The same is true of the free exercise of religion, inasmuch as it is a civil right cognate with other more general civil rights. The question is to know the criteria which must govern the action of the public powers in limiting the free exercise of religion. This is the crucial issue in the constitutional question of public care of religion. We shall turn to it later.

For the moment, it is to be noted that the free exercise of religion remains a freedom *sui generis*, even though it is cognate with other civil rights. The reason is that in all its forms it raises the issue of man's relation to God, as conceived by doctrine, affirmed by conscience, socially organized, and proclaimed in public utterance. In contrast, other civil rights have only to do with man's relation to other men or to society.[13]

The foregoing analysis presents the answer which the contemporary consciousness, personal and political, gives to the first conceptual question, what is religious freedom. (There may be a difficulty about the proper classification of the three freedoms listed, but it is of minor importance.) Moreover, the foregoing understanding of religious freedom is substantially in accord with the understanding contained in the pertinent declarations of the World Council of Churches.[14] The fact is of some importance for the ecumenical dialogue.

The second conceptual question, what is constitutional government, is likewise complex. For our purposes, which concern constitutional government as the political correlate of the juridical notion of religious freedom, it will be sufficient rapidly to recall four basic principles which combine to make government constitutional, scil., limited in its powers.

The first principle is the distinction between the sacred and the secular orders of human life. The whole of man's existence is not absorbed in his temporal and terrestrial existence. He also exists for a transcendent end. The power of government does not reach into this higher sacred order of human existence. It has no share in the *cura animarum* or in the *regimen animorum;*[15] it is not the judge or the representative of transcendent truth with regard to man's eternal destiny; it is not man's guide to heaven. Its powers are limited to the affairs of the temporal and terrestrial order of man's existence. And they are not to be used as instruments for the spiritual purposes of the Church, the maintenance of her unity or the furtherance of her mission.

The second principle is the distinction between society and state. Historically, this distinction developed out of the medieval distinction between the *ecclesia* (*christianitas*) and the *imperium*. The imperial power played a role within Christendom—a limited role; it was charged with limited functions within the Great Society inasmuch as the *ecclesia* was a socio-temporal reality. Today, in the developed constitutional tradition, the state is an agency that plays a role within society—a limited role. The purposes of the state are not coextensive with the purposes of society. The state is only one order within society—the order of public law and political administration. The public powers, which are invested with the power of the state, are charged with the performance of certain limited functions for the benefit of society—such functions as can and must be performed by the coercive discipline of law and political power. These functions are defined by constitutional law, in accord with the consent of the people. In general, "society" signifies an area of freedom, personal and corporate, whereas "state" signifies the area in which the public powers may legitimately apply their coercive powers. To deny the distinction is to espouse the notion of government as totalitarian.

The third principle is the distinction between the common good and public order. It follows from the distinction between society and state. The common good includes all the social goods, spiritual and moral as well as material, which man pursues here on earth in accord with the demands of his personal and social nature. The pursuit of the common good devolves upon society as a whole, on all its members and on all its institutions, in accord with the principles of subsidiarity, legal justice, and distributive justice. Public order, whose care devolves upon the state, is a narrower concept. It includes three goods which can and should be achieved by the power which is proper to the state—the power inherent in the coercive discipline of public law. The first is the public peace, which is the highest political good. The second is public morality, as determined by moral standards commonly accepted among the people. The third is justice, which secures for the people what is due to them. And the first thing that is due to the people, in justice, is their freedom, the due enjoyment of their personal and social rights—those empowerments and immunities to which the people, individually, collectively, and corporatively, lay rightful claim. John of Salisbury spoke for the tradition of constitutionalism when he said: "The prince [the constitutional monarch, in contrast to the tyrant] fights for the laws and for the freedom of the people."[16] The power of the state is therefore limited to the maintenance of public order in this threefold sense. (We omit here, as not relevant to our subject, the function of the state with regard to the good of "prosperity," the material welfare of the people.)

The foregoing three principles belong to the order of political truth. When government is based on them, it is based on the truth. The fourth principle is at once a substantive political truth and also the primary rule of political procedure. It is the principle and rule of "freedom under law." The freedom of the people is a political end, prescribed by the personal consciousness among the people. The freedom of the people is also the higher purpose of the juridical order, which is not an end in itself. Furthermore, freedom is the political method *per excellentiam*, prescribed by the political consciousness among the people. In so far as a political society must depend on force and fear to achieve its ends, it departs both from political truth and from the true method of politics. Finally, freedom under law is the basic rule of jurisprudence, which runs thus: "Let there be as much freedom, personal and social, as is possible; let there be only as much restraint and constraint, personal and social, as may be necessary for the public order." In all these ways, the principle and rule of freedom under law sets limits to the power of government.

The Question of Judgment

In reply to this question, the Second View affirms the validity of religious freedom, in the sense explained, as a legal institution, a juridical notion, a civil and human right. Correlatively, it affirms the validity of constitutional government, within whose structure religious freedom, in the sense explained, finds its necessary place. Two things about this compound affirmation must be noted.

First, the Second View undertakes to justify religious freedom, not to idealize it. It is not a question of affirming an ideal instance of constitutional law, after the manner of the First View. The Second View maintains that an ideal instance of constitutional law is a contradiction in terms. In the Second View, therefore, religious freedom is not thesis; neither is it hypothesis. The Second View abandons these categories of systematization. It does not accept, as its basic systematic notion, the abstract notion of the exclusive rights of truth, which creates the disjunction, thesis and hypothesis. Instead, it posits, as the basis for a systematic doctrine of religious freedom, the concrete exigencies of the personal and political consciousness of contemporary man—his demand for religious freedom, personal and corporate, under a limited government. This demand is approved by reason; it ought to be approved by the authority of the Church. Hence the Second View affirms the validity of an order of constitutional law in which public care of religion is limited to public care of religious freedom in the complex sense already described.[17]

In negative terms, the Second View rejects the opinion that public care of religion necessarily means, per se and in principle, a political and legal care for the exclusive rights of truth and a consequent care to exterminate religious error. In positive terms, it holds that public care of religion is provided in both necessary and sufficient measure when the order of constitutional law recognizes, guarantees, and protects the freedom of the Church, both as a religious community and as a spiritual authority, at the same time that it gives similar recognition, guarantee, and protection to the general religious freedom— personal, ecclesial, associational, and practical—of the whole body politic. Within the new perspectives of today, the Church does not demand, per se and in principle, a status of legal privilege for herself. The Church demands, in principle and in all situations, religious freedom for herself and religious freedom for all men.

Second, the Second View makes its affirmation of religious freedom in full awareness that this affirmation is at once new and traditional. It represents a growth in the understanding of the tradition, which corresponds to the growth of the personal and political consciousness of men today, to the enlargement of the pastoral solicitude of the Church today, and to the self-understanding of the Church in the world of today, as the missionary Church, in the diaspora, the sign of truth, justice, love, and freedom lifted among the nations. Therefore the Second View speaks to the ancient constitutional question of public care of religion in a new historical state of the question. The answer must be new, because the question is new. The answer must also be traditional, because it is the answer of the Church. However, only the elements of the answer are to be found in the tradition, not the answer itself in explicit and systematized form.

There are therefore two tasks: (1) to present the arguments for the affirmation of religious freedom; (2) to review the tradition, within the new perspectives of today, in order to show that the affirmation represents a valid growth in the understanding of the tradition. Since the concept of religious freedom is complex, the argument for affirming its validity must be made part by part. Moreover, since the juridical notion has a political correlate, the political and juridical arguments will be adduced co-ordinately with the theological and ethical arguments. All the arguments will be summarily indicated, not fully developed.

Freedom of Conscience

The theological argument[18] is the tradition with regard to the necessary freedom of the act of faith which runs unbrokenly from the text of the New Testament to the Code of Canon Law (can. 1351). This tenet of Catholic doctrine is held no less firmly by all who bear the name of Christian. In fact, even the atheist holds it. It is part of the human patrimony of truth, embedded in the common consciousness of mankind. The ethical argument is the immunity of conscience from coercion in its internal religious decisions. Even the Church, which has authority to oblige conscience, has no power to coerce it. The political argument is the common conviction that the personal internal forum is immune from invasion by any powers resident in society and state. No external force may coerce the conscience of man to any form of belief or unbelief. The juridical argument enforces the same conclusion; it is contrary to the nature of civil law to compel assent to any manner of religious truth or ideology. The distinction between the sacred and the secular is binding on law and government; and the personal conscience is a sacred forum. Moreover, for the argument here, it does not matter whether the conscience be true or erroneous. It is not within the competence of society or state to judge whether conscience be true or erroneous. And jurisprudence declares the distinction to be irrelevant for the purposes of civil law.

The Free Exercise of Religion

This, as we have seen, has three component elements.

Ecclesial or Corporate Freedom The theological principle here is "the freedom of the Church," the doctrine celebrated by Gregory VII and restored to its centrality by Leo XIII. The pregnant phrase expresses the whole supernatural reality of the Church, as the community of the faithful and as a spiritual authority *sui iuris*. It expresses her distinction from civil society in origin, constitution, and purposes; it likewise expresses her transcendence to all political forms. In the present connection, the phrase asserts the internal autonomy of the Church in the face of the public powers—her right to define her own statute of existence on the basis of the divine will, to determine her own form of organization and government and her own norms of ecclesial life and action, to elect or appoint her own rulers, to educate her own clergy, and to communicate across national boundaries. In all her internal affairs the Church is immune from interference by the public powers. This same claim to internal autonomy is likewise made by other Christian churches, which today reject all forms of Erastianism. Political and legal philosophy acknowledges this ecclesial freedom. The powers of the state are limited to the purposes and interests of the body politic; civil law can deal only with civil affairs. Internal ecclesiastical affairs are no more the concern of the public powers than the affairs of the internal forum of conscience.

Corporate religious freedom also includes the religious freedom of the family and the freedom of the religious school. The Napoleonic concept of *l'état enseignant* and the consequent doctrine of the monopoly of education by the state are contrary to the tradition of constitutionalism and its distinction between society and state.

Freedom of Religious Association First, freedom of affiliation with a religious community is inseparable from personal freedom of conscience. And it is supported by the same arguments. A man's religious affiliation or nonaffiliation is no more the concern of the state than his internal religious decision to believe or not to believe. In both respects he enjoys the same immunity from coercion. The political axiom *Cuius regio, eius et religio,* whereby religious freedom became the prerogative only of the prince, not of the people, is now recognized to be incompatible with both Christian and political principle. Second, freedom of association for religious or charitable purposes derives, on the one hand, from freedom of conscience, and on the other hand, from the general right of voluntary association. This latter right is based on the social nature of man, whose sociality is not exhausted by his citizenship in a body politic. It is likewise based on the principle of subsidiary function as a principle of social organization. The Jacobin revolutionary principle, which abolished all social institutions intermediate between the individual citizen and the state, was a violation of the constitutional tradition.

Freedom of Religious Expression This, as we have seen, is the free exercise of religion in the most formal sense. It is both a personal and also an ecclesial freedom, whose exercise is public, within society, chiefly in the forms of worship, witness, and the teaching of religious doctrine in itself and in its implications for society and state. The argument here is the indissolubility of the link, first, between the internal freedom of the Church and her external freedom to fulfil her apostolic office, and second, between personal freedom of conscience and social freedom of religious expression. The indissolubility of this link is established by a convergence of arguments.

First, the Church, as a community and as an authority, is immune from coercion by the public powers in the discharge of her religious mission, which looks both to the salvation of souls and also, by way of overflow (in the classic Augustinian doctrine), to the creation here on earth of conditions of peace and justice among men and nations. The nineteenth-century rationalist-individualist theory, which would confine the Church "to the sacristy" (in the famous phrase), is incompatible both with the theological doctrine of the freedom of the Church and also with the traditional principles of constitutionalism. These latter confer no power on the state to inhibit the free and public exercise of the Church's mission, much less to define what the mission of the Church is. The French Law of Separation of 1905, for instance, was a flagrant violation of sound political and legal principles. It was a sign, among others, of the final corruption of the constitutional tradition in Europe, which had begun with the rise of absolutism and its twin doctrines of the indivisibility of sovereignty and the complete identity of society and state.

Second, within the complex juridical notion of religious freedom, external freedom of religious expression is inseparably linked with internal freedom of conscience. Lest there be misunderstanding, the exact structure of the argument is to be noted.

The argument does not assert that freedom of religious expression is a logical deduction from freedom of conscience. This manner of argument would imply a hidden premise which is false, namely, a rationalist-individualist conception of man, as if the human person were somehow first an individual and only in the second instance a social being, in such wise that a logical inference could be drawn from individual rights to social rights. Second, the argument makes no appeal to any theory about the rights of the erroneous conscience, whatever may be the value of such a theory. The Second View does not base the juridical notion of freedom of religious expression on such a theory, for the reason already stated, namely, that the truth or error of conscience is not relevant to the constitutional question of public care of religion. Finally, the argument here does not raise the issue of tolerance. Tolerance is a concept of the moral order. It implies a moral judgment on error and the consequent adoption of a moral attitude, based on charity, toward the good faith of those who err. Our present discussion, however, has nothing to do with moral attitudes; it concerns freedom of religious expression as an integral part of the larger juridical notion of religious freedom.

Two lines of argument converge to establish the relation between freedom of conscience and freedom of religious expression. First, a true metaphysic of the human person affirms that human existence is essentially social-historical existence. It is not permitted to introduce a dichotomy into man, to separate his personal-interior existence and his social-historical existence. Hence it is not permitted to recognize freedom of conscience and to deny freedom of religious expression. Both freedoms are given in the same one instance; they are coequal and coordinate, inseparable, equally constitutive of the dignity and integrity of man. A dichotomy between them would rest on a false metaphysic of the human person. From the moral point of view, the dichotomy would be a sort of Kantianism, a separation of the personal-moral and the social-juridical orders. From the political point of view, it would introduce a schism in the body politic, an inequitable classification of citizenship on the basis of religious belief.

The political-legal argument reaches and enforces the same conclusion. In the constitutional tradition, no public official is empowered, by virtue of his public office, to inquire into the theological credentials of any religious body, and to decide whether it exists *iure divino*, whether its doctrine and polity are in conformity with divine revelation, whether it is divinely authorized to conduct public worship, give public witness to its faith, and teach those who are willing to listen. It is not within the competence of the public powers to consign churches to the sacristy, or to exterminate religious opinions from the public domain. The Erastian doctrine that the public powers are the arbiter of religious truth and the architect of church polity is not only contrary to Christian doctrine but also contrary to political principle. Civil law, which has no power to coerce the religious conscience, has no power to coerce the social expressions of the religious conscience. To bring force to bear, in restraint of freedom of religious expression, is to bring force to bear on conscience itself, in restraint of its freedom.

This argument, which is based on metaphysical, ethical, and political principle, is re-enforced by a historical argument. As a matter of historical fact, coercion or constraint of religious worship, witness, or teaching has inevitably resulted in the destruction or diminution of freedom of conscience, from the days of Diocletian to our own day of more subtle and damaging pressures on conscience.

The Limits of the Free Exercise of Religion

Here is the crucial question. From a practical point of view, society must have some way of protecting itself and its members against abuses committed in the name of the free exercise of religion. And it is the function of the state to provide this protection. From a more theoretical point of view, the free exercise of religion, like the exercise of other cognate civil rights, takes place in the public domain. It is therefore somehow amenable to regulation by the powers which preside over the public domain. Therefore we confront again the crucial issue in the constitutional question of public care of religion. What is the competence of the public powers with regard to passing judgment on forms of religious expression in society? Whence does this competence derive? What are the norms which should govern the action of the public powers in imposing limits, in particular cases, on freedom of religious expression?

The question has had a long history, as we shall indicate. And its history is not yet ended. The Second View maintains that the question admits no ideal solution, that it cannot be settled a priori, *more ge-*

ometrico, down to the last detail. It is, however, possible to state certain principles of solution.

First, the care of religion, in so far as it implies the care of souls, is not in any sense a function either of civil society or of the state. Second, the care of religion, in so far as religion is an integral element of the common good of society, devolves upon those institutions whose purposes are religious—the Church and the churches, and various voluntary associations for religious purposes. The school too, in its own way, can make a contribution to the religious element in the common good. Third, the care of religion, in so far as it is a duty incumbent on the state, is limited to a care for the religious freedom of the body politic.

It is not exact to say flatly that the state is incompetent in religious matters, as if this were some sort of transtemporal principle, derivative from some eternal law. The exact formula is that the state, under today's conditions of growth in the personal and political consciousness, is competent to do only one thing in respect of religion, that is, to recognize, guarantee, protect, and promote the religious freedom of the people. This is the full extent of the competence of the contemporary constitutional state. From another point of view, constitutional law has done all that is necessary and all that is permissible, when it vindicates to the people what is due to them in justice, namely, their religious freedom. That religious freedom is due to the people in justice is precisely what the personal and political consciousness of contemporary man affirms. Thus it is possible to define, in principle, the functions of constitutional law in our day of the written constitution.

First, freedom of conscience, freedom of religious association, and ecclesial freedom (in the sense of internal autonomy) are to be recognized as absolutely intangible by all legal or extralegal forces. (Obviously, when corporate religious bodies or voluntary associations perform civil acts, such as ownership of property, making contracts, etc., they are subject in these acts to the reasonable regulations of civil law.) Second, personal and corporate freedom of religious expression in worship, witness, teaching, and practice is likewise to be recognized, as inherently related to freedom of conscience and to internal ecclesial freedom. This freedom of religious expression, however, is not absolutely intangible, for the reasons given. Therefore the question arises, what is the criterion which makes limitation of this freedom legitimate.

First, the criterion cannot be theological, scil., the objective theological truth or error involved in some form of public worship, witness, teaching, observance, and practice. The public powers are not competent to make theological judgments. Nor may their action be instrumental in the public enforcement of theological judgments made by the Church. Second, the criterion cannot be ethical, scil., the rightness or wrongness of the personal or collective conscience that prompts particular forms of religious expression. The public powers are not competent to inquire into the norms whereby conscience is formed and to judge their truth or falsity. Third, the criterion is not social, scil., the common good of society. In the first place, the public powers are not the sole judge of what is or is not for the common good. This is a social judgment, to be made by the people, either through a constitutional consent (*consensu iuris*) or through the channels of public opinion. In the second place, in consequence of the distinction between society and state, not every element of the common good is instantly committed to the state to be protected and promoted. Under today's conditions of growth in the personal and political consciousness, this is particularly true of the spiritual goods of the human person, primary among which is religion. Therefore, fourth, the criterion can only be juridical, scil., the exigencies of public order in its threefold aspect—political, moral, and juridical.

This is the criterion which governs the action of law and the power of the state in regulating or limiting the exercise of the general civil rights of the citizenry, with which freedom of religious expression is cognate. Hence the public powers are authorized to intervene and to inhibit forms of religious expression (in public rites, teaching, observance, or behavior), only when such forms of public expression seriously violate either the public peace or commonly accepted standards of public morality, or the rights of other citizens.[19] The public powers are competent to make judgments only with regard to the essential exigencies of the public order and with regard to the necessity of legal or police intervention in order to protect the public order.

Evidently, this juridical criterion is quite general in its manner of statement. The practical problem lies in its application in given cases. And the casuistry is endless. What chiefly matters is that the application should never be arbitrary. In what concerns religious freedom, the requirement is fourfold: that the violation of the public order be really serious; that legal or police intervention be really necessary; that regard be had for the privileged character of religious freedom, which is not simply to be equated with other civil rights; that the rule of jurisprudence of the free society be strictly observed, scil., as much freedom as possible, as much coercion as necessary.

For the rest, the issues of casuistry, as they arise, will call for a continual dialogue between the public powers and the personal and political consciousness of the citizenry, with a view to finding equitable solutions. In the end, the value of civil law in matters of religion is severely limited. What chiefly matters is that the free exercise of religion should always be responsible—before God, before the rights of others, before the community and its legitimate sensibilities, before the state and its necessary empowerment to effect harmony of rights in cases of conflict. What further matters is the spirit of tolerance, as a moral attitude, among the citizenry, a spirit of reverence and respect for others, which issues in an abhorrence of coercion in religious matters.

One problem in casuistry requires special mention. It centers on the notion of proselytism. In ecumenical thought today a distinction is made between evangelism and proselytism, between responsible evangelical witness or teaching and an irresponsible caricature thereof. The former is regarded as a legitimate exercise of religious freedom; the latter is regarded as the corruption of religious freedom into license. It is, however, difficult to draw the line sharply between these two forms of religious expression (just as it is difficult to draw the line between the legitimate influence of the Church in the temporal order and illegitimate interference of the Church in political affairs). At that, certain characteristics of proselytism can be discerned: the self-assertive aggressiveness that always characterizes propaganda; purely destructive attacks on religious beliefs, institutions, and devotional practices; language or action offensive to the religious sensibilities of the community; the employment of means of seduction, by appeal, for example, to materialist motives; perhaps in particular, efforts to undermine religious faith in the young.

Proselytism is recognized by its style, which is infraevangelical, unsuited to the gospel of love, contrary to the manner of God's own approach to man, which is full of respect. Proselytism does not stand at the door and knock; it rushes rudely into the house. It is hardly possible to formulate a legal definition of proselytism; it is even less possible to cope with it by the rough instrument of law. Historically, for instance, the problem of the Anabaptists was never equitably solved. Proselytism creates a dilemma for the Christian and political conscience. At bottom, it represents an unchristian use of force in religious matters. Shall it therefore be met by force? The Christian would prefer to show forbearance.

The Tradition

The history of public care of religion as a theological, ethical, political, legal, and jurisprudential problem has been lengthy and involved. Only the most meager outline of it is possible here, sketched chiefly with a view to indicating the changes in the state of the question that have taken place.

The beginnings of the argument go back to the pagan Roman Empire, in which the citizen was permitted his freedom of conscience but compelled to offer sacrifice to the Emperor. The argument assumed Christian form with St. Augustine. He always held firmly to freedom of conscience, the necessary freedom of the Christian act of faith. Nevertheless, he consented to the use of the imperial power to take coercive care of the Donatists. No one today, however, argues the question in his terms, scil., the pragmatic religious value of "salutary constraint," imposed by the public power, as a means for assisting the return of the heretic to the Church. This is not the state of the question today, even in the First View.

The medieval argument was more complicated. The great Hildebrand [Pope Gregory VI, 1073–84] declared the state of the question in the pregnant phrase that is forever connected with his name, "libertas ecclesiae." Imperial care of religion (the phrase was not medieval but the thing itself was) was limited by the principle of the freedom of the Church, that is, the freedom of the Roman Pontiff and the freedom of the Christian people. The first imperial care of religion was to be a care for the freedom of the Church, a respect for the immunity of the Church from imperial intervention in her internal affairs and in her apostolic office. The essential question was obscured in the Later Middle Ages, when the Gregorian principle of the freedom of the Roman Pontiff was expanded by canonists to the dimensions of the papal prerogative as finally formulated in the doctrine of the two swords and in the system, for instance, of Giles of Rome. The Gregorian state of the question, however, has been restored to full actuality in our present day; it has also been amplified and adapted in the light of new historical circumstances. The question today, as we have seen, is whether public care of religion is not only limited *by* a necessary care for the freedom of the Church, but also limited *to* a care for the freedom of the Church together with a care for the religious freedom of all peoples and all men.

The other pertinent medieval argument dealt with the question, who is to enjoy the "freedom of the Christian people" (*libertas populi christiani*). The argument was made in terms of a distinction between Jews, pagans, and heretics, and it yielded different conclusions. Care of religion meant limited freedom for the Jew, tolerance for the pagan, intolerance for the heretic. The ultimate premise of the argument was concrete and historical, namely, the principle that in the Christian commonwealth the Christian faith was the basis of citizenship, the foundation of all *droit de cité*, the title to the freedom of the Christian people. From this principle the juridical axiom followed, "Extra ecclesiam nullum ius." The axiom did not state an abstract ethical theory (error has no rights); its sense was concrete, historical, constitutional. No one today argues the constitutional question in these terms. The medieval state of the question is archaistic. (A third great medieval argument, about the relation between conscience and the truth, need not detain us here.)

In the post-Reformation era the constitutional question became not only complicated but highly confused. The basic Hildebrandine principle was lost from view. The care of religion by the prince, Catholic or Protestant, came to be determined by the territorial principle (first enunciated by Luther) and by the view, common to Catholics and Protestants (as an afterimage of the medieval doctrine of the two swords), that the power of the prince is to further the cause of religious truth (either Catholic or Protestant, as the case might be) and to persecute error. Gradually, however, the principle of freedom of conscience came to be commonly accepted: "Nec est quisquam puniendus propter conscientiam." But the principle of the free exercise of religion was not accepted. The question therefore arose, what modes of coercion and constraint were or were not incompatible with freedom of conscience. What did the function of public care of religion empower the prince to do with regard to the suppression of public expressions of erroneous religious faith, Catholic or Protestant, as the case might be?

At first, the dichotomy between freedom of conscience and the free exercise of religion was maintained. Gradually, however, the conviction began to penetrate the common consciousness, Catholic and Protestant, that the link between the two freedoms was more intimate than had been supposed in that individualistic age. Men began to feel that freedom of conscience became meaningless when its public expressions were inhibited. They also began to see that, when outward religious conformity was enforced, freedom of conscience itself was damaged or lost.[20] This growing conviction did not support any concept of religious freedom, but it did enlarge the scope of tolerance.

The conviction seems to have been largely a matter of common sense. In this respect it resembled the gradual recognition of the principle of reciprocity, so called, the political adaptation of the golden rule to the controversy between Catholic and Protestant. At that, common sense is not a bad guide in matters of politics and law. And the fact was that the political and legal aspects of the constitutional question of public care of religion, rather than its theological and ethical aspects, were causing the trouble, in consequence of the unprecedented confusions of the time. Never was there a more disastrous blurring of the classic distinctions made by the constitutional tradition—between the sacred and the secular, between society and state, between the common good and public order. As for the classic rule of jurisprudence, it was stood on its head, to read, "As much coercion as possible; as much freedom as necessary."

In particular, three conceptions of political sovereignty prevailed, which forbade an equitable solution of the constitutional question as a political and juridical question. First, the nation or principality was conceived on the analogy of the family, and the prince was conceived to be *pater patriae*, whose paternal power extended to a care for the total welfare of his subject-children, including their religious welfare. Second, the prince was conceived to be *praecipuum membrum ecclesiae*, whose power was somehow ecclesial in that it extended to a care for the religious unity of his subjects, which was generally considered to be essential to their political unity. Third, the false principle of the indivisibility of sovereignty had become established, and in consequence the religious prerogative of the prince was considered to be simply an essential attribute of his political sovereignty. Care of religion was not the prince's duty; it was his inherent right. And the scope of its exercise was left to his own arbitrary determination. The constitutional question was hopelessly bogged down in this political and juridical morass.

The state of the constitutional question was altered by the ratification of the American Constitution (1789) and its Bill of Rights (1791). The question ceased to be asked in terms of political and legal support of the exclusive rights of truth, with consequent intolerance of error. The question was asked, and answered, in terms of religious freedom—personal, ecclesial, associational, practical. The premise of the answer was the restoration, in a new form adapted to new circumstances, of ancient and medieval constitutionalism. Religious freedom as a legal institution, which was formally created by the First Amendment, stood in harmonious relation with the political conception of government as limited in its powers, which was stated in the Constitution. Public care of religion by the state became legal care of "the free exercise of religion" in society. By establishing a form of government and an order of constitutional law that were both new and also a renewal of traditional principles, the people of the United States altered the state of the historic constitutional question of public care of religion. The alteration was effected by a consensual act of the people; this in itself was a singular historical event.

At the time, no *raison d'église* obliged the Church to reckon with the new development. There were less than 30,000 Catholics in the new Federal Republic. Moreover, the Church was immediately plunged into the lengthy and bitter conflict with the French Revolution. Prominently at issue in the conflict was a concept of religious freedom that was totally different—in its premises, meaning, import, and purport—from the concept embodied in the First Amendment to the American Constitution. No one, then or later, took official notice of the difference. The attention of the Church, from Pius VI to Pius IX, was totally engaged in the condemnation and containment of the new European revolutionary ideology.

The next constructive phase of the constitutional question was inaugurated by Leo XIII. He read the signs of the times, as every Pope does. Two were decisive for the orientation of his doctrinal instruction and pastoral solicitude. They were visible in the traditionally Catholic nations of Europe. The first was the phenomenon of the "illiterate masses" (*imperita multitudo*), which was basic to the doctrine of *Libertas*, as the same phenomenon in the form of the "people in misery" (*miserum vulgus*) was basic to the doctrine of *Rerum novarum*. The statistics of illiteracy at the time are well known. The masses were also religiously untutored, politically inert, economically powerless, deficient in both the personal and political consciousness. The second sign of the times was the spread of totalitarian democracy (as it is called today), both as a quasi-religious ideology and also as a political regime, whose purpose was to effect the apostasy of the masses, the destruction of traditional Catholic culture, the establishment of a new morality, a new politics, a new historical-social order.

The basic philosophical tenet was the theory of the "outlaw conscience" (*conscientia exlex*), the absolute autonomy of the individual human reason.[21] The political transcription of this basic tenet of rationalism was the theory of the juridical omnipotence and omnicompetence of the state.[22] Implicit in the theory was the unity and indivisibility of the national sovereignty. Consequent on the theory was the obliteration of all distinction between society and state. The whole of social life was subsumed under the power of the totalitarian state.

The state conceived its religious prerogative in terms of its own omnicompetence. Like the autonomous individual reason of which it was the political embodiment, it became the supreme arbiter of religious truth and church polity. Its theological judgment, based on the rationalist principle, was that all religions are equally true as equal expressions of the individual outlaw conscience. On the basis of this judgment, the state promulgated the *ius commune*, the statute of religious freedom. All religions are to be equal in their rights within society, because they are all equal in their inherent truth. The *ius commune* was an act of omnipotent sovereignty, which positively authorized the existence of all religions within the society-state on an equality of legal footing which corresponded to their equality in theological truth. Moreover, the indivisibility of sovereignty permitted no other public authority to exist in society. Hence the Church and the churches were assigned the equal statute of purely voluntary associations, whose right to existence and action derived solely from the juridically omnicompetent state. Thus the Church was incorporated into the juridical order of the state and made subject to the "unlimited and lawless government" (*principatus sine modo sine lege*), in Leo's phrase, of rationalist political theory. In technical law, the Church had no public existence. Public religion was a *contradictio in adiecto*. Officially, the state—that is, the whole of public life—was atheist. Religion was a purely private affair.

This was the conception of religious freedom as a legal institution, and the corresponding conception of the state as a totalitarian power, that confronted Leo XIII. Like his predecessors, but on the basis of a far more acute analysis of historical and political reality, he condemned both the legal institution and the ideology that inspired it. It was not possible then to make a distinction between the institution and the ideology. The institution was vicious in its principle; it was condemned in itself and in its principle.

What Leo XIII confronted was the post-Reformation confessional nation-state *à rebours*. It was the lineal progenitor of the people's democracy of contemporary Communist theory. The public philosophy was atheism; it alone had public rights. Religion had no public rights; it was to be exterminated from the public domain by the power of the state. This juridical order and this form of polity were characterized in rationalist theory as "ideal." To the rationalist mentality, which is untouched by historical consciousness, discourse about "ideals" in law and politics is congenial. The rationalist deals in theses, in ideological propositions that are not derived from historical reality but are to be imposed upon it.

Leo XIII was not untouched by the logic of contradiction; no controversialist ever is. Hence he constructed his own conception of the confessional state. He made his defense of the *status quo ante*. In common with the whole European Church in the nineteenth century, he formed part of what is called the Conservative Reaction. (Today, when we have come to understand better the price of revolution, this movement receives more kindly judgment at the hands of historians.) Five aspects of the Leonine theory of the confessional state require comment.

First, he adopted the theory of the ethical society-state (*Kulturstaat*), proper to the postmedieval era, whose roots are in Plato. It is difficult to find in Leo XIII the classic distinction between society and state (except in *Rerum novarum*). The distinction had been lost from view during the absolutist era. Correlatively, nowhere in some eighty-eight documents that deal with political or religio-political affairs did Leo XIII ever develop a complete philosophy of law and jurisprudence, in the style of St. Thomas' treatise *De lege*. He was a moralist, not a lawyer. As portrayed in his text, the society-state had the four classic characteristics. It was built upon a conception of the common good. The total care of the common good was committed to the *principes* (Leo's favorite word); hence the disappearance of the distinction between society and state. The social order was to be constructed from the top down, by the action of the rulers. The citizen appears simply as subject, whose single duty is obedience to rule. The cachet of the theory is in the maxim that Leo quotes: "Qualis rex, talis grex." This theory met the needs of the time, specified by the phenomenon of the illiterate, inert masses.

Second, against the lawless and unlimited government of rationalist theory, Leo XIII developed the true notion of political authority, derivative from God, subject in its uses to the divine law, directed in its action to the common good. In his own idiom and for his own day he wrote a *Speculum principis christiani*. In this great *aggiornamento* of the medieval *Fürstenspiegel*, the ruler appears as the servant of God, the architect of the social order, the supreme agent responsible for the Christian quality of social life.

Third, Leo XIII accepted the analogy, common in post-Reformation theory, between civil society and domestic society. The ruler appears in *Libertas* as pater-familias, who is "to govern in kindly fashion and with a sort of fatherly love."[23] In *Immortale Dei* the subjects appear as children, who are "to be obedient to their rulers and show them reverence and loyalty, with a certain species of that *pietas* which children show their parents."[24] In this paternal conception of rule, the power of the ruler extends to a care for the total welfare of his children-subjects, the illiterate masses. His *patria potestas* is to protect them, since they cannot protect themselves, in their possession of the patrimony of Christian truth that has been their heritage in the traditionally Catholic nation. To this end the ruler is to repress the "offenses of the unbridled mind," which are like "injuries violently wrought upon the weak."[25]

Fourth, Leo XIII accepted an adaptation of the territorial principle of the post-Reformation era, the principle that in one "city" (*civitas*) only one faith should be publicly professed.[26] This, incidentally, is not the dogma of faith that all men are called by God through Christ to unity of religious faith in the one Church. The dogma states a thesis whose realization is to be eschatological. Leo XIII "temporalized" the thesis; his premise was historical—the traditional unity of faith in the Catholic nations of Europe. In the one "city" the one public faith should obviously be the true faith, certainly in those "cities" which have been traditionally Catholic. The Catholic faith ought to enjoy the favor of the law and the protection of the ruler, as part of his paternal care for the common good and for the total welfare, including the religious welfare, of his subject-children. Certainly, little support of the Church could be expected from the illiterate masses; it was they who needed the protection of the ruler. With complete realism, Leo XIII saw that the reliance of the Church had to be on the heads of state.

Fifth, Leo XIII permitted the ruler to tolerate the legal institution of religious freedom, in given circumstances, for the sake of gaining or guarding some greater good or for the sake of avoiding some greater evil. Nothing more than tolerance could be granted to the institution in the only historical sense in which Leo XIII understood it—the sense given to the institution by Continental sectarian Liberalism. In this sense, the institution was not a legitimate exigence of the personal and political consciousness, which at the time did not exist in the illiterate masses. It was an outrageous act of totalitarian sovereignty, based on a rationalist ideology that was, in effect, the destruction of human dignity.

Thus Leo XIII brought to its final term of development the theory of the confessional state. Nothing has been added to it since his day, except perhaps its qualification as the "ideal instance" of constitutional law. Leo XIII never uses the word "ideal." What impresses the student of his doctrine is not any quality of idealism, but a strong sense of historical realism. As the whole tenor of his pontificate shows, Leo XIII was not lacking in the historical consciousness.

In another respect, Leo XIII laid the foundations for a new development of doctrine, a new growth in the understanding of the Christian tradition which Vatican Council I laid as an enduring imperative on the Church.[27] The Leonine development was accomplished, as all legitimate development must be accomplished, by a *ressourcement*, a creative return to the sources of the tradition, a review of traditional doctrine within a new perspective created by history. The Leonine perspective was created by the fact that totalitarian democracy, in the style of Continental sectarian Liberalism, had renewed in a more vicious form than ever the confusion of the sacred and the secular orders of human life which had been the disastrous legacy of the post-Reformation era. Hence Leo XIII recalls the tradition of the dyarchy, which is the first principle in Christian constitutionalism.

Moreover, he states the doctrine in a developed form of understanding that was unprecedented, a new thing in papal utterances. The dyarchy is not left in its medieval form of understanding—the doctrine of the two powers in the one Great Society, the *ecclesia*. In Leo's understanding, there are two societies, two orders of law, and two powers. There are seven major texts, which cover his whole pontificate. They are found in *Arcanum* (1880), *Nobilissima Gallorum gens* (1884), *Immortale Dei* (1885), *Officio sanctissimo* (1887), *Sapientiae christianae* (1890), *Praeclara gratulationis* (1894), and *Pervenuti* (1902).

This reiterated statement of the dyarchy, in developed form, is the very heart of Leo's doctrine on constitutionalism. He emphasized in a new way the transcendence of the Church, both as a spiritual authority and as the People of God, who are ruled by His law, revealed in Christ. He also emphasized in a new way the relative autonomy of the secular order of human life—the proper autonomy of the People Temporal, who are ruled by a civil law, under a government whose powers are limited by a higher order of law not of its own making.

Leo XIII did not pursue the consequences of this latter emphasis. It would have been inappropriate, as well as impossible, to pursue them in a day when the People Temporal were so largely illiterate, culturally and religiously, and consequently incapable of asserting their rightful autonomy, their empowerment to judge, direct, and correct the processes of political rule and legal action. In any case, Leo XIII opened the door to the developments which became visible in Pius XII and John XXIII. For the rest, his statement of the autonomy of the socio-political order dissipated the afterimage of medieval *christianitas,* which for so long had hung more or less heavily over the Catholic nation-states. Thereafter *christianitas* on the medieval model would be archaism. His statement also condemned the confusion of religion and politics that still existed, not least in the Catholic nation-states.[28] Finally, the statement of Leo prepared the way for a change in the state of the question of public care of religion. Implicit in the statement was a declaration of the freedom of the people, once the people had fulfilled the conditions of freedom, which are the growth of the personal and political consciousness. And implicit in the freedom of the people is religious freedom as a juridical institution correlative with constitutional government as a form of polity.

In another respect, the Leonine statement of the dyarchy at once effected a development of doctrine and opened the door to further developments. It restored to its proper centrality the Gregorian doctrine of the freedom of the Church, which had been lost from view in the post-Reformation era.

It would not be consonant with the evidence of the texts to say that Leo XIII's master idea, in what concerns public care of religion, was the notion of the exclusive rights of truth and the rightlessness of error. He does indeed blast the silly rationalist notion that all ideas are equally true and rightful, because they are all equally free as expressions of the autonomous reason. He insists on the tautology that truth is truth and error is error. He also insists that the criterion of truth and error is not freedom. He further insists that truth and error, right and wrong do not enter the juridical order on an equal title, which was the other rationalist sophism. What is true or right may receive positive juridical authorization; what is false or evil can receive only juridical tolerance. This, incidentally, is the only concrete juridical sense that can possibly attach to the otherwise unhelpful abstraction, that error has no rights. No sensible man would quarrel with this concrete sense. The point at the moment, however, is that this Leonine doctrine, directed against the basic tenet of rationalism, was not his central notion in the question of public care of religion.

His central notion was "the freedom of the Church." One could begin to appreciate its centrality by counting the number of times that the phrase, or an equivalent of it, appears in his writings (some eighty-one times in sixty documents). A more positive proof emerges from a study of the texts on the dyarchy. It is clear that the doctrine of the freedom of the Church is equally as central as the doctrine of the dyarchy itself. Freedom is the first property of the Church; and freedom is the first claim that the Church makes in the face of society and state: "This freedom is so much the property of the Church, as a perfect and divine work, that those who act against this freedom like-wise act against God and against their duty."[29]

The decisive proof results from an understanding of the structure of Leo XIII's controversy with Continental sectarian Liberalism, and with its notion of religious freedom as a legal institution that stood in correlation with a form of polity in which government was "lawless and unlimited." The essential vice of the system was not that the lib-eralist state granted equal rights to truth and error and dethroned the Church from its historic status of legal privilege. The essential vice was that this political and juridical system destroyed the freedom of the Church. Thus it attacked the very nature of the Church as a community, an order of law, and a spiritual authority. The basic line of battle was drawn by Proposition 39 of the *Syllabus:* "The state, inasmuch as it is the origin and source of all rights, possesses a power of jurisdiction that knows no limits."

The texts are numerous and formal. They begin with *Inscrutabili* (1878) and its indictment of what Leo later will call the "new regal-ism," which "makes [the Church] subservient to the sovereignty of political rulers."[30] So too *Immortale Dei:* "In this kind of political or-der, presently so much admired, it is a deliberate policy either to drive the Church wholly out of public existence or to hold her bound and fettered to the regime."[31] So again *Libertas* and its protest against the politicization of the Church: "Accordingly, they falsify the nature of this divine society; they diminish and inhibit her authority, her teaching, all her action. At the same time, they aggrandize the power of civil government to the point of subjecting the Church of God to its sovereign rule, as if the Church were just another voluntary associ-ation of citizens."[32] *Et alibi pluries.*

Proposition 39 of the *Syllabus* was the destruction of the freedom of the Church. Hence Leo XIII was led to restore this doctrine to the rightful centrality that it had in the tradition. He was Hildebrand redivivus. The essential care of religion that devolves upon the public powers is not a care for the exclusive rights of truth and for the exter-mination of error. It is a care for the freedom of the Church. The phrase is pregnant with multiple meanings, which Leo XIII specified. It is not, however, pregnant with the concept of "establishment," the status of legal privilege for the Church, with the consequent status of legal disadvantage for other religious bodies. Leo XIII never draws this conclusion from his central doctrine. He does indeed draw the conclusion, but from other premises of a more historically conditioned kind.

Proposition 39 of the *Syllabus* was also the destruction of the essential dignity of man, which resides in his freedom. Leo XIII did not greatly attend to this aspect of the matter; it did not lie within his historical problematic. However, by his central emphasis on the freedom of the Church he at once reinstated the Gregorian state of the question of public care of religion and thus also opened the way to a widening of the question, thus stated, to include the issue of the freedom of the human person—the issue of religious freedom as a legal institution within a system of constitutional government, correspondent to the legitimate exigencies of the personal and political consciousness.

Pius XII, in his turn, read the signs of the times and discerned two that gave direction to his doctrine and pastoral solicitude. The first was totalitarian tyranny on the Communist model. Now the threat was not simply to the freedom of the Church in the traditionally Catholic nations of Europe; the new threat was to the freedom of the people everywhere. An ideology and a system of rule were abroad, "which in the end rejected and denied the rights, the dignity, and the freedom of the human person."[33] The problematic that had been only implicit in Leo XIII's time had now become terribly explicit. The full implications of Proposition 39 of the *Syllabus* had been realized. The second sign of the times was the rise of the personal and political consciousness: "The people have been awakened, as it were, from a lengthy dormancy. In the face of the state and in the face of their rulers they have assumed a new attitude—questioning, critical, distrustful. Taught by bitter experience, they oppose with increasing vehemence the monopolistic reaches of a power that is dictatorial, uncontrollable, and intangible. And they demand a system of government that will be more in accord with the dignity and freedom of the citizenry."[34]

The mission of the Church, therefore, must include the vindication of the "dignity of man."[35] The goal of Pius XII's pontificate, which he recommended as a goal for all men of good will, was "to give back to the human person the dignity with which he was en-

dowed by God from the beginning."[36] To this end, a new social order
had to be constructed, based on this principle: "The purpose of all
social life remains always the same, always sacred and obligatory,
namely, the development of the personal values of man as the image
of God."[37] Proceeding from these premises, Pius XII made his first
contribution to the development of doctrine in the matter of religious freedom. It consisted in his development of the concept of government as constitutional, that is, limited in its powers.

He abandons Leo XIII's ethical concept of the society-state, with
its four classic characteristics. Instead he adopts the juridical concept
of the state (*Rechtsstaat*), whose genesis owed more to Christian inspiration. The state is only one order of action within society; it is an
agent of society for certain limited purposes. Society and state are not
built on a generic conception of the common good, but on a concrete
conception of the human person in the present historical moment,
marked by the rise of the personal and political consciousness. The
basic notion in Pius XII's sociopolitical philosophy is thus stated:
"Man as such is by no means to be considered the object of social life
or a sort of inert element in it; on the contrary, he is the subject,
the foundation, and the end of social life."[38] The Pope revalidates the
fundamental insight that gave rise to the constitutional tradition, the
"free man, bound by duties, endowed with inviolable rights, who is
the origin and end of human society."[39]

Therefore the primary function of government is a function with
regard to the juridical order: "To protect the inviolable rights that
are proper to man, and to have a care that everyone may more readily
discharge his duties—this is the chief function of the public power."[40]

Therefore too the function of government with regard to the common good is limited:

> Does not this principle [the juridical function of govern-
> ment] bring out the genuine meaning of the common
> good which the state is called upon to promote? From this
> principle it follows that the care of the common good does
> not imply such an extensive power over the members of
> the community that, in virtue of it, public authority would
> be allowed to restrict the expansion of individual human
> action, as described above, or to make direct decisions
> with regard to the beginning or the termination (except in
> the case of legitimate punishment) of human life, or to
> determine on its own cognizance what should be the

movement of human life—physical, spiritual, religious, and moral—in such a way as to come in conflict with the personal rights and duties of man.[41]

Here, as elsewhere, Pius XII shows his awareness of the distinction between society and state, between the total common good of society and the elements of the common good that are committed to the power of the state. In his own idiom, the distinction is between the wider order of "social life" and the narrower "juridical order" of society.

Therefore, again, Pius XII abandons completely the Leonine notion of government as paternal. The relationship between ruler and ruled is only political, not familial. The citizen is not a child. Still less is he the mere passive object of rule. He is to be an active participant in the fashioning of his own social and political destiny. In Pius XII's conception, society and state are to be built, as it were, from the bottom upon the human person and by the human person, or, in more formally political terms, on the consent of the people and by the consent of the people.

Therefore, finally, the nineteenth-century polarity of the illiterate masses and the *principes* is dissolved. Now the terms of political life are the "true people" (as distinct from the "masses") and the public powers as representative of the people, united with the people in the traditional political effort to achieve an "ideal of freedom and equality."[42]

Thus Pius XII effected a badly needed *aggiornamento* of the official political philosophy of the Church. He relinquished the elements in Leo XIII's philosophy that had become archaistic. He brought the Church abreast of the developments in the constitutional tradition that were demanded by the new personal and political consciousness.

Constitutional government, limited in its powers, dedicated to the defense of the rights of man and to the promotion of the freedom of the people, is the political correlate of religious freedom as a juridical notion, a civil and human right, personal and corporate. By advancing the doctrine of constitutional government, Pius XII moved along the way opened by Leo XIII, towards a change in the state of the question of public care of religion. Moreover, if his doctrine is considered as a whole, in itself and in its tendency, within the perspectives set by his insight into the signs of the times, it may be maintained that he helped to constitute the ancient question in a new state. He took a step beyond Pius XI, who was himself in the Gregorian tradition that had been renewed by Leo XIII.

Pius XI rejected the formula "freedom of conscience," because to his ears it still bore connotations of the rationalist theory of the outlaw conscience. However, against the invasions of the Fascist totalitarian state, he undertook "to fight the good fight for freedom of consciences."[43] In the context, it would seem, he was continuing the ancient fight for the freedom of the Church, as the community of the faithful. This is what he defended against the operations of Proposition 39 of the *Syllabus* which were still visible in Mexico: "As a society of men, the Church has absolute need of a just freedom of action for the enjoyment and growth of her own life; and the faithful have the right to live in civil society according to the dictates of reason and conscience."[44]

Pius XI was in the Gregorian tradition, as Pius XII would also be: "Wherefore We . . . address all civil rulers and all those who are in any way in charge of public affairs, and We solemnly assert that the Church must always enjoy a due freedom, in order to pursue her work of education, to impart truth to the mind, to impress justice on the spirit, and to refresh both mind and spirit with the divine love of Jesus Christ."[45] Again, when Pius XII comes to declare the essential exigencies of the Church within society and state, to be recognized in a concordat, the declaration takes this form: "Concordats ought therefore to assure to the Church a stable condition in law and in fact in the state with which they are concluded, and guarantee the Church a full independence in the fulfilment of her divine mission."[46] The formulation is in terms of the Gregorian-Leonine principle. Nothing is said about a situation of legal privilege as per se a claim of the Church. Nor is it implied that only such a legal situation of establishment as the one religion of the state would assure the requisite legal and social stability and freedom of the Church.

Already under Pius XI the problematic of religious freedom began to widen in consequence of the crudities of Nazi totalitarianism and its sweeping attack on all manner of religion, Catholic and Protestant. Therefore Pius XI took the forward step of assuming the patronage of the freedom of all religious men: "The man of religious faith has an inalienable right to profess his faith and to practice it in appropriate ways. Laws which repress or render difficult the profession and practice of religious faith are in contradiction with a law of nature."[47] This statement rests on a general premise, "that man as a person possesses God-given rights which must remain immune from any invasion on the part of society that would deny, annul, or diminish them."[48] The problematic is developing. The freedom of the Church as the community of the faithful is not the sole object of the Church's concern. The freedom of the human person in his belief in God is also to be recognized and protected against unjust encroachments by legal or social forces.

Pius XII accepts this wider problematic of religious freedom. Among the "fundamental rights of the person," which are to be recognized and promoted by the juridical order of society, he includes the "right to private and public worship of God, including also religious action of a charitable kind."[49] Religious freedom as a juridical notion, which required legal recognition and protection, has emerged into clarity. In this juridical sense, religious freedom is an integral element in the freedom of the people, which sets limits to the powers of the state. It is a freedom in which all the people equally share, without discrimination on the score of particular forms of religious belief. Moreover, religious freedom in its universal juridical sense is a proper object of legal and social care. In the constitutional order of a society in which the personal and political consciousness is active, public care of religion becomes a care for the religious freedom of the Church and likewise a care for the religious freedom, personal and corporate, of the human person as such.

This affirmation, presently being made by the Second View, is fully in consonance with the doctrine of Pius XII. It is also fully in continuity with the growth in the understanding of the tradition which had been inaugurated by Leo XIII's renewal of the Gelasian and Gregorian tradition. The two essential junctures of ideas have, in effect, been made. The first juncture is between the two correlative exigencies of the personal and political consciousness—between constitutional government (Pius XII's juridical state), limited in its powers by a necessary respect for human rights, and the concept of religious freedom as a general civil and human right, claiming the protection of the juridical order of society. The second juncture is between the ancient historic defense of the freedom of the Church and the newly necessary defense of the freedom of the people. In the present moment of history the freedom of the people of God is inseparably linked with the freedom of the peoples of the world. What the pastoral solicitude of the Church today demands, the developed doctrine of the Church likewise proclaims and authorizes, namely, a universal care for religious freedom in society and state.

One document of Pius XII requires special attention, the Allocution to the Congress of Italian Catholic Jurists of December 6, 1953.[50] The document must be regarded as one of the Pope's occa-

sional deliberate efforts to fall short of complete lucidity. The purpose was achieved in the present case; this document has been cited
by both parties to the present controversy, between the First and the
Second Views. In any event, the major doctrinal intention of the document is plain, namely, to clarify an issue of jurisprudence with regard to the legal institution of intolerance. The Pope's chosen
universe of discourse is the problem of public care of religion as a
problem within the international juridical community presently being
formed. Four propositions immediately emerge with adequate clarity..

First, throughout the document the Pope uses the vocabulary of
"tolerance." However, what he is talking about is the immunity of the
citizen from coercion by the public powers in his religious profession
and practice. This is precisely the definition of religious freedom in
its contemporary juridical sense, explained above. Hence it cannot be
maintained that the Pope refuses to acknowledge the concept of religious freedom. The issue of vocabulary is trivial.

Second, the Pope asserts that the theological question of objective
religious truth, and the moral question of the obligations of conscience toward what is objectively true and good, are not proper matters for political discussion or legal decision by individual states or by
the international community. What confronts the statesman or jurist
is the constitutional question, namely, the question of the use of legal
coercion in religious matters.[51]

Third, the Pope implies that a statute of religious freedom
throughout the international community, subject to restriction only
by the exigencies of the public order, would be acceptable to the
Church and ought to be acceptable to the Catholic state. By religious
freedom he means the immunity of the citizens from coercion in "the
free exercise of their own ethical and religious beliefs and practices,
in so far as these do not violate the penal laws of the state in which
they dwell."[52]

Fourth, in continuity with all his predecessors the Pope rejects the
solution of the constitutional question, and the consequent concept
of religious freedom, that were proper to nineteenth-century European sectarian Liberalism. The solution, as we have seen, took the
form of an act of sovereignty whereby the state positively authorized
the existence and action of religious error and positively conferred
upon truth and error an equal social and legal mandate. This solution
and this concept of religious freedom, as we have likewise seen, are
outlawed not only by Catholic theological and ethical principle but
also by the political and legal principles of constitutionalism.

With these simple matters out of the way, the Pope approaches with considerable delicacy his central issue, which is the jurisprudence of legal intolerance. His question is, what is the ultimate and most general rule of jurisprudence in terms of which the legal institution of intolerance is to be justified. The question is theoretical, a *quaestio iuris.*

Is it to be maintained that this ultimate rule of legal action is a duty, per se incumbent on the state, to repress religious and moral deviations? If this is so, it follows that such deviations are to be repressed by the state, whenever and as far as it is possible for the state to repress them. The state would fail in its duty, if it were to tolerate religious and moral errors in circumstances in which their repression was possible. Such tolerance would be immoral.

The Pope denies both the premise and the conclusion of this system of jurisprudence. He denies the premise: "The duty to repress moral and religious deviations cannot therefore be considered an ultimate norm of action."[53] He denies the conclusion: "Hence the affirmation: Religious and moral aberration ought always to be suppressed, as far as repression is possible, because tolerance of them is in itself immoral, cannot be sustained in its unconditioned absoluteness."[54] The Pope goes on to assert that this rule of jurisprudence is unknown to the civil and Christian tradition: "Neither the common conviction of men, nor the Christian conscience, nor the sources of revelation, nor the practice of the Church recognize such a rule."[55] Thus the Pope fulfils his severely limited doctrinal intention, which was to make clear that the possibility of legal repression of error and evil is not the juridical criterion that justifies such repression.

However, he carries his doctrine one step farther. The rule of jurisprudence, that religious and moral deviations are always to be repressed by the state, as far as it is possible to repress them, rested for its validity on an ethical premise: "That which does not correspond with truth and the norm of morality has, objectively, no right either to existence or to dissemination or to action." Here the Pope grants the premise, but still refuses the conclusion. The premise merely asserts the obvious truth that there is an objective distinction between truth and error, good and evil. It also implies that truth and goodness may receive the positive sanction of law, whereas error and evil may not. This too is obvious. The question is whether one may draw from this ethical axiom the jurisprudential conclusion that, whenever the state can repress error and evil, it ought to repress them, as a matter of primary and ultimate duty. The Pope refuses this conclusion. The

only legitimate conclusion is that the state may never positively authorize the existence, dissemination, or activity of what is erroneous
or evil.

For the rest, the Pope does not deny that the state has a duty to
repress religious and moral deviations, or, in broader terms, that care
of religion is a duty incumbent on the state. No one who is ac-
quainted with the civil and Christian tradition of constitutionalism
will deny this. The question has always been, and still is, what is the
rule of jurisprudence which justifies the use of coercive measures in
fulfilment of this duty. In more general terms, what is the competence of the state with regard to religious matters? In reply to this
positive question, the Pope is content to make three general affirmations.

First, he affirms that the question cannot be decided in the abstract; there is need always to consider the relativities of history, the
diversity of factual circumstances. A priori discourse about duties
that per se devolve upon the state is illegitimate and useless, for one
simple reason: "It can happen that in determinate circumstances He
[God] does not confer upon man any mandate, does not impose any
duty, does not even give any right to inhibit or repress that which is
erroneous and false."[56] The *quaestio iuris*, about the duties and rights
of the state with regard to the care of religion, is inherently a historical question, not an abstract one. Every answer to it is necessarily
hypothesis, an answer conditioned by circumstances, an application
of principles within a determined situation of fact. The disjunction
between thesis and hypothesis is factitious.

Second, he affirms that, from the standpoint of the Church, the
supreme juridical principle that governs the constitutional question
is the common good of the Church, both as a national and as an
international entity.[57] From his other writings it is clear that the good
of the Church consists essentially in two things: first, exact observance of the requirements of the Gelasian-Leonine dyarchy, and second, full assurance of the freedom of the Church. From the
standpoint of the statesman, the juridical criterion for the limitation
of religious freedom is the exigencies of public order, as specified in
penal laws.[58]

Third, he affirms the competence of the "jurist" with regard to the
quaestio facti, scil., what are the determinate exigencies of the good of
the Church and of the public order of society in given circumstances.
Since the *quaestio facti* is a question of constitutional law, whose justice must rest on the consent of the governed, the "jurist" here is the

citizen, or better, the people as a whole. Finally, the Pope affirms the necessity of a dialogue between the Church and the jurist-people in the process of reaching a mutually satisfactory solution of the *quaestio facti.*

It is not difficult to assemble from the vast corpus of Pius XII all the principles that were marshaled above in support of the Second View: (1) the theological principles—the dyarchy, the freedom of the Church, the freedom of the act of faith; (2) the ethical principles—religious freedom as the rightful exigence of the contemporary personal and political consciousness; the insight that the free man, bound by duties and endowed with rights, is the origin and end of the social order; (3) the political principles—that the public power is not the judge of religious truth or of the secrets of conscience; that the primary function of the public powers is the vindication of the juridical order of human and civil rights, i.e., the fostering of the freedom of the people; (4) the juridical principle—that the criterion for public restriction of religious freedom is some necessary requirement of public order; (5) the jurisprudential principle—that necessity, not possibility, is the further criterion for coercive inhibition of the free exercise of religion.

The principles are all stated, but they are not systematized, and the conclusion to which they point is not explicitly drawn. At that, the basic concept for a work of systematization has gradually emerged, beginning with Leo XIII—the freedom of the Church as allied, in the present historical juncture, with the freedom of the peoples of the world. At the same time, the ancient problem of public care of religion has emerged in a new state of the question.

The state of the question proper to the post-Reformation and Liberalist eras is now archaistic—the care of religion as the care for the exclusive rights of truth and for the consequent extermination of error. There has been a return to the traditional theological state of the question, in its Gregorian form, public care of the freedom of the Church. Today, however, in the new circumstances of our own age, marked by the growth of the personal and political consciousness, the Gregorian state of the question, reinstated by Leo XIII and confirmed by Pius XII in the line of Pius XI, has necessarily been widened. The public care of religion which the doctrine and pastoral solicitude of the Church today require and authorize is care of religious freedom, in the complex sense approved by the common consciousness of men.

This affirmation, to which the Second View concludes after a review of the tradition within the new perspectives created by the historical moment, is strongly confirmed by John XXIII. He situated himself firmly within the Gregorian tradition. Moreover, with the historical consciousness that was his mark, he broadened even more explicitly than Pius XII the problematic of religious freedom in the light of the signs of the times.

Speaking of the work of the coming Council, he voices the primary traditional concern and claim of the Church, to which the Council would turn its attention:

> What is to be said about the relations between the Church and civil society? We live in the face of a new political world. One of the fundamental rights which the Church cannot renounce is the right to religious freedom, which is not simply freedom of worship. The Church claims and teaches this freedom, and for the sake of it she continues to suffer grievous penalties in many countries. The Church cannot renounce this freedom, because it is of the essence of the service which she is bound to render. This service is not offered as a collective or a complement of that which other institutions are required to render or have appropriated to themselves. It is an essential and irreplaceable element of the design of Providence, in order to set men on the way of truth. Truth and freedom are the foundation stones upon which the edifice of human civilization is erected.[59]

The centrality of the Gregorian principle is evident. Moreover, the last sentence adumbrates in advance the theme of *Pacem in terris*.[60] This Encyclical consciously builds on Pius XII and his conception of the juridical state as the servant of the free man and the free society. What concerns us here is that John XXIII makes more explicit the new state of the question of public care of religion and speaks more directly to the question in its new state. It will be sufficient briefly to indicate the two major contributions that he made to the development of Catholic doctrine on the subject.

First, the juncture between the two correlative exigencies of the personal and political consciousness is made explicit in the very structure of the Encyclical. The concept of constitutional government is more sharply described than in Pius XII,[61] even to the point of recommending, for the first time in papal documents, the written constitution.[62] And this concept of the limited functions of the state is brought into explicit correlation with a fully developed description of the juridical order of human and civil rights and freedoms, whose protection and promotion is the primary function of the state.[63] This is Pius XII, of course, but speaking with a new accent—more affirmative, more confident that the present moment in history is the term of a progress that has been real, even though not unambiguous.

Moreover, within the juridical order of human and civil rights the right to religious freedom is firmly situated: "This too is to be numbered among the rights of man, that he should be able to worship God in accord with the norm approved by his conscience (*ad rectam conscientiae suae normam*) and to profess his religion privately and publicly."[64] The declaration is not ambiguous, as some have maintained. It is to be understood within the context of the Encyclical and its concept of the juridical state. Obviously, the Pope cannot espouse the theory of *conscientia exlex;* he asserts that conscience must be formed by higher norms (*conscientia recta*). But for the purposes of civil life, in order that conscience may possess the status of personal and civil right in the face of the public power, it is not required that the norms whereby conscience is formed should be true (*conscientia vera*).

The reason is the traditional one, namely, that the public power is not the judge of the truth or falsity of the norms whereby conscience is formed. The public power is obliged to respect the personal or corporate conscience as such, for the precise reason that conscience is subject to higher norms which the public power cannot legislate. To deny this is to affirm Proposition 39 of the *Syllabus, quod absit.* John XXIII touches the tradition in speaking of the mode of action of public authority: "Since all men are equal in their natural dignity, no one has the power to force another to act out of inner conviction. Only God can do this, since He alone scrutinizes and judges the secret counsels of the heart."[65]

Religious freedom is a human freedom in the external forum of society. It is a personal and corporate right to immunity from coercion by any legal or extralegal forces in the profession and practice of religion. This right is grounded in the law of nature—or, if you will, in the exigence of reason—which manifests itself, in today's social historical context, both through the mature personal consciousness which claims the right and also through the mature political consciousness which forbids the state to deny or diminish it. It is evident that John XXIII's whole discussion of human and civil rights, including religious freedom, is commanded by the historical consciousness, by a sense of man's "spiritual aspirations" (*animorum appetitiones*)[66] which reason approves as expressions of man's growing consciousness of his own self-in-society—or, if you will, his own personal and social nature.

This is not liberalist individualism or any sort of false personalism. The Pope's thought reveals the methodology of natural-law thinking at its best, both in ethics and in politics. For him, religious freedom is not some sort of Platonic idea that has had no history but has been always somehow "there," to be seen by anyone who cared to look at it. Religious freedom is the reasonable affirmation of the contemporary human consciousness. In the Second View, which is that of John XXIII, it is also an affirmation of the Christian consciousness that has become aware of the essential link between a government of limited powers (Pius XII's "system of government that will be more in accord with the dignity and freedom of the citizenry") and religious freedom as a juridical notion, a civil and human right, to be protected by a legal institution written into constitutional law (John XXIII's more consequent affirmation).

John XXIII's second contribution to the new statement of the question of religious freedom, and to its solution, lay in his tetradic diagram of the spiritual forces that sustain human society: Leo XIII had endlessly reiterated the triad—truth, justice, and love; so too had Pius XII. John was the first Pope to add the fourth spiritual force, freedom, as coequally essential. The new tetrad was new; it was also fully traditional. The tradition has always asserted that the human quality of society depends on the freedom of the Church. In a new and more profound understanding of the tradition, John XXIII affirms that the human quality of society depends on the freedom of the people. The second juncture of ideas has been formally effected. In our age (the reiterated phrase in which John XXIII reveals his historical consciousness) the two freedoms are inseparable—in fact, they are identical. They stand or fall together. The doctrine of the Church affirms both of them. Her pastoral solicitude extends to each of them.

The spiritual order of society is founded on truth—on the true view of man, his dignity, his duties and rights, his freedoms and obligations. This order must be brought into being under fidelity to the precepts of justice, whose vindication is the primary function of the public power as well as the primary civic duty of the citizenry. This order needs to be animated and perfected by love; for civic unity cannot be achieved by justice and law alone; love is the ultimate force that sustains all human living together. Finally, this order is to achieve increasingly more human conditions of social equality, without any impairment of freedom.[67]

Truth, justice, and love assure the stability of society; but freedom is the dynamism of social progress toward fuller humanity in communal living.[68] The freedom of the people ranks as a political end, along with justice; it is a demand of justice itself. Freedom is also *the* political method whereby the people achieve their highest good, which is their own unity as a people: "A society of men achieves its unity (*coalescit*) by freedom, that is, by methods that are in keeping with the dignity of its citizens, who are by nature men of reason and who therefore assume responsibility for their own actions."[69] Society is bound to the usages or methods of freedom (*libertatis consuetudinem teneat*)[70] in its constant effort to base itself on truth, govern itself with justice, and permeate itself with civic friendship.

When the freedom of the people is unjustly limited, the social order itself, which is an order of freedom, is overthrown. The problem of political refugees, for instance,

> shows that the rulers of certain nations impose excessive limits on the just measure of freedom within which each citizen should be allowed to live a life worthy of a man. In fact, in this kind of state the very right to freedom is at times called into question or wholly denied. When this happens, the right order of civil society is overthrown in its very foundations; for by its nature the public power looks to the protection of the good of the community, and its chief duty is to recognize the legitimate reaches of freedom and to keep inviolable the rights of freedom.[71]

By this accent on the freedom of the people, new in modern papal utterances, the historical problematic of the nineteenth century is completely dissolved. The rightful autonomy of the people, implicit in Leo XIII's statement of the dyarchy, has received explicit affirmation. In particular, the state of the question of religious freedom has been altered. The distinction which Leo XIII could not make has now been made—between religious freedom as a juridical notion and a legal institution in a free society, and the false ideology and the resultant form of political regime that once inspired the notion and the institution.[72] Now religious freedom has a new basis in each of the four dynamic spiritual forces that sustain society. It is an exigence of truth, justice, and civic friendship or love. In particular, it is acknowledged to be an integral element of the freedom of the people.

It is not now a question of tolerating the institution as a lesser evil. John XXIII is not enlarging the hypothesis of the First View. He is quietly bidding good-bye to both thesis and hypothesis in the sense of the *opinio recepta*. He represents the present term of a new development of the genuine tradition, *eodem sensu, eademque sententia*. Now the Church positively affirms the validity of the institution of religious freedom. It embodies a civil and human right, personal and corporate. It also embodies a recognition by government of one of the "legitimate reaches of freedom" (*honestos libertatis fines*)[73] which are immune from restriction by any legal or extralegal force.

The Second View must undertake the task of showing that it is the traditional view—the view that represents a valid and necessary growth in the understanding of the tradition. The foregoing pages illustrate a way in which this task may be accomplished. There may be other ways.

The Issues

Only the beginnings of an effort to initiate an intramural dialogue on religious freedom were made in the second and third conciliar sessions, in the speeches in the conciliar aula, and later in the comments, criticisms, and emendations sent in to the Secretariat for the Promotion of Christian Unity. A few illustrations will show the difficulties involved in setting afoot a dialogue between the First and Second Views.

For instance, the First View asks the question, whether a man has a natural right to found a false religion. It answers the question in the negative and considers that it has dealt a mortal blow to the Second View. The trouble is that the Second View does not answer the question in the affirmative. In fact, it is not inclined to answer the question at all. In the manner of its asking, under complete abstraction from all historical reality, the question is irrelevant to the issue of religious freedom in its contemporary sense, which supposes a given historical-social-political context. Hence no dialogue ensues.

Again, the First View asks the question, whether error is to be granted the same rights as truth. It returns a negative answer and again considers that it has cut the ground from under the Second View. The trouble is that the Second View does not stand on this simplistic ground. It clarifies the question to mean, whether the public power may positively authorize the existence and dissemination of religious error on the same footing on which it positively authorizes the existence and dissemination of religious truth. To the question thus framed, it answers again that the question itself is irrelevant to the contemporary issue of religious freedom. What is more, the fallacy of the previous question, so called, appears. Is it in any sense the function of government to authorize the public existence of any religion, true or false? The answer is no.

To give an example, the first Amendment to the Constitution of the United States does not positively authorize the existence and propaganda of Jehovah's Witnesses. Fortunately too, it does not positively authorize the existence and propaganda of the Catholic Church—fortunately, for such an authorization by the public power would be a monstrous violation of the freedom of the Church, which neither requires nor tolerates any such authorization. The legal institution of religious freedom in its contemporary sense is not a positive authorization of either truth or error. This institution does not "grant" rights, that is, confer empowerments in the matter of religion. Its essential premise is that the public power is not competent to confer such empowerments. In other words, its essential premise is a denial of Proposition 39 of the *Syllabus*. The First Amendment is simply the recognition of an immunity. By it the people of the United States, inspired by the personal and political consciousness, declared that the free exercise of religion is to be immune from coercive restriction by the power of the state or by any power within society. The First Amendment is a limitation imposed by a free people on the public power; it is not an assertion of the power of the state over the people, in the sense of Continental sectarian Liberalism. The issue, whether error is to be granted the same rights as truth, simply does not arise. Hence again there is no dialogue.

For a final example, the First View asks the question, whether the erroneous conscience has rights in the public forum. To illustrate its negative answer, it gives an example. If I mistakenly think you owe me five dollars, does my erroneous conscience give me the right to demand five dollars from you? Again the Second View declares the question to be irrelevant. As for the example, it limps badly. First, it is taken from the sphere of juridical relations between men, as ruled by commutative justice, whereas religious freedom has to do with man's relation to God. What is more important, it confuses the notion of right as an empowerment and as an immunity. My erroneous conscience gives me no empowerment to demand from you money that you do not owe me. On the other hand, my religious conscience, whether erroneous or not, confers on me an immunity from coercion, whether legal or extralegal, within limits defined by the exigencies of public order. Once again the dialogue dies.

In its turn, the Second View asks some questions. It inquires, for instance, whether the whole issue of human rights is to be argued on the premise that the nature of man is a historical nature, whose rational exigencies manifest themselves progressively, under the impact of the continually changing social-political context, and in response to the growing personal and political consciousness. In the face of this question, the First View tends either to look blank or to launch the accusation that this is juridical modernism. In either case, there is no dialogue.

Again, in what concerns the interpretation of papal documents, the Second View asks the question (apropos of Leo XIII, for instance), is not the historical context of the document and its doctrinal, polemic, and pastoral intentions to be considered, with the result that particular assertions may be regarded as historically conditioned and therefore subject to further development in what concerns their manner of conception and statement, under altered circumstances and with the rise of new questions which affect the perspectives in which the truth is viewed. The First View replies that Leo XIII did indeed speak within a historical context but that his utterances transcended the context. What matters is what he said—the propositions that he put down on paper. These propositions stand forever, true, certain, and immutable. The Second View may urge the issue, citing the assertion of Pius XII that Boniface VIII's doctrine of the sun and the moon and the two swords was historically conditioned and is today archaistic.[74] In reply, the First View changes the subject, raising the issue of the doctrinal authority of papal encyclicals, with appropriate citations. This issue is important, but it would seem to suppose an answer to the prior question. Again the parties fail to join in dialogue.

At that, this abortive dialogue seems to indicate where the real issue lies. The First and Second View do not confront each other as affirmation confronts negation. Their differences are at a deeper level—indeed, at a level so deep that it would be difficult to go deeper. They represent the contemporary clash between classicism and historical consciousness.[75] This, however, is a subject too vast to be dealt with here. It will be sufficient further to illustrate the clash by considering the objections that each view brings against the other.

The First View accuses the Second View of doctrinal errors—Liberalism and neo-Liberalism, subjectivism, relativism, indifferentism, Rousseauism, laicism, social and juridical modernism, humanistic personalism, existentialism, situation ethics, false irenicism. These, at any rate, were the accusations brought against the incomplete and badly organized version of the Second View that appeared in the original text of Chapter Five of the Decree on Ecumenism. And there were others. It is not difficult to show that all these accusations rest upon misunderstanding. The Second View needs only to explain itself in order to show that these accusations of doctrinal error are groundless.

The Second View is less harsh in its judgment. It does not accuse the First View of doctrinal errors but of theological fallacies.

The first is archaism—the fallacy which maintains that the Church's understanding and manner of statement of her faith, and of doctrines of reason related to faith, can and ought to be halted in some particular stage, under denial of the possibility and legitimacy of further development. The first historic victim of the fallacy was Eusebius of Caesarea during the controversy over the new Nicene formula of the Church's faith in the Son and Word. The scriptural formulas, said he and the men around him, are definitive; it is not permitted to go beyond them. These men refused to consider the fact that Arius had asked a new question which could not be answered, without ambiguity, in scriptural formulas. Similarly, the First View would fix the doctrine of the Church on religious freedom in its nineteenth-century stage of conception and statement. It refuses to consider the fact that the state of the question has been altered and the nineteenth-century answer is inadequate.

Archaism therefore consists in the rejection, on principle, of the more recent synthesis or systematization, and in the effort to adhere or return to the synthesis or systematization of a prior age, which is judged to be simple and more pure. History has known scriptural archaism, in the original Protestant Reform; patristic archaism, in Baius and Jansenius; medieval archaism, in various kinds of Scholastic Talmudism. The First View is a sort of political archaism. As Boniface VIII's doctrine was archaistic after the emergence of the autonomous nation-state in the fifteenth century, so the First View is archaistic after the growth of the personal and political consciousness in the twentieth century. With this growth in man's understanding of himself as a free man in a free society, Catholic doctrine on religious freedom must likewise grow in its understanding of itself. Pius XII glimpsed the fact and reckoned with it in his doctrine on the juridical state, but he drew back, with his wonted caution, from its full implications. With all the penetration of his extraordinary insight, John XXIII saw the fact with full clarity. His insight found expression in his articulated concept of the freedom of the people as a political end and as *the* political method, and in the correlative concept of religious freedom as a necessary and integral element of the freedom of the people. What remains is simply the fuller conceptualization of religious freedom as a social faculty, a human and civil right (personal and corporate), and a legal institution. What remains too is the recognition that the First View is archaistic, because all sense of the personal and political consciousness is absent from it.

The second fallacy is misplaced abstractness; it is the contrary of the famous fallacy of misplaced concreteness, identified by Alfred North Whitehead. It is the fallacy which creates ideologies. On the face of it, the First View presents itself as a theory conceived with full abstractness, the pure creation of the *conscience survolante*. In fact, however, it is an apologetic for the nation-state of largely Catholic population which began to take shape, under more or less absolutist rule, in the post-Tridentine era, and then felt the religious and political shock of the French Revolution. This special kind of political-legal realization began to receive recognition in a series of concordats in the nineteenth century, of which the first was with the Kingdom of the Two Sicilies in 1818. It is, of course, entirely legitimate to construct an argument in favor of this historical realization. However, the argument would have to be constructed as Leo XIII constructed it—with concreteness and complete historical realism. The fallacy enters when the Leonine argument is transposed into an abstract thesis which proposes an abstract "ideal instance" of constitutional law, per se and in principle obligatory on an abstraction called "the state."

Here is the neuralgic point in the intramural dialogue on religious freedom. It may be that the intramural segment of the dialogue is not the most important today, given the world-wide character of the problem. Nevertheless, the intramural dialogue has priority. Until it is conducted to a conclusion and a Catholic consensus takes form, the ecumenical dialogue is impossible and so too is the dialogue between Christian and non-Christian. It has often been pointed out that, if the First View stands as the immutable formulation of Catholic doctrine, the whole dialogue *ad extra* is cut off before it can begin.

It has been alleged that the Second View implies a rejection of the classic concept of the Catholic confessional state. In its generality, this allegation is false. Obviously, the "Catholic state" is not a univocal concept. This fact will be admitted by anyone who is familiar with political history and with the variant content of concordats. The concept covers a whole variety of historical realizations, from the *ancien régime* with its Gallicanized Union of Throne and Altar, to contemporary Portugal, in which (according to some jurists) there is a mode of separation of Church and state. Some of these historical realizations were sufficiently ambiguous. In any case, the whole issue needs to be argued with great care and with due regard for all the necessary distinctions.

The primarily necessary distinction is between society (or the people) and state (or the order of public law and administration). From this distinction another follows immediately—between the public profession of religion by society (*officium religionis publicae*) and the care of religion by the public power (*cura religionis*). Neither of these distinctions is clearly and consistently maintained by Leo XIII. The result has been confusion.

Obviously, the Second View acknowledges, in common with all Catholics, that an obligation to profess faith in God and to worship Him is incumbent on society—on the people as such as well as on individuals. This obligation, however, is not fulfilled by legislative or executive action by the public power. It is fulfilled by occasional public acts of worship, usually on so-called state-occasions—the opening of the legislature and judiciary, national days of thanksgiving and prayer, etc. These acts of worship are organized by the Church, not by the government, which has no competence in liturgical matters. Moreover, they are to be voluntary acts, since they are formally acts of religion. No legal coercion may be exerted to force either individuals or the people to participate in these occasional acts of public faith and worship. All this is clear. The Second View rejects the sectarian Liberalist notion of religion as a purely private affair, against which Leo XIII insisted on the *officium religionis publicae*.

Obviously too, the Second View embraces the notion of the Christian society, described in the modern papal encyclicals. The development of the Christian social conscience is a duty of the highest order; so too is the effort to permeate all the institutions of society—economic, social, cultural, political—with the Christian spirit of truth, justice, love, and freedom; so too is the growth of the personal and political consciousness among the people. The helpless and inert *imperita multitudo* of Leo XIII's time was not a Christian people in the high sense of the word. The Second View rejects the notion of the laicized society in the sense of Continental sectarian Liberalism. In particular, it regards the religious unity of a particular society or people as a good of the highest order—an order so high that it transcends the political order. The emergence of such Catholic societies in history has been a work of divine providence. All this too is clear.

The difficulty begins when the distinct constitutional issue of public care of religion arises, scil., the function of the public power with regard to religion in society and among the people. Only here does the issue of the "Catholic state" become controversial. The word "state" has its proper political-legal meaning.

The First View maintains that there is an abstract idea of the order of constitutional law and an abstract idea of the religious competence of the public power that are distinctively Catholic. In this abstract conception, the Catholic order of constitutional law contains two related institutions, first, the establishment of Catholicism by law as the single religion of the state (i.e., the one religion recognized by law, which alone has the civil right of public existence, guaranteed and supported by the power of the state), and second, intolerance of other religions (i.e., the empowerment of the state to use its legal and police powers to exterminate from public existence all other religions). These twin institutions are of the legal order, matters of constitutional law. Establishment is not a profession of faith in the Catholic religion as the one true religion. It is a legal enactment whose force is felt in the public life of the people. Establishment is not an act of religion; it is a political act of the public power. (Historically, it normally found its place in the *constitution octroyée*, so called, which was not in any sense an act of the people but only of the ruler.) Moreover, the First View maintains that these two legal institutions, establishment and intolerance, constitute the "ideal instance" of constitutional law. Where they exist, the ideal "Catholic state" exists.

The ideal may be seen, for instance, in the Concordat with the Republic of Ecuador (September 26, 1862): "The Catholic Apostolic Roman religion shall continue to be the single (*unica*) religion of the Republic of Ecuador, and it shall always be maintained in the possession of all the rights and prerogatives which it ought to enjoy according to the law of God and the dispositions of canon law. In consequence, no other dissident cult and no society condemned by the Church can ever be permitted in Ecuador."

Under allowance for some differences of opinion among its proponents, the general position of the Second View may be stated in the following five propositions.

1) It is not at all incompatible with the doctrine and practice of religious freedom that there should exist an "orderly relationship" (*ordinata colligatio,* in Leo XIII's phrase) between the public power, as the representative of the people, and the Church, which has authority over the community of the faithful. Moreover, this relationship may be made formally legal by a concordat. (A concordat would normally require ratification by the elected legislature in democratically organized countries, since it is an international convention.) Furthermore, out of respect for historical custom, where it exists, it is not inappropriate or contrary to religious freedom that the people of a particular nation should declare their common allegiance to the Catholic Church in some sort of constitutional document. This declaration has no juridical consequences; it has the value of a statement of fact.

2) In order that the relationship between the two powers may be orderly, the requirements of religious freedom must be observed. There are three.

First, there must be no infringement or inhibition of the freedom of the Church as a spiritual authority and as the community of the faithful. Her internal autonomy must remain inviolable and the free exercise of her apostolic mission must be unimpeded. Moreover, the Church is not to be used by the public power as *instrumentum regni.*

Second, there must be no confusion of the religious and the political—in particular, no confusion of religious unity and political unity. As the public power has no share whatever in the care of souls (*cura animarum*) or in the control of thought (*regimen animorum*),[76] so it has no share whatever in the care of the unity of the Church. The unity of the Church is a unity of the supernatural order; the care of it is committed exclusively to the Church, and this care is to be exercised by the purely spiritual means proper to the Church. Even when the theological concept of the unity of the Church is historicized or temporalized to mean the religious unity of a given people or ethnic group in the one true faith, this fact must imply no politicization of the national Church, no empowerment of the state to protect or promote the unity of the national Church by coercive means. This would be an infringement of the freedom of the Church and a violation of the exigencies of the Leonine dyarchy; it would also be action *ultra vires* by the public power. Moreover, the functions of the state with regard to the national culture, whatever they may be, imply no empowerment of the state with regard to the religious welfare of the people, which remains exclusively the duty and prerogative of the Church.

Third, the relationship between the Church and the national government must be so conceived and so executed that it will not result in the alienation of the people from the Church that was a prominent feature of the post-Tridentine and sectarian Liberalist eras. This would be, in effect, an infringement of the freedom of the Church as the community of the faithful.

3) The legal institution of religious intolerance is incompatible with religious freedom as an integral element of the freedom of the people. The right to religious freedom, personal and corporate (in the sense described above), is a rational exigence of the contemporary personal and political consciousness. The correlative exigence is that the public power should have no empowerment to use coercive measures to exterminate any religion from public existence and public action. Exceptions to this rule occur only in particular cases in which there is a clear violation of public order which makes demonstrably necessary the intervention of the public power. Moreover, this third proposition is not hypothesis in the sense of the First View. It is a matter of principle—theological, ethical, political, legal, jurisprudential. It is not a lamentably necessary concession to *force majeure,* made in order to avoid a greater evil or to gain a greater good. Religious freedom is a personal and political good. It is part of that "establishment of freedom" which, as Acton said and John XXIII in effect repeated, represents the "highest phase of civil society."

4) There is no such thing as an "ideal instance" of Catholic constitutional law. In particular, the twin institutions of establishment and intolerance do not represent the ideal instance. There may be some constitutional orders which are good and others which are bad. The first Catholic criterion of judgment was proposed by Pius XII, scil., whether the constitutional order assures the Church a stable condition in law and in fact and full freedom in the fulfilment of her spiritual ministry. (The centrality of the freedom of the Church is visible in the new series of concordats initiated by the Concordat with Latvia in 1922.) The second Catholic criterion was proposed by John XXIII, scil., whether the constitutional order assures the citizen the secure possession of all his personal rights and protects and promotes in full measure the legitimate freedom of the people.

These two criteria are to base the Catholic judgment, no matter what may be the religious composition of the citizenry—whether conditions of religious unity or conditions of religious pluralism obtain. There are not two standards of judgment on constitutional law—one for a Catholic people and another for a religiously pluralist people. The fact of the religious unity of a particular people in the Catholic faith does not make obligatory the legal institution of establishment, as if a situation of legal privilege were a Catholic constitutional ideal. Still less does the religious unity of the people authorize the legal institution of intolerance, as if this institution were also a Catholic ideal.

In its turn, the Second View does not propose the legal institution of religious freedom as a constitutional ideal, an abstract thesis, conceived a priori, under abstraction from historical-social reality. It discards the categories of the ideal and the tolerable, thesis and hypothesis, as invalid categories of discussion about constitutional law. It goes back to the Jurist for its category of legal discussion. It is the function of law, said the Jurist, to be useful to the people.[77] Its categories of political discussion are taken from John XXIII—truth, justice, love, and the freedom of the people. As for its category of socio-religious discourse, it would prefer to abandon the ambiguous neologism, "the Catholic state," and go back to the noble medieval phrase, "the Christian people." This is not archaism; it is *ressourcement*.

5) As the historical consciousness precludes the fallacy of archaism, so also it precludes the fallacy of anachronism. This latter fallacy consists in the assumption that a later and more perfect stage in the Church's understanding of her own tradition existed before it actually did exist. The Second View presents itself as the contemporary stage in the growing understanding of the tradition. This understanding cannot be found in ecclesiastical documents of the nineteenth century. It was brought into being by a dynamism proper to the twentieth century, the growth of the personal and political consciousness, first noted by Pius XII and more fully developed in its implications by John XXIII. The notion of religious freedom as a human and civil right, personal and corporate, is not to be sought in theologians of the nineteenth century, since it is explicitly the product of a twentieth-century insight into the exigencies of the personal and political consciousness. The link between religious freedom and limited constitutional government, and the link between the freedom of the Church and the freedom of the people—these were not nineteenth-century theological-political insights. They became available only within twentieth-century perspectives, created by the "signs of the times." The two links were not forged by abstract deductive logic but by history, by the historical advance of totalitarian government, and by the corresponding new appreciation of man's dignity in society.

The complex notion of the freedom of the Church had indeed always stated the question of public care of religion in its proper terms. It had also stated the essential claim that the Church perennially must make on the public power, as the essential requirement of positive divine law that is binding on the public power. But the tradition had been obscured by history—by the decadence of the constitutional tradition after the *quattrocento* broke with the medieval conception of kingship, and by the involvement of the Church in the politics and power struggles of the late medieval period, the post-Tridentine era, and the century of sectarian Liberalism in Europe and Latin America.

However, what history had obscured, history would also clarify. History brought forth Proposition 39 of the *Syllabus*, brutally incarnate in a form of totalitarian society-state. In the light of history Leo XIII began to restate the question of public care of religion in its traditional terms and to restore the traditional centrality of the Church's ancient claim to freedom in the face of the public power. Pius XI and Pius XII began to work out the wider political implications of the tradition in the altered historical context of the twentieth century. By his fuller acceptance of the context, John XXIII renounced all archaism, confirmed the new problematic of religious freedom, and began to apply to its resolution the newly developed tradition, theological and political.

If archaism is now forbidden, so too is anachronism. The rejection of this latter fallacy controls the thought of the Second View in two major ways.

First, it controls the interpretation of papal documents of the past. The Second View does not search in the Leonine corpus or elsewhere for "proof-texts," that is, for explicit earlier statements that will textually confirm the explicitness of its own later statements. Nor does it undertake to "read back" into the text of Leo XIII its own synthesis of the tradition. Both of these procedures would be vitiated by anachronism, a violation of good theological method. As Leo XIII cannot be "read back" into Innocent III, so John XXIII cannot be "read back" into Leo XIII.

The theological task is to trace the stages in the growth of the tradition as it makes its way through history. Scylla is archaism; Charybdis is anachronism. The task is to discern the elements of the tradition that are embedded in some historically conditioned synthesis that, as a synthesis, has become archaistic. The further task is to discern the "growing end" of the tradition; it is normally indicated by the new question that is taking shape under the impact of the historical movement of events and ideas. There remains the problem of synthesis—of a synthesis that will be at once new and also traditional. This is the problem faced by the Second View.

Second, the rejection of anachronism controls judgments on past situations. To return to the example already given, the Second View does not denounce the Church or the Republic of Ecuador for a violation of religious freedom in 1862. More in general, in judging all past or present realizations of the Catholic state, so called, the historical situation needs to be considered. The historical institutions of establishment and intolerance are to be judged *in situ*. They might well be judged valid *in situ*. The function of law, said the Jurist, is to be useful to the people. These institutions might well have been useful to the people, in the condition of the personal and political consciousness of the people at the time. This was Leo XIII's judgment. It would be anachronistic to question it.

But if anachronism is outlawed, so too is archaism. Leo XIII himself rejected the latter fallacy by his restatement of the Gelasian dyarchy and the Gregorian principle of the freedom of the Church. It may still be useful for the people of God in certain countries of the world today that the Church should be recognized by law as the common religion of the people. This would validate the judgment that the institution of establishment should be retained in those countries. But nothing can validate the judgment that this legal status is "ideal" because it enlists the coercive power of government in the service of the exclusive rights of truth. To say the least, this view is archaistic. The argument would have to be that establishment is useful for assuring the freedom of the Church, as the people of God and as a spiritual authority. This argument might be more difficult to make. In any case, its conclusion would not be that establishment is a constitutional ideal.

On the other hand, no argument can be made today that would validate the legal institution of religious intolerance, much less canonize it as a Catholic ideal. The institution cannot even be tolerated today as a harmless archaism. Nor is it even permissible to raise the question, whether legal intolerance may be useful to the people—either to the people of God or to the civil people. The fact is that legal intolerance stands condemned today by the common consciousness of the peoples of the world. The condemnation is binding today on all civilized states, which, as such, must reject Proposition 39 of the *Syllabus*. Today, religious freedom, as a human and civil right, personal and corporate, which requires the protection of a legal institution, has emerged as an exigence of the personal and political reason. As such, it claims the sanction of Catholic doctrine.

These five propositions suggest the position taken by most proponents of the Second View with regard to the complicated issue of the "Catholic state," so called.

It is now possible to state the issues in the controversy.

There seems to be a basic agreement between the First and Second Views that the controversy concerns the constitutional question, the technical question of public care of religion by the public power, as a theological, ethical, political, legal, and jurisprudential question. This antecedent agreement is important, since it rules out irrelevant issues. There are, for instance, a number of issues involved in the larger problem which is customarily called, not without some ambiguity, the problem of "Church and state." These issues, however, are not directly relevant to the narrower question of public care of religion. From the foregoing exposition it is clear that the First and Second Views, in dealing with this question, make affirmations that are either contradictory or contrary.

1) The state of the question.—Has it altered in consequence of a Christian discernment of the new signs of the times (the Second View), or is it somehow by definition immutable (the First View)? This question seems to have first priority. Unless there can be agreement on the state of the question, further argument is futile. Moreover, all other disagreements seem to stem from this one.

2) The basic concept in the question of public care of religion.—Is it the exclusive rights of truth (the First View) or the freedom of the Church as inseparably allied, in the present moment of history, with the freedom of the civil people (the Second View)?

3) Public care of religion in constitutional law.—Is there an ideal instance of Catholic constitutional law (the First View), or not (the Second View)? Furthermore, is there a dual standard for Catholic judgment on orders of constitutional law, one for the Catholic nation and another for religiously pluralist peoples (the First View), or is there a single standard equally applicable to any order of constitutional law (the Second View)? More in particular, are the categories of judgment the ideal and the tolerable, thesis and hypothesis, principle and expediency (the First View), or are they the good and the bad, the just and the unjust, the more or less just and the more or less unjust (the Second View)?

4) The competence of the public power with regard to religion.—

Does it extend to public care of religious truth (the First View), or is it limited to public care of religious freedom (the Second View)? Does it extend to a care for the Church herself—her doctrine, authority, prestige (the First View), or is it limited to a care for the freedom of the Church (the Second View)? Does it extend to a care for the religious unity of the people as related to their political unity (the First View), or is it limited to a care for the religious freedom of the people as related to their civil and political freedom (the Second View)?

5) The rule of jurisprudence for repressive intervention by the public power in what concerns the free exercise of religion.—Is it the possibility of such intervention without serious disturbance of the public order (the First View), or is it the necessity of such intervention in order to maintain the essential exigencies of the public order (the Second View)?

6) The state and positive divine law.—What is the essential requirement of positive divine law which is binding on the state, that is, on the public power? Is the public power bound to establish the Church by law as the one religion of the public power, that is, the one religion whose right to public existence and action is recognized by the public power (the First View), or is this a misunderstanding of the whole matter (the Second View)? On the other hand, is the essential requirement of positive divine law satisfied when the public power recognizes and protects the freedom of the Church (the Second View), or is this a minimalizing of the whole matter (the First View)?

7) The legal institution of intolerance.—Is it the logical and juridical consequence of the legal establishment of the Church, in such wise that the two institutions stand or fall together (the First View), or is it possible to maintain an organic and even a legal relationship between the Church and the public power, and at the same time abolish the legal institution of intolerance and introduce the legal institution of religious freedom (the Second View)? More in particular, what are the correct premises on which to validate the legal institution of establishment? And are there today any premises on which the legal institution of intolerance can be validated?

8) The issue of the Catholic confessional state.—This issue runs through all the foregoing seven issues, in such wise that the answer to it will depend on the answers to them. Here one general question may be added. To what extent is this kind of state—that is, this conception of the order of constitutional law and this conception of the religious competence of the public power—the creation of post-Tridentine history, and to what extent is it the creation of transtemporal doctrine?

9) The issue of theological judgment.—Is the Second View infected with doctrinal errors (as the First View maintains), or is the First View infected with theological fallacies (as the Second View maintains)? How successfully does each View contend with the objections brought against it by the other?

The basic issues in the controversy seem to come to expression in the foregoing series of nine interrelated topics. The node of the controversy also appears. It is the notion of the ideal. This is the "fighting word." But is the fight necessary? The Second View fights against the notion, because public care of religion is a constitutional question; it has to do with legal institutions, to which the notion of an ideal is inapplicable. The First View fights for the notion, because public care of religion has to do with the maintenance of the religious unity of a Catholic people, which is an ideal. If this is the issue, it is no issue at all. The Second View can grant that the religious unity of a Catholic people is an ideal to be pursued. The First View need only grant that the legal institutions of establishment and intolerance are not ideal means of pursuing it. In any event, until the false issue of the ideal is disposed of, there is little possibility of getting on with the real argument. The ideal has become a King Charles's head, or, if you will, a red herring across the trail.

There are also three other sets of issues that must be briefly mentioned.

1) Religious freedom, as a concept and as an affirmation.—Has the concept been adequately described? And has the affirmation of it been reasonably made in terms of argument, and theologically made in terms of a genuine growth in the understanding of the tradition? Many particular issues arise under this general topic.

2) The mode of argument for the validity of religious freedom as a human and civil right, embodied in a legal institution.—The basic issue here concerns the different mentalities with which the whole question of public care of religion is approached—the extrinsecist-abstract-logical-deductive-ahistorical mentality (the First View), and the historical consciousness (the Second View). The cognate issue concerns the development of doctrine concerning public care of religion. Has there been a genuine growth in the understanding of the tradition from Gelasius I to John XXIII (the Second View), or did the growth come to a stop at some determined stage (the First View)?

3) Certain theological principles and pastoral considerations that

are relevant to the whole problem. The general question is, which of the two Views more adequately reckons with these principles and considerations.

First, religious divisions are not simply brute fact but theological fact. That is to say, the fact of them is inherent in the supernatural economy of salvation. The economy hangs suspended from the divine predilection and predestination; faith is a gift offered to man's freedom; the economy is a divine action that unrolls in time and space; the eschatological division (Mt 25:31–46) is prefigured in history; Christ did not come to bring peace but division (Lk 12:51–53). No historical-geographical realizations of Catholic unity escape this theological fact. Religious pluralism is theologically the human condition.

Second, there is the mode of God's governance of men—its disposition to "overlook" (Acts 17:30), its "forbearance" (Rom 3:26), its respect for human freedom, its adamant resistance to the "divine temptation," as it has been called—the temptation to coerce men for their own good (cf. Mt 4:7).

Third, there is the evangelical consciousness of the Church—the *pusillus grex*, the pilgrim Church which is "poor," that is, dependent only on spiritual means to win wayfaring man to herself; the missionary Church, forever engaged in a work of discernment, seeking in the historical succession of human cultures for their truly human elements, striving always to save the institutions of men by filling them with a content of truth, justice, love, and freedom; willing always to recognize the reality of human progress, despite its ambiguities.

Fourth, there is the fact of the great sin of our times—carelessness and even contempt for the dignity of the human person and its birthright of freedom. Against this sin, the Church has sharpened her emphasis on man as the image of God and also enlarged her pastoral solicitude for human freedom.

Fifth, there is the contemporary need for ecumenical dialogue on the issue of religious freedom, and the further need for dialogue between Christian and non-Christian. For this dialogue the Church needs a common doctrine; she also needs a doctrine that can be made intelligible to the contemporary man of good will.

These considerations, and others too, are relevant to the question of judgment on the two Views. Which of them is more in consonance with these theological truths? Which of them better reflects the contemporary pastoral solicitudes of the Church?

Notes

1. EDITOR NOTE: Mimeographed versions of this article were first distributed to the American bishops at the Council in the summer of 1964, then translated into four languages and distributed to all conciliar participants in the late summer or fall of that year. A briefer version was published as "The Problem of Religious Freedom," *Theological Studies* 25 (December 1964):503–75. The text presented here is from *The Problem of Religious Freedom*, Woodstock Papers, number 7 (Westminster, Md.: The Newman Press, 1965). It was also published as "Le probleme de la liberté religieuse au Councile," in *La liberté religieuse: exigence spirituelle et problème politique* (Paris: Centurion 1965), pp. 9–112; and "Die religiöse Freiheit und das Konzil," *Wort und Wahrheit* 20 (1965):409–30, 505–36; as "Il problema della libertà religiosa al concilio," *Il Nuovo Osservatore* 54 (1966):686–734; and "La libertà religiosa: Un grave Problema di oggi ereditato dalla storia di ieri," in *Cattolicesimo e libertà*, ed. F. V. Joannes (Milano: Mondadori, 1969), pp. 157–254.

2. EDITOR NOTE: Richard Regan, S.J.'s *Conflict and Consensus* (1967) is the most comprehensive study available of the various drafts and development of the Declaration. Mention should also be made of Donald Pelotte's *Theologian in Conflict* (1976), chapter 3: "Vindication: 1960–67," pp. 74–114. Murray outlines that development more completely in his 1965i, the introduction to his translation of *Dignitatis Humanae Personae* (*DH*) in 1966i, and, especially, 1966d.

3. Apr. 17, 1964; *AAS* [*Acta Apostolica Sedis*] 56 (1964) 389.

4. *Ci riesce*, *AAS* 45 (1953) 788–89.

5. Ibid.

6. *Libertas*, *ASS* [*Acta Sanctae Sedis*] 20 (1887–88) 605.

7. Ibid., p. 609.

8. *Pacem in terris*, *AAS* 55 (1963) 279.

9. Ibid., p. 265.

10. Cf. Ibid., p. 260.

11. Cf. Ibid.

12. EDITOR NOTE: In a description of why the Council delayed debate on religious liberty, Murray cites canonist opposition but also disagreement with what he called the French-speaking school of those who were willing to affirm religious freedom. The French thought their theologically grounded justification to be "richer and more profound," in contrast with Murray's view, which they considered "superficial." For this discussion, see 1966i, especially p. 42.

13. EDITOR NOTE: In the preceding two pages, Murray claims that contem-

porary consciousness grants a special, privileged position to religious freedom, that is nonetheless cognate with other social freedoms. To me he seems to be here importing Christian constitutionalism into his "natural" argument. For my discussion of the possible theological premises in Murray's argument, see the general introduction "The Ongoing Argument," above.

14. Cf. A. F. Carrillo de Albornoz, *The Basis of Religious Liberty* (New York, 1963), esp. pp. 16–26, 155–62.

15. Cf. Leo XIII, *Sapientiae christianae*, ASS 22 (1889–90) 396.

16. *Polycraticus* 8, 17 (*PL* 199, 777).

17. EDITOR NOTE: See Murray's struggle with religious freedom as an empowerment in the third article of this volume.

18. EDITOR NOTE: Murray here and elsewhere throughout this article presents five distinct arguments and their resulting principles that support religious freedom. These arguments between two distinct orders "link," "converge," or form "junctures" that yield an affirmation of civil religious freedom (see also pp. 150–51, 169, 173, 176, 187). The last of the principles is the "jurisprudential" ("as much freedom as possible, as much coercion as necessary"). As we will see in the last article in this book (1968), he later moved the content of this last principle closer to a core definition of the human person.

19. EDITOR NOTE: Murray developed most of his public order criteria in American arguments over censorship of adult books. See his 1956f (chapter 7, "Should There Be a Law?" in *WHTT*), 1956a, and 1965f.

20. Cf. J. Lecler, *Toleration and the Reformation* 2 (tr. T. L. Westow; London, 1960) 197, 235, 250, 253, 279, 355, 362, 377, 379, 400, 426.

21. Cf. *Syllabus*, prop. 3 (*DB* 1703). [EDITOR NOTE: "Syllabus" in *Enchiridion Symbolorum: Definitionum et Declarationum de Rebus Fidei et Morum*, edited by Henry Denziger and Clement Bannwart, S.J. (Freiburg: Herder, 1922), para. 1703.]

22. Cf. *Syllabus*, prop. 39 (*DB* 1739).

23. *Libertas*, ASS 20 (1887) 605.

24. *Immortale Dei*, ASS (1885) 163.

25. *Libertas*, ASS 20 (1887) 605.

26. Cf. Ibid., p. 604.

27. Cf. *DB* 1800.

28. Cf. *Cum multa*, ASS 15 (1882) 242.

29. *Officio sanctissimo*, ASS 20 (1887) 269.

30. *Praeclara gratulationis*, ASS 26 (1893–94) 712.

31. *Immortale Dei*, ASS 18 (1885) 171.

32. *Libertas*, ASS 20 (1887) 612.

33. *Divini redemptoris*, AAS 29 (1937) 72.

34. Radio message, Dec. 24, 1944; *AAS* 37 (1945) 11–12.

35. Ibid., p. 22.

36. Radio message, Dec. 24, 1942; *AAS* 35 (1943) 19.

37. Ibid., p. 14.

38. Radio message, Dec. 24, 1944; *AAS* 37 (1945) 12.

39. Ibid., p. 15.

40. Radio message, June 1, 1941; *AAS* 33 (1941) 200.

41. Ibid.

42. Cf. Radio message, Dec. 24, 1944; AAS (1945) 13–16.

43. *Non abbiamo bisogno, AAS* 23 (1931) 302.

44. *Firmissimam constantiam,* AAS 29 (1937) 196.

45. *Summi pontificatus, AAS* 31 (1939) 445.

46. *Ci riesce, AAS* 45 (1953) 802.

47. *Mit brennender Sorge, AAS* 29 (1937) 160.

48. Ibid., p. 159.

49. Radio message, Dec. 24, 1942; *AAS* 35 (1943) 19.

50. *AAS* 45 (1953) 794–802.

51. Cf. Ibid., p. 798.

52. Ibid., p. 797.

53. Ibid., p. 799.

54. Ibid.

55. Ibid. 4a.

56. Ibid., pp. 798–99.

57. Cf. Ibid., p. 801.

58. Cf. Ibid., p. 797.

59. Radio message, Sept. 11, 1962; *AAS* 54 (1962) 682.

60. *AAS* 55 (1963) 257–304.

61. Cf. Ibid., pp. 273–79.

62. Cf. Ibid., p. 278.

63. Cf. Ibid., pp. 259–69.

64. Ibid., p. 260.

65. Ibid., p. 270.

66. Ibid., p. 279.

67. Ibid., p. 266.

68. Cf. Ibid., p. 265. [EDITOR NOTE: Freedom as the driving force for social betterment anchors Murray's principal argument to common good concerns. By offering a social betterment grounding for liberty, he bypassed individualistic interpretations of Western freedoms. See also 1963j, p. 613; 1966b, p. 574; and the fourth article in this book.]

69. Ibid., p. 266.

70. Ibid., p. 297.

71. Ibid., pp. 285–86.

72. Cf. Ibid., p. 300

73. Ibid.

74. Cf. Allocution *Vous avez voulu,* Sept. 7, 1955; *AAS* 47 (1955) 678.

75. EDITOR NOTE: The classicism versus historical consciousness distinction is from Lonergan. Murray had been in contact with Lonergan, particularly after 1958, and had an advance copy of the latter's "Transition from a Classicist World-View to Historical Mindedness" in 1966. For Murray the Council's affirmation of religious freedom entailed also an affirmation of "historical consciousness," parallel to the Nicene Council's affirmation of a dogmatic way of knowing along with its affirmation of "homoousion" (see 1964c, 1966j). He also appealed to historical consciousness in support of the majority report, which recommended changes in the church's policy toward artificial contraception, accusing the minority report as being caught in "classicism" (see 1967g).

76. Cf. Leo XIII, *Sapientiae christianae,* ASS 22 (1889–90) 396.

77. Cf. 1–2, q. 95, a. 3.

3

The Issue of Church and State at Vatican Council II[1]

This article is the least finished of the arguments in this volume. Here Murray struggles with what *Dignitatis* and *Gaudium et Spes* ("The Church in the Modern World") said—and did not say—about the "changing state" of the church/state question. He also struggles with notions of religious freedom as an empowerment and religious pluralism as somehow normative within the modern world. His problems with *Dignitatis* and *Gaudium et Spes* were occasioned by the reduction of the argument he presented in "The Problem" to a secondary position within the Declaration. His problems with freedom as an empowerment and with religious pluralism were sparked by the Council's admission that non-Catholic religions contain at least elements of salvific truth, that they are legitimate actors within salvation history.

Murray suggests that Catholics ought to develop an attitude of equality and respect in ecumenical discourse. He further suggests that attitude might be analogous to the attitudes of equality and respect that are required for civil discourse. To my reading, he does not satisfactorily ground that ecumenical attitude in this article, much less does he follow through its implications for the discussion of theological truth claims. Likewise he suggests that religious pluralism is the "normative context" for civic living and ecumenical discourse, without explaining how or why it is normative.

At issue here is the Catholic church's approach to truths it finds beyond its borders and to the truths that it possesses. At each point in his discussion of empowerment and pluralism Murray is stopped by a notion of Catholic truths as timeless and eternally complete. With such a notion, it is difficult to see how ecumenism could call for anything more than tolerance on the Catholic side.

The issues of empowerment and pluralism continue to dominate ecumenical and religious liberty discussions. In my notes, I will suggest forms of analysis in Murray's late treatment of other issues that might contribute to a resolution of the impasse that he was encountering.

No formal document on the relations between Church and state issued from Vatican Council II, although the issue had appeared in the legislative history of the Council. The original schema of the Constitution on the Church, distributed on November 10, 1962, contained a chapter (9) "On the Relations of Church and State." It was a revision of a prior text, also written by the Theological Commission, "On the Relations of Church and State and on Civil Tolerance." Also during the preconciliar period—in December, 1960—a schema on religious freedom was prepared by a subcommission of the Secretariat for Promoting Christian Unity, meeting in Fribourg. It was recognized that the particular issue of religious freedom needed to be clarified, if there was to be any hope of instituting proper ecumenical relationships between the Catholic Church and the other Christian churches and communities.

In June, 1962, Cardinal Bea presented to the Central Commission a revision of the Fribourg schema, containing three brief chapters, the third of which was entitled "On the Relations between the Church and Civil Society." At the same time the Theological Commission presented its own schema—the first of the two mentioned above. A lengthy discussion of the two schemata proved inconclusive; their respective tendencies were quite diverse. The matter was referred to Pope John XXIII, who created in July, 1962, a mixed committee whose function would be to effect a reconciliation of the two tendencies. (In the end, this committee—composed of Cardinals Ciriaci, Ottaviani, and Bea, Msgr. Willebrands, and Fr. Tromp—never met.) In that same month the Secretariat schema was revised, to take account of certain views expressed in the schema of the Theological Commission. In February, 1963, the Secretariat decided further to revise its schema and to leave aside the Church-state issue. This new revision, approved by the Secretariat in May, 1963, was presented to the Co-ordinating Commission in July, and the decision was reached that it should be chapter 5 of the schema on ecumenism to be presented by the Secretariat. (The details of the long delay in getting the text printed need not concern us here.) Chapter 9 was omitted from the revised schema on the Church. And thus it came about that only the issue of religious freedom was discussed by the Council.

The explicit intention of the Declaration on Religious Freedom was narrowly defined in the final text, namely, "to develop the doctrine of recent popes on the inviolable rights of the human person and on the constitutional order of society" (n. 1). Nevertheless, in the course of fulfilling this relatively restricted doctrinal intention, the Declaration made certain significant contributions towards a development of doctrine in regard to the Church-state issue. In its turn, the Constitution on the Church in the World Today confirmed, and in certain respects advanced, this development. The purpose of this article is to analyze the development.

The New Problematic

In general, the development consisted in a transformation of the state of the question. A movement in a new direction had already been begun by Leo XIII. From early Christian times, through the medieval era, through the later era of the French classical monarchy, and through the post-Reformation epoch of confessional absolutism, the primary issue had been stated in terms of the relationship between the two powers, spiritual and temporal—pope and emperor, pope and king or prince. This issue retained a mode of its validity for Leo XIII. He did not indeed contend for "union of Church and state" on the model of the *ancien regime,* wherein the Union of Throne and Altar entailed an enclosure of the national Church within the national kingdom and some consequent manner of subordination of Church to state. However, against the dogma of "separation of Church and state" in the sense of Continental laicism, he consistently contended for an orderly relationship between ecclesiastical and political authority. At the same time he transformed this ancient issue of the dyarchy by including it within a broader statement of the question, to which the conditions of the time, the progressive laicization and also industrialization of society in Continental Europe, led him.

The new terms were the "Church," both as a spiritual authority and also as the community of the Christian faithful, and "human society" in the whole range of its institutional life—social, economic, and cultural, as well as political. Within this broader context, the issue of the dyarchy tended to appear, less as a formally juridical issue of structural relationships between the two powers, than as the wider issue of their reciprocal co-operation toward the integral good of the "same one man, both Christian and citizen," whom they both encounter—and thus encounter each other—in the concrete life of society. What supremely mattered to Leo XIII was the establishment of a Christian order in the whole of society. The orderly relationship between the two powers was simply a subordinate aspect of this larger goal. The issue of the dyarchy as such had begun to lose its ancient primacy.

Vatican Council II pursued and prolonged this line of development. The chief witness here is the whole Constitution on the Church in the World Today. Of particular significance are Part 1, chapter 3, "On Human Activity in the Whole World," and chapter 4, "On the Function of the Church in the World Today." The basically Leonine inspiration of these two chapters is instantly visible; but so too is the development of doctrine beyond its Leonine stage. And again the source of the development lies in a broadening of the perspectives in which the question is viewed.

For Leo XIII, "human society" meant concretely the Europe of the nineteenth century. His religious interests did indeed range much farther afield. But the focus of his political and social teaching, as of his diplomacy, was obviously on the European nations, chiefly the so-called Catholic nations, as these underwent the shattering impact of the French Revolution, Continental laicism, and the Industrial Revolution. In contrast, for Vatican II, "human society" meant quite literally the whole world—and the whole world as it is everywhere undergoing the more shattering impact of the technological revolution of the twentieth century.

Again, both Leo XIII and Vatican II were concerned with religion as the basic dynamic element—both salvific and civilizational—in the life of the world, whether in the broader or in the narrower sense of the term "world." For Leo XIII, however, religion uniformly meant Christianity and Christianity uniformly meant the Catholic Church, which he conceived to be not only the unique but also the exclusive ecclesial form of Christianity. The Christian religion in this Catholic sense was for him the "teacher and nurse of Christian civilization," that is, the civilization of Europe. (He also firmly supported the religio-political privileges of France with regard to missionary activity in the East and Far East, which dated from the days of Francis I, and which resulted, in effect, in the identification of Catholic expansion and the expansion of French national culture—a result not altogether happy in its confusion of Christianization and Europeanization.) In particular, the Christian religion in its Catholic sense was, for Leo XIII, the origin and support of the unity of the Catholic

European peoples. In so far as he paid attention to the religion and to the ecclesial communities which emerged from the Reformation, it was to regard them as representing, not only religious error, but also a solvent of traditional European culture. (Be it noted, on the other hand, that he was the first Pope to use the phrase "separated brethren"[2].)

In this sense his religio-civilizational outlook was related to his historical outlook, which was simple and narrow. The key to it is in the famous once-upon-a-time passage ("Fuit aliquando tempus . . . ") in *Immortale Dei*.[3] The medieval era was the golden age of Christian unity, of harmony between the two powers, and of the obedience of princes and peoples to the authority of the Church. Then came the Reformation, which was a revolt against the authority of the Church, the rupture of Christian unity, and the origin of profound civilizational change. Later, by virtue of logical as well as historical sequence, came the Revolution, which was a revolt against the sovereignty of God Himself, a schism within the Catholic nations, a disruption of the relationship between the two powers, and the beginnings of the laicization of European culture. Within these historical perspectives, whose focus of origin was in the past, Leo XIII could not but call for a return to a Christian unity once possessed, to an ecclesiastical obedience once rendered, to the matrix of a culture once fertile of Christian forms.

Vatican II, however, relinquished this retrospective view of history and adopted a prospective view. Its perspectives open out from the present. They are set by the signs of the times, which are chiefly two. The first is a rising consciousness of the dignity of the human person; correlative with it is a mounting movement toward the unity of the human family. Therefore the problem for the Church, as for man himself, is an increasing realization, in all manner of institutional forms, both of human dignity and of human unity. "As we undertake our work therefore," said the Council in its Message to Humanity on October 20, 1962, "we would emphasize whatever concerns the dignity of man, whatever contributes to a genuine community of peoples." Hence the work of the Church, as the work of man himself, looks to the future. It implies a movement forward—not a return but a renewal.

Moreover, the doctrinal perspectives of Vatican II are ecumenical, whereas Leo XIII's were not. Not only did the Council gratefully acknowledge the "heritage of faith handed down by the apostles" as found in the Eastern Churches, and the Christian and ecclesial elements retained in the separated churches and ecclesial communities in the West, and the religious values in non-Christian religions, and in particular the community of tradition between Christianity and Judaism. In the same spirit it also recognized that the future of civilization on this earth depends, not solely on the Church, but on the widest possible co-operative effort. The Council reiterated the Leonine position, as in this text from the Constitution on the Church in the World Today: "The Church believes that she, through each of her members and through the entirety of her community, can contribute greatly toward making the family of men and its history more human" (n. 40). But there is a new development: "In addition, the Church gladly sets a high value on the contributions which other Christian churches and ecclesial communities have made and are making, in a united effort, toward the fulfilment of the same task" (*loc. cit.*). Leo XIII never said that. Nor did he rise to the humility of the further statement: "At the same time, [the Church] holds firmly that she can be assisted to a great extent and in a variety of ways by the world itself, by individual men and by human society, through their endowments and efforts, in preparing the way for the gospel" (*loc. cit.*).

Continuity, however, is here visible. Leo XIII took the first decisive step toward healing the breach between the Church and the European world of his day, which had been his unhappy legacy from the pontificate of Pius IX. He offered to this limited "world" the assistance of the Church for the healing of the ills of the time. Vatican II took a much longer step in the same direction. It repeated Leo's offer—on a more generous scale—and thus reaffirmed an ancient tradition. It also did something new. In its turn it asked the world—conceived in all its global sweep and growing complexity—for its own assistance, not merely for the healing of the ills of the times (upon which, in the spirit of John XXIII, the Council did not lengthily dwell), but more importantly for the fulfilment of the signs of the times. The Council repeatedly insisted that the inherent sense of the gospel summons the Church to the task of lifting man to his true dignity and of knitting the bonds of human community. It also insisted that the world must know itself to be summoned to the same task by the stirrings within its own consciousness.

It is not the intention of this essay to pursue in detail, or to estimate the adequacy of, the Council's solution to its own developed version of the Leonine problematic. The first point here is the new conception of the problematic. Its terms are not now, as they were for Leo XIII, the Catholic Church and human society in Europe. The terms are wider—religion in its full ecumenical sense and human society throughout the wide world. The second point is that, again in continuity with Leo XIII, the Council situated the narrow issue of Church and state within the context of its own widened problematic. Thus it effected a further transformation of the state of the narrower question. And in consequence it opened the way to a development of doctrine on the matter. It can hardly be said that the Council itself wrought out the development. Nevertheless, it offered certain guidelines. They may be gathered both from the Declaration on Religious Freedom and from the Constitution on the Church in the World Today.

Dignitatis Humanae

In the first place, in accordance with the world-wide outlook of the Council, the Declaration acknowledges the fact of the religiously pluralist society as the necessary historical context of the whole discussion. The acknowledgment is implicit in the intention of the document to deal with a universal human right. It becomes more explicit in the section on corporate religious freedom (n. 4) and in the concluding pastoral exhortation (nn. 14–15). Leo XIII, in contrast, by reason of his restricted and retrospective view of history, had tended to assume, as the historical premise of the Church-state question, the religious unity of the Catholic nations, so called, and the historic rights acquired by the Church within this limited geographical context. His thought was still, in a sense, tributary to the view, developed largely in the post-Reformation era and accepted then by both Catholic and Protestant rulers and by their respective churches, that the introduction of religious pluralism into a religiously unitary society was illegitimate; that it was to be resisted by the power of government; that government could do no more than tolerate it, and then only when religious dissent had so established itself as a social force that the attempt to eradicate it by force would do more harm than good.

In the second place, the Declaration embraces the political doctrine of Pius XII on the juridical state (as it is called in Continental idiom), that is, on government as constitutional and as limited in function—its primary function being juridical, namely, the protection and promotion of the rights of man and the facilitation of the performance of man's native duties. The primacy of this function is based on Pius XII's personalist conception of society—on the premise that the "human person is the foundation, the goal, and the bearer of the whole social process,"[4] including the processes of government. In contrast, Leo XIII had held a more statist and moralist view of society. In his classic encyclicals, up to *Rerum novarum*, the traditional distinction between society and state is obscured; the foundation and bearer of the social process is the ruler (or, if you will, the state); and the goal of the ruler-state is the common good considered as an ensemble of virtues in the body politic, notably the virtue of obedience to rule. It is not until *Rerum novarum* that the dignity of the human person and the inviolability of his rights begins to emerge as determinant of social and political doctrine, thus affording the point of departure for the doctrine of Pius XII, John XXIII, and the Council.

In the present matter, the significance of the political doctrine of the Declaration (as also of the Constitution on the Church in the World Today) lies in its disavowal of the long-standing view of government as sacral in function, that is, as invested with the function of defending and promoting religious truth as such. This view of government is visible even in Leo XIII. Its disavowal by the Declaration follows on its intention to develop the doctrine of more recent popes on the constitutional order of society. In this development the function of government appears as the protection and promotion, not of religious truth, but of religious freedom as a fundamental right of the human person. This is a secular function, since freedom in society—notably religious freedom—is a secular value, as are the values of justice and love or civic friendship. All three of these values are rooted in the truth about the human person, which is the truth upon which the whole social and political order rests.[5] Hence the tutelage of these values is proper to the notion of government as secular in the full range of its purposes. It is true that the final text of the Declaration is inadequate in its treatment of the limitations imposed on government by sound political doctrine. Nevertheless, the disavowal of the old notion of government as sacral in function is sufficiently clear, both from the firm statement of the essentially juridical function of government (n. 6), and also from the earlier statement that the proper purpose of government is to have a care for the common temporal good[6] and that it would exceed its limits were it to presume to direct or impede religious acts (n. 3). These statements, jejune though they are, exclude the notion that government is to be the judge of religious truth, the defender of the true faith, or the guardian of religious unity.

In the third place, in systematic harmony with its own doctrine on the universal right to religious freedom and on the limitations of governmental power in matters religious, the Declaration makes the statement: "The freedom of the Church is the fundamental principle in what concerns the relations between the Church and governments and the whole civil order" (n. 13). The import of this statement is considerable. It opens the way to a new structure of Catholic doctrine on Church and state—to a renewal of the tradition whose great exponent was Gregory VII: "In moments of considered solemnity, when their tone was passionate and their religious feeling at its deepest, Gregory VII and his contemporaries called the object toward which they were striving the 'freedom of the Church.' "[7] In modern times Leo XIII powerfully effected a renewal of the Gregorian tradition: "A major significance of Leo XIII in the history of doctrinal development lies in his great effort to rescue the Church from the regalist tradition—from that servitude to the state under which it had lain for nearly half a millennium of regalism. The servitude dated from the triumph of Philip the Fair's lawyers over Boniface VIII, which had been solidified by the rising centralized monarchies, especially in France. In a full view, Leo XIII appears as the Gregory VII of the nineteenth century, returning under the stress of the times [as regalism reappeared in laicist garb] to the splendid device under which the great Hildebrand fought his battle, 'the freedom of the Church.' "[8] The phrase occurs in well over a hundred texts in the Leonine corpus, of which perhaps one fourth have to do with the Roman question. One providential result of this tragic impasse was that it drew the attention of the papacy to the "fundamental principle."

The implications of the principle were not worked out in the post-Leonine canonist systematizations. Oddly enough, the inarticulate major premise controlling these systematizations seems to have been the civilist formula, the "unity of the Church." In the late medieval view of the civilists the formula stressed the role of the prince in the construction of the *ecclesia,* that is, *christianitas,* the Christian world. The role of the prince, now understood as the "Catholic state," in the construction of the Christian society, now contracted to the dimensions of the "Catholic nation," seems likewise to have been a major preoccupation of the modern canonists. The text of *Dignitatis humanae,* however, made vital contact with the profound doctrine of Leo XIII, and through him with the genuine tradition.

After the vote on the fifth conciliar schema (*textus recognitus,* which was presented on October 25, 1965), an amendment was submitted by three Fathers, suggesting that in n. 13 the text should read "fundamental condition" instead of "fundamental principle," in referring to the freedom of the Church. The reasons for the change were not given. At any rate, the substitute text would have been in harmony with the received opinion in the canonist school, according to which the freedom of the Church is merely the fundamental condition of right relationships between Church and state, whereas the fundamental principle is the Church's exclusive right to a situation of legal privilege. The amendment was rejected. The laconic reason advanced by the Secretariat read: "It is a question of a true principle." The response was not wholly adequate.

The text of the schema was, in fact, an implicit citation from the Encyclical Letter of Leo XIII to the French Cardinals, *Notre consolation* (May 3,1892). In it he defends himself against the charge that his policy of *ralliement* in France was inconsistent with the policy of opposition that he was adopting toward the government of Italy—the former policy being religious in inspiration; the latter, political. The policies, he replies, are profoundly consistent, since "the question which concerns us in Italy is also eminently religious in as much as it is related to the fundamental principle of the freedom of the Church,"[9] which was also the principle at stake in France. The freedom of the Church is not merely a true principle; it is the fundamental principle governing the relations of the Church with all governments.

This is not the place to explain in detail what the formula "the freedom of the Church" meant to Gregory VII within the context of medieval Christendom. The Vatican Declaration, however, gives an adequate explanation of what the freedom of the Church concretely means today. In an implicit citation from Pius XII it is said to mean "that stable condition of right and of fact [which guarantees] the necessary independence [of the Church] in the fulfilment of her divine mission" (n. 13). Moreover, a proper distinction is made between the Church as an authority and as a community. And in both senses the Church claims freedom as a strict right. In the sense of the Declaration the object or content of the right is negative—an immunity from coercive constraint or restraint by any human power in society or state, whether in the exercise of spiritual authority or in the communal living of the Christian life.

It should be noted here that the freedom of the Church is understood in this same sense in *Christus dominus,* the Decree on the Pastoral Office of Bishops: "In the performance of their apostolic office, which looks to the salvation of souls, bishops per se possess full and perfect freedom and independence of any civil power. Wherefore it is not permissible to impede, directly or indirectly, the exercise of their ecclesiastical office or to prohibit their free communication with the Apostolic See, with other ecclesiastical authorities, and with their subjects" (n. 19). Here the freedom of the Church as a spiritual authority is presented as an immunity. This concept, here as in *Dignitatis humanae,* is technically correct.

A more detailed description of the meaning of the freedom of the Church is given in the section of the Declaration which deals with religious freedom as a corporate right. This section was written with a view to satisfying the requirements both of the freedom of the Catholic Church (as set forth, for instance, in Leo XIII) and also of the freedom of the churches and ecclesial communities (as set forth in the declarations of the World Council of Churches, notably at Amsterdam in 1948 and at New Delhi in 1961). Two general areas of freedom are distinguished. The first includes the internal affairs of the community—its organization, manner of rule, worship, religious nurture, the selection, training, appointment, and transferral of ministers, communications *ad extra,* the erection of churches, the possession of property. The second includes the external action of the community—its public witness to its own faith as such, and its further witness to the values of its faith in their relation to the affairs of the temporal order. The Declaration makes no concessions to an "angelist" conception of religion or to the notion of churches as being shut up "in the sacristy."

Furthermore, the Declaration makes sufficiently clear—without being altogether as precise as might be desired—that the foundation of the Catholic Church's right to freedom is twofold. The theological foundation is the mandate of Christ to preach His gospel and to observe His commandments (n. 13). This unique theological title, however, cannot be urged in political society and against government. The mandate of Christ to His Church is formally a truth of the transcendent order in which the authority of the Church is exercised and her life as a community is lived. Therefore it is not subject, or even accessible, to judgment by secular powers as regards its truth or falsity. The authorities and faithful of the Church are indeed conscious that their freedom is of divine origin—a participation respectively in the freedom of the Incarnate Word and in the freedom of the Holy Spirit. In political society, however, and in the face of government, only that title to freedom may be urged which the powers of the secular order are able, and are obliged, to recognize. This title is the basic truth about the dignity of the human person and about the necessary freedom of his life—especially his religious life, both personal and corporate—in society.

This distinction between the Church's two different titles to freedom is of the highest importance. If the unique theological title is not asserted, the way is opened to indifferentism—the reduction of the Catholic Church to one of many ecclesial communities, whose respective rights to freedom rest on univocally the same foundation, namely, a divine mandate. On the other hand, if the theological title is asserted against secular powers in society and state, the way is opened to a confusion of the two orders of human life to a negation of the transcendence of the Church and to a violation of the due autonomy of the secular order, as this autonomy was defined by the Council rather more sharply than ever before (a matter to be dealt with later).

The Church would abdicate her transcendence, were she to present her theological title to freedom in society for judgment by any organs of secular government. As has been said, the Declaration itself makes sufficiently clear that secular government today—given the developed differentiation of the secular and sacral orders—is not empowered to make judgments *de meritis* in matters of theological truth. At the same time, the due autonomy of the secular order would be violated, since this autonomy requires that the powers which rule the secular order should make judgments on the secular grounds proper to that order—the truth which is its foundation, the justice which is its goal, the love or civic friendship which is its motivating and unifying force, the freedom which is at once its goal and its method of pursuing the goal of justice. Hence the autonomy of the secular order requires that, within this order and in the face of its constituted organs of government, the Church should present her claim to freedom on these secular grounds—in the name of the human person, who is the foundation, the end, and the bearer of the whole social process.

It should be noted too that the distinction here in question is of the highest ecumenical importance. On the one hand, it establishes the churches and ecclesial communities on a basis of reciprocity, both with regard to the object or content of their right to freedom in the social and political order, and also with regard to the foundation of this right as asserted within this order. On the other hand, this reciprocity, precisely because it is an affair only of the political and social order, implies no blurring or leveling of the doctrinal differences among the churches, which are of quite another order. As the Decree on Ecumenism says, and as all convinced Christian believers agree: "Nothing is so foreign to the spirit of ecumenism as a false irenicism which harms the purity of Catholic doctrine and obscures its assured genuine meaning" (n. 11). At the same time, the rules of the dialogue must be such that "each can treat with the other on a footing of equality" (n. 9). This reciprocity in the ecumenical dialogue is a matter of love and respect, not only for the other as a person, but also for the truth as possessed by each, to be understood by both. An analogy is visible here. The civil community in its most profound meaning and manner of action is itself a form of dialogue. The dialogue does not disguise, but brings to light, differences of view. But in order that it may be a proper dialogue, it is essential that each should treat with the other on a footing of equality. In the civil dialogue, which is carried on under conditions of constitutional order, this reciprocity is a matter of strict right. And the constitutional right—in our case, to equal religious freedom—is the necessary condition and firm support of the ecumenical dialogue.[10]

A certain uneasiness or discontent was felt by some of the conciliar Fathers and theologians over the "negative" notion of religious freedom put forward by the Declaration.[11] They would have wished it to be said that the freedom of the Church is a "positive" freedom. But surely there is here some failure to make the necessary distinction between two orders of discourse and reality.

The mandate of Christ empowers the Church to preach the gospel to every creature—to every man as a creature of God, to whom the divine message of salvation is addressed. To this empowerment or freedom of the Church there corresponds on the part of all men and all peoples an obligation to hear the word of God and to respond to it by faith as assent and consent. In this sense the content of the freedom of the Church is positive; it is a freedom "for" the preaching of the gospel. This discourse, however, moves in the transtemporal order of the history of salvation—the order of man's vertical relation, so to speak, to God acting and speaking in history through His Church. On the other hand, the technical issue of religious freedom rises in the juridical order, which is the order of horizontal interpersonal relations among men, between a man and organized society, and especially between the people—as individuals and as associated in communities, including religious communities—and the powers of government. As asserted in the interpersonal order of human rights, the freedom of the Church, whether as a community or as an authority, is and can only be negative in its content; it is a freedom "from" any manner of coercive constraint imposed by any secular power. As further guaranteed in the constitutional order of civil rights, the freedom of the Church consequently appears as an immunity. To confuse these two distinct orders of discourse, and the modes of freedom proper to each, is to run into inextricable difficulties.

One may be mentioned. Government is a power whose mode of action, like that of law, is ultimately coercive. If the freedom of the Church in the juridical order is rightly taken to be no more than an assurance against the use of governmental power, or any other secular power, in restraint of her divine mission, no difficulty arises. On the contrary, this self-denying ordinance on the part of government is a matter of obligation. This is obvious. On the other hand, if the freedom of the Church in the juridical order is taken to be some manner of positive claim on government, the claim can only be that government should use its power in furtherance of the Church's divine mission. *Quod absit.* No other positive content to the claim can be assigned. The Church cannot ask governments, as she asks men, for faith in the word of God. What she asks—all she can ask—of governments was immortally stated by Paul VI, in fidelity to the tradition and in authentic confirmation of the doctrine of *Dignitatis humanae,* when he spoke to statesmen in his discourse of December 8, 1965: "And what is it that the Church asks of you, after almost two thousand years of all manner of vicissitudes in her relations with you, the powers of earth—what is it that she asks of you today? In one of the major texts of the Council she has told you what it is. She asks of you nothing but freedom—freedom to believe and to preach her faith, freedom to love God and to serve Him, freedom to live and to bring to men her message of life."[12]

It is clear therefore that the Council renewed traditional doctrine on the relations of Church and state by restoring, in continuity with Leo XIII, the principle of the freedom of the Church to its fundamental place in the structure of the doctrine. By the same token, it is clear that the issue may no longer be argued in terms of "union" and "separation" of Church and state, or in terms of "thesis" and "hypothesis." The words "union" and "separation" can mean, and in the course of history have meant, many things. In the modern canonist school, however, union of Church and state has at least meant the legal establishment of Catholicism as the religion of the state, to which constitutional status certain privileges normally accrue, and from which, in the case of other cults, certain civil disabilities logically follow.[13] Union in this sense is the thesis, the ideal prescribed by Catholic doctrine. In turn, separation, which means at least a constitutional situation of nonestablishment and of equal religious freedom for all, is hypothesis, a concession to circumstances, to be no more than tolerated.[14]

In the legislative history of the Declaration the issue of establishment was first mentioned in the *Relatio de animadversionibus Patrum* which was included in the fascicle with the third conciliar schema (*textus emendatus*) presented in November, 1964. There it was said:

> The institution of religious freedom prohibits such legal intolerance as would reduce certain citizens or certain religious communities to a condition of inferiority in what concerns their civil rights in matters religious. But it does not forbid that the Catholic religion should be recognized by human law as the common religion of the citizens in a particular country—in other words, that the Catholic religion should be established by public law as the religion of the state. In such a case, however, care must be taken that from the institution of a state-religion no juridical or social consequences should be derived that would infringe the equality before public law of all citizens in religious matters. In a word, together with the institution of a state-religion the institution of religious freedom is to be maintained.

The purpose of this note was to respond to the objection of some Fathers that a declaration of general religious freedom would be at odds with the institution of establishment as approved by the Church, in practice and—according to some—by doctrine.

In response to the wishes of some Fathers, a sentence on establishment was inserted in the text of the fourth conciliar schema (*textus reemendatus*) presented in September, 1965. It read: "The institution of religious freedom does not stand in the way of special recognition being given to one religious community in the constitutional order of a society, under consideration of historical circumstances among peoples, in such wise, however, that at the same time the right of all citizens and religious communities to religious freedom be acknowledged and maintained."

This statement proved controversial. The *Relatio* of the Secretariat on the changes made in the fifth conciliar schema (*textus recognitus*) presented in October, 1965, distinguished four positions: (1) that no mention of establishment be made; (2) that the text should clearly affirm that special constitutional recognition must be given to the true religion whenever this is possible; (3) that, if the Declaration deals with establishment, it should do so in a conditional sentence; (4) that the Declaration should deal with establishment but in a conditional sentence. The Secretariat voted to accept the fourth proposal as the *via media*. Hence the fifth schema was made to read thus: "If, under consideration of historical circumstances among peoples, special civil recognition is given to one religious community in the constitutional order of a society, it is necessary at the same time that the right of all citizens and religious communities to religious freedom should be acknowledged and maintained" (n. 6).

After the vote of October 26, 1965, some sixteen *modi* dealing with this sentence were submitted. One of them, signed by three Fathers, asked that the whole sentence be stricken out. Another, signed by twenty-eight Fathers, asked that the sentence be changed from its conditional form back to its former declarative form. The rest proposed merely verbal alterations. The two significant changes were rejected by the Secretariat on grounds of the overwhelming vote of approval given to the section in question (2,034 to 186). Hence the final text retains the conditional form.

It is therefore clearly the mind of the Council that the establishment of Catholicism as the religion of the state is no more than a matter of historical circumstances, and not a matter—or even a consequence—of doctrine. It is not thesis but hypothesis. In fact, the conditional form of the conciliar statement, taken in its full force and in the light of the interventions of the Fathers who recommended it, reveals the unwillingness of the Council to approve the institution of establishment even as a matter of purely historic right. On the other hand, it is even more clearly the mind of the Council that the institution of religious freedom is not hypothesis but thesis—a matter of doctrine, not of historical circumstances. To put the whole thing more simply, it is time now to drop the categories of thesis and hypothesis completely out of the Catholic vocabulary. The future systematization of Catholic doctrine on Church and state will not have the disjunctive structure characteristic of the once-received opinion. Its structure will be unitary.

Moreover, it will have to be more than a doctrine on "Church and state" in the theological sense of "Church" and in the classical sense of "state." The traditional rubric accurately defined the issue only in the days when the Church was, or was considered to be, conterminous with society, and when a single structure of spiritual authority confronted a single structure of temporal authority. The Council, by its recognition of religious pluralism in the world (in the conciliar sense of "world"), acknowledged that this historical situation no longer exists, if it ever really did exist. The same acknowledgment is implicit also in the very notion of the "pilgrim Church," which was a dominant conciliar theme. The traditional rubric may still be useful to designate the contemporary issue, if its terms are invested with a symbolic meaning and used to designate the poles of that permanent tension in human society which reflects the tension inherent in the dual nature of man, who is a creature both of time and of eternity. However, after *Dignitatis humanae* and *Gaudium et spes*, the literal terms of the issue are rather "religion and government," religion in a historical-pluralist sense, and government in the constitutional sense accepted by these two conciliar documents, following *Pacem terris*. This narrow issue, moreover, exists at the interior of, and in subordination to, the larger problematic of "religion and human society," already described.

The relationship of religion and government was regarded by *Dignitatis humanae* both as a theological-religious issue and also as a constitutional and legal issue. And the relationship was primarily defined in terms of freedom—the freedom of the human person and the freedom of religious communities, including the Church. The Declaration, in effect, affirmed the independence of "Church" and "state." But the notion of independence does not exhaust the issue of the relationship between these two social magnitudes, which are also structures of authority (in diverse ways, of course). Does their independence imply their separation—and what is the meaning of "separation"? Does it imply the neutrality of government toward religion, and what kind of "neutrality"—a neutrality of indifference or of general benevolence? Does it imply reciprocal co-operation and mutual support—and to what extent and in what forms? These are complex questions, and the Declaration did not undertake to deal with them adequately.

There was, however, among some of the Fathers a fear that the Declaration might be interpreted in the separationist sense of Continental laicism, which implied either hostility or at best indifference toward religion on the part of government. There was little, if any, basis for this fear, unless the concept of religious freedom in the Declaration were to be egregiously misunderstood. At any rate, in order to preclude the possibility of misinterpretation, a half sentence was added in the sixth and final conciliar schema: "Government, whose proper function is to care for the common temporal good, ought indeed to recognize the religious life of its citizens and to favor it . . . " (n. 3). Later, moreover, when it is a question of the duties of government, two are noted. The primary duty is toward the religious freedom of all citizens. The second duty is "to supply conditions favorable to the cultivation of religious life, in such wise that citizens may in fact be enabled to exercise their religious rights and to discharge their religious duties, and that society itself may enjoy the values of justice and peace which ensue upon the fidelity of men toward God and His holy will" (n. 6).

It must be admitted that this second duty is not phrased with entirely luminous clarity. Nevertheless, the intention of the statement is clear enough. It is primarily negative, that is, it is meant to exclude either a hostile or an indifferent attitude toward religion on the part of government. However, the positive meaning of the statement was deliberately left vague. What do governmental "recognition" and "favor" of religion in society concretely mean? In particular, what manner of constitutional or statutory transcription of such recognition and favor should be made? Again, what is concretely meant by "conditions favorable to religious life"? The text leaves these concrete questions open, because the answer to them would largely depend on variant circumstances.

The positive intention, however, is not in doubt. It was to affirm the traditional doctrine that religion is a social good, a fundamental element of the common temporal good of society. This was the doctrine upon which Leo XIII endlessly insisted. Religion is not simply an affair of the internal forum of conscience or even of the sacristy. It is formally a matter of public interest. Consequently it claims the recognition and the favorable attention of government. Leo XIII was speaking, of course, about the Catholic religion, in the face of the laicizing governments of Continental Europe. The Declaration develops his doctrine by clearly stating that governmental recognition and favor of religion in society are to be accorded under safeguard of the principles of religious freedom and of the equality of all citizens before the law—an equality which "itself is integral to the common good of society" (n. 6). Therefore not only are hostility and indifference excluded; so too is "discrimination" on religious grounds (n. 6). This latter exclusion was necessary in order that the Declaration might be faithful to the Pian and Johannine (not Leonine) notion of the common good—that its primary component is juridical.

For the rest, it would seem to be in the sense of the Declaration to say that governmental favor of religion formally means favor of the freedom of religion. Similarly, conditions favorable to religious life should be understood to mean conditions favorable to the free profession and practice of religion. Government does not stand in the service of religious truth, as an instrument for its defense or propagation. Government, however, must somehow stand in the service of religion, as an indispensable element of the common temporal good. This duty of service is discharged by service rendered to the freedom of religion in society. It is religion itself, not government, which has the function of making society religious. The conditions favorable to the fulfilment of this function are conditions of freedom. In the way of sheer principle, it seems not possible to say more than this. And this much the Declaration says.

Gaudium et Spes

The Constitution on the Church in the World Today reveals a sharper sense of the distinction between society and state than can be found in Leo XIII, or perhaps even in Pius XII, though the latter, in virtue of his concern for the juridical order of society, began to sort out the confusions visible in the former. The Constitution deals with our question roughly in terms of this distinction. In Part 1, chapter 4, there is the question of the relation of the Church to human society and of her function in human society. In Part 2, chapter 4, the narrower question comes up, "Church and state." In neither case is the treatment systematic; but some important principles are stated.

In dealing with the Church-and-society problematic, two major concerns seem to pervade the Constitution. One is to reaffirm the Leonine distinction between the two societies and likewise to reaffirm the transcendence of the Church to the temporal order. The mission of the Church, it is said, "is not of the political, economic, or social order; the purpose which [Christ] set for it is of the religious order" (n. 42). In consequence, the Church "is not bound to any particular form of human culture, or to any political, economic, or social system" (loc. cit.). In further consequence, her ardent wish is "that, standing in the service of the good of all, she may be able to develop freely under any form of government which recognizes the fundamental rights of the person and of the family, and also recognizes the exigencies of the common good" (loc. cit.).

The statement adds a new breadth and an important qualification to Leo XIII's oft-repeated thesis of the indifference of the Church to political forms. Leo XIII, in the face of the French Catholic Right, was endeavoring to disentangle the Church from the institution of monarchy, without at the same time committing the Church to democratic institutions, about which he knew nothing, except in so far as these institutions appeared, in vitiated and unacceptable form, in the laicist republics of Continental Europe. The Council, in contrast, accepting and prolonging the views of Pius XII and of John XXIII, makes a political commitment, however discreet, to constitutional government—or, if you will, to the juridical state whose basic inspiration is a consciousness of the dignity of the person and a recognition of human rights. Only under this manner of government is the freedom of the Church, together with the freedom of man himself, assured. Hence the Council utters one of its few rebukes: "Disapproval is voiced of (*reprobantur*) those forms of government, to be found in some countries, which fetter civil and religious freedom . . . " (n. 73). And again: "It is inhuman that political authority should assume totalitarian or dictatorial forms which do injury to the rights of the person or of associations" (n. 75).

To the transcendence of the Church are linked both the universality of her mission and her freedom in its accomplishment. However, transcendence to the world does not mean isolation from the world. The second major concern of the Constitution is to make this clear. The Council espouses the thesis of St. Augustine, developed in his treatise *De civitate Dei,* which Leo XIII had summed up in the opening paragraph of *Immortale Dei* and thereafter had endlessly repeated: "That immortal work of a merciful God, which is the Church, does indeed, per se and of its very nature, look to the salvation of souls and to their achievement of happiness in heaven. Nevertheless, in the world of mortal man it is the source of so many and such great benefits that it could not have brought forth more or greater benefits if it had been instituted, primarily and chiefly, to further the prosperity of life here on earth."[15] This is the traditional paradox.

The Constitution points to the resolution of it in the notion of the Church as "the leaven and, as it were, the soul of human society, which is to be renewed in Christ and transformed into the family of God." The relationship between the two Cities is described by the word "compenetration." And it is forthrightly stated that this dynamic relationship "can be perceived only by faith; it is, in fact, the mystery of human history" (n. 40).

At least the structure of the mystery can be described in these terms: "In pursuit of her salvific purpose, the Church communicates the divine life to men—but not only that; a reflection of her light somehow streams forth over the whole world, and its effect is chiefly shown in that it heals and elevates the dignity of the human person, strengthens the bonds of human society, and invests the daily activity of man with a deeper meaning and import" (n. 40). The terms are Augustinian and Leonine, but with a difference. The theme of human dignity has now become central in a new way: "By no human law can the personal dignity and freedom of man be so adequately safeguarded as by the gospel of Christ committed to the Church" (n. 41). Or again: "In virtue of the gospel committed to her, the Church proclaims the rights of man; she also acknowledges and holds in high regard the dynamism of today, whereby these rights are everywhere promoted" (*loc. cit.*).

There is more than a hint of triumphalism in the first part of this last sentence, though it is qualified by the second part. It would be fair to say that the Church—that is, the hierarchy and the Holy See—did nothing to advance the struggle for the political rights of man in the eighteenth and nineteenth centuries—those rights, notably the right of free speech, which safeguard the person against the encroachments of the state and also secure for citizens a share in the processes of government. Only rather late—with *Rerum novarum* in 1891—did the papacy enter the battle for the socio-economic rights of man. And it was not until Vatican II, of course, that the Church proclaimed the right to religious freedom. The victories won in the West for the cause of constitutional government and the rights of man owed little to the Church, however much the "leaven of the gospel," as *Dignitatis humanae* insinuates (n. 12), may have contributed to the rise of the secular dynamism which, in fact, brought the "free world" into existence.

In any event, the statements in *Gaudium et spes,* like those in *Dignitatis humanae,* represent *aggiornamento.* And they are programmatic for the future. From now on, the Church defines her mission in the temporal order in terms of the realization of human dignity, the promotion of the rights of man, the growth of the human family towards unity, and the sanctification of the secular activities of this world.

This mission in the temporal order, however, still remains a mission of the religious order—a spiritual mission. It is limited in its scope as it is limited in the means of its accomplishment. These are entirely of the spiritual order: "The power which the Church is able to impart to human society today consists in faith and love made operative in life. It does not consist in any sort of external control exercised by merely human means" (n. 42). Here, of course, would be the place to outline the doctrine of the Decree on the Apostolate of the Laity, *Apostolicam actuositatem,* on the laity as the proper agent for the accomplishment of the mission of the Church in the temporal order. However, a mere reference to this doctrine must here suffice.

The discourse of *Gaudium et spes* on the life of the political community (Part 2, chapter 4) is uninspired and inadequate. For instance, there is no mention of the cardinal political principle of the consent of the governed, which is as old as Aristotle and Cicero, and which was central to the political thought of the High Middle Ages, even though the institutions to make it operative were lacking at that time. So too the section on the political community and the Church (n. 76) does no more than state a few general principles. At that, these are stated in such a way as to exhibit nuances of development.

Mention is made of the "pluralist society" (an almost last-minute addition to the text). It is suggested that this type of society gives rise to today's problem of the relations of Church and state. There is, however, no firm affirmation that the pluralist society presents not only the normal but also the normative context for any theory of these relations. The wider state of the question, "religion and government," which was implicitly adopted by *Dignitatis humanae,* is here contracted to the dimensions exhibited in the introductory rubric, "the political community and the Church." The narrowness of this view was probably necessary, but it was also regrettable.

The first assertion, here as earlier, bears on the transcendence of the Church to the political community and its various forms. The earlier idea of "compenetration" also appears, if only implicitly, in the statement that the Church "is at the same time the sign and safeguard of the transcendence of the human person" (n. 76). It is characteristic of *Gaudium et spes* that it occasionally strikes off a brilliant phrase, pregnant with implications, in the midst of a passage of otherwise prolix and uninspired prose. This is such a phrase. Its implications are extensive. It suggests the central significance of the Church for the political order. It suggests the *locus standi* of the Church in the face of the state; the order of public law and administration. It suggests the essential basis of the Church's claim to freedom in the face of all public powers. It implies that the Church may neither be enclosed within the political order nor be denied her own mode of spiritual entrance into the political order. It indirectly asserts the rightful secularity of the secular order, at the same time that it asserts the necessary openness of the secular order to the transcendent values whose pursuit is proper to the human person. If one were looking for a single phrase in which to resolve the whole problematic of *Gaudium et spes*—the dynamic relation of the Church to the world—this might well be the phrase, especially if it were understood that for the Church to signify and safeguard the transcendence of the human person is for her likewise to signify and further the unity of the human family.

The text does not fully draw out all these implications. It goes on briefly to reaffirm the Leonine principle: "The political community and the Church are independent of each other, and are autonomous, each in its own field" (n. 76). It further proceeds to reaffirm the principle, likewise Leonine, of their necessary harmony—except that it uses the word "co-operation" instead of the favorite Leonine word "concord." There is, however, an interesting nuance in the statement of the necessity for this concord or co-operation. For Leo, the reason lay in the fact that the two structures of authority, for all their independence as structures, held command and rule over the same body of men; the same one man who is "at once citizen and Christian." As Libertas puts it: "Utriusque est in eosdem imperium."[16] For Leo XIII, authority is rule. For the Council, however, authority is service: "Both [authorities], though on a different title, stand in the service of the personal and social vocation of the same men" (n. 76). This restatement of the Leonine doctrine reflects the more personalist conception, to call it such, both of the People of God and of the People Temporal.

The principle of co-operation of Church and state in the service of the human person is thus stated as a principle. However, the concrete forms of co-operation are to be instituted "under regard for circumstances of place and time" (n. 76). Implicit, here again, is a rejection of the disjunctive theory and its assertion of an abstract "thesis." Explicit is a recognition that the contingent relativities of history, and not any logical deductions from abstract principle, must determine the institutional forms of Church-state co-operation. Moreover, the rest of the paragraph makes it clear that the co-operation, both as a matter of principle and in the various forms of its realization, is not required by some sort of *raison d'eglise* but by the dual nature of the human person: "Man is not confined to the temporal order alone; rather, living his life in human history, he has a care for his eternal vocation in its wholeness" (n. 76).

Therefore, it is implied, the care of the Church extends in diverse ways to both aspects of man's destiny, since man is a unity and his destiny is somehow unitary. However, the limitations of the mission of the Church in the temporal order are again stated and all manner of clericalism is again rejected by this assertion: "Those who give themselves to the ministry of the word of God must make use of ways and means which are proper to the gospel; and these differ in many respects from the means at the disposal of the earthly city" (n. 76).

Finally, the Constitution comes to the principle of the freedom of the Church:

> It is always and everywhere necessary that [the Church] should preach the faith with true freedom, teach her doctrine about society, exercise her function among men without hindrance, and pass moral judgment even on affairs that belong to the political order, when such judgment is required by concern for the fundamental rights of the person or for the salvation of souls, under use of all those means, and only those means, which are in harmony with the gospel and with the good of all, having regard for diversities of time and place (n. 76).

This statement of what the freedom of the Church means is not as extensive and complete as the statement made in *Dignitatis humanae*. However, in accord with its own context, it lays emphasis on the point less emphatically made in *Dignitatis humanae*, namely, the Church's freedom of spiritual entrance into the order of politics. The mode of entrance is purely spiritual, since it takes the form simply of moral judgment on political affairs, and since the grounds of judgment are metapolitical, having to do with the rights of man and the salvation of souls. Moreover, nothing is here said about the execution of these moral judgments in terms of law, public policy, social action, etc. On this crucial point the Constitution is content to have recalled a necessary distinction, "between those affairs which Christians, whether alone or in association, undertake as citizens, under the guidance of their Christian conscience, and those affairs which Christians undertake in the name of the Church and in union with their pastors" (n. 76). This distinction, one may think, is rather distinctively European in its origin and import. It began to come into currency in the twenties, under Pius XI, when there began to be talk of Catholic Action (with the initial letters in upper case), which is a form of organized apostolate not common outside the Latin countries.

In the context of discourse both about the evangelical character of the Church's resources and about the freedom of the Church, the Constitution makes a further important point, both of principle and of practice: "The Church does not put her trust in privileges granted by civil authority. More than that, she will renounce the exercise of certain legitimately acquired rights, when it shall have become clear that their exercise may call into question the disinterested character of her witness, or when new circumstances of life require different arrangements" (n. 76). The implicit disavowal of the ancient recourse to the secular arm is clear enough. The notion that certain rights of the Church can be merely historic—therefore contingently legitimate but not exigencies of doctrine—is likewise clear enough. But the privileges in question are not specified. Perhaps it may be permissible to see a reference to the modern right to legal establishment asserted within the nation-state, and to other consequent legal privileges. Thus the doctrine of *Dignitatis humanae* would be fittingly completed.

In any event, the sharpened awareness of the purely spiritual character of the Church's mission, even in the temporal order, which is visible all through the Constitution, leads necessarily to a new disposition on the part of the Church to impose self-denying ordinances on the whole range of her action within the temporal order.[17] This new disposition is part of that spirit of evangelical poverty about which the conciliar Fathers frequently discoursed.

It is in place here to cite the invitation issued by *Christus dominus* to civil authorities that they should likewise pass some self-denying ordinances:

> Consequently, in order rightly to protect the freedom of the Church and more fittingly and effectively to promote the good of the faithful, the Council desires that in the future no rights or privileges regarding the choice, nomination, presentation, or designation for the episcopal office should be granted to civil authorities. Moreover, civil authorities themselves, whose obedient disposition toward the Church the Council gratefully acknowledges, are courteously asked to renounce, of their own accord and after consultation with the Holy See, rights of this kind which they presently enjoy by compact or custom (n. 20).

The premise of this request was the stated doctrine that "the right of nominating and installing bishops is the proper, peculiar, and per se exclusive right of competent ecclesiastical authority" (*loc. cit.*).

The tendency of the request itself is to realize more perfectly the implications of the principle stated by Leo XIII: "It cannot be doubted, under safeguard of the faith, that the governance of souls was committed to the Church alone, in such wise that powers of the political order have no share whatever in it."[18] The historic privilege of governments to nominate bishops was, however remotely and subtly, a share in the governance of souls. It was always per se an abuse, a confusion of the secular and sacral orders, and, as the Council clearly implied, an infringement of the freedom of the Church, an invasion of her immunity from political interference in all that concerns her own internal government and her care of souls.

The simple conclusion here is that the two conciliar documents, *Dignitatis humanae* and *Gaudium et spes,* have made a joint contribution toward the renewal of traditional doctrine with regard to the ancient issue of Church and state. Previous confusions of the historical with the doctrinal have been sorted out. The systematization based on the distinction between thesis and hypothesis has been dismantled. The relevant principles have been stated with a new purity, which was made possible by the new perspectives in which the whole issue was viewed. New theological insights into the concrete reality of the pilgrim Church, and other new insights made available by secular experience (notably the experience of the relation between religious freedom as a human right and the freedom of the Church), have resulted in genuine and fruitful development of doctrine. This doctrinal work was inspired by the maxim of Leo XIII, "Vetera novis augere et perficere." A work of systematization remains to be done under the same inspiration.

Notes

1. EDITOR NOTE: This article was published as "The Issue of Church and State at Vatican II," *Theological Studies* 27 (December 1966):580–606. As far as I know, it was never republished.

2. Lettre á Mgr. Satolli á propos du Congrés des Religions, 8 septembre 1895 (*Lettres Apostoliqes de S. S. Léon XIII, Texte latin avec la traduction française en regard* [Paris: Maison de la Bonne Presse, n.d.] 257). This edition is hereafter cited as "Bonne Presse," with volume and page.

3. Bonne Presse 2, 32.

4. Cited by John XXIII in *Pacem in terris* (*AAS* 55 [1963] 263) from Pius XII's Radio Message, Christmas, 1944.

5. EDITOR NOTE: To the traditional three supports for the political order—namely, truth, justice, and love—John XXIII had added, according to Murray, the notion of freedom as essential for civic living (see 1963j, p. 613; 1964f, p. 62; 1966b, p. 574).

6. EDITOR NOTE: Murray had strenuously rejected the notion that the full common good was rightly the concern of the modern state. The people had restricted the state to the public order portion of the common good, taking to themselves concern for the common good. That the terminology remained in *Dignitatis* and that Murray was forced here to curtail a broad interpretation of the state's legitimate concerns, indicates how much the Declaration was a compromise document and highlights the grounds out of which some argue that the Council did not repudiate the canonical argument for establishment.

7. G. Tellenbach, *Church, State and Christian Society at the Time of the Investiture Contest* (tr. R. F. Bennett; Oxford: Blackwell, 1940) p. 126.

8. John Courtney Murray, S.J., "Leo XIII: Separation of Church and State," *Theological Studies* 14 (1953) 192.

9. Lettre encyclique aux Cardinaux Français, 3 mai 1892 (Bonne Presse 3, 127).

10. EDITOR NOTE: Murray's normal stylistic clarity appears here to have slammed against a conceptual wall. Obviously he is trying to make the case that ecumenical dialogue must move well beyond the virtue of tolerance, as he understood that term. Participants must approach those conversations with attitudes of equality and reciprocity, with humility and a willingness to learn from others. Murray had uncovered these virtuous attitudes in his study of modern democratic cultures. First, he discovered that not only the institutions, but even the very principles that direct civic life are open to historical development and decline. To keep development going, Western societies had made "a great act of faith" in the moral powers of the people to "judge, correct, and direct" social institutions and the principles that guide institution formation. This was all within the arena of natural law discourse. That is, it was all within the temporal order.

Murray is here talking about *theological*, revelationally based discourse in the civic, temporal order. As I mentioned in the general introduction, for much of his life Murray kept theological truth claims locked up inside the Roman church, thereby allowing him to deal with them in a conceptualist, ahistorical manner (even while he discovered the historicity of natural law claims and insisted that his church face valid developments outside its borders). With the conciliar insight that valid, salvific insight can and will arise outside the Roman church, that non-Catholic churches are themselves agents of salvation, theological discourse is thrown into the historical stream. Are, then, the same virtues called for in ecumenical discourse as in civic moral discourse? If so, are those same virtues in ecumenical discourse grounded in a manner similar to that of civic discourse, namely, in a generalized right (and obligation) to judge, correct, and direct theological truth claims? Without the admission that all churches have an obligation to judge, direct, and correct ecumenical, revelationally based truth claims, it appears impossible to move beyond theological intolerance to the virtues of equality and reciprocity. The analogy dissolves.

Murray more satisfactorily developed an analogy between civil and ecclesiological discourse in his discussion of the role of the press within the church. In a first talk ("Information and the Church," 1964a), he tried to transfer the right of the civic people to a free press to the internal life of the church. But he ran afoul of the civil people's right to judge, correct, and direct governmental activities. There was, he claimed, no right of the believer to judge, correct, and direct the magisterium. In a second argument ("Freedom, Authority, Community," 1966g), he grounded the right to a free press and accurate information within the church on the social need that the church has to build bonds of love, mutual commitment, and understanding.

In that second article, he used the spatial imagery of a vertical relationship to the truth and a horizontal relationship to other human beings. We will see in the next few paragraphs of this present article that he attempts to use that spatial imagery to distinguish requirements for adherence to Catholic doctrine within the church from requirements for external, ecumenical discourse. The difference between his use of that imagery here and in 1966g is, of course, that here the requirements for social discourse are applied to a conversation that he still conceives as essentially outside the Roman church; in 1966g they are applied to the internal life of that church. For my discussion of this dialectic shakedown, see my discussion in Hooper, 1986, pp. 181–90.

11. EDITOR NOTE: For the next few pages Murray will attempt to remove any hint of religious freedom as an empowerment from *Dignitatis*'s understanding of the civil order. He does so here by placing the empowerment to preach the Gospel in a transtemporal order, the latter differentiated sharply from the civil order. Three pages further on, he will try to restrict the active role of the state vis-à-vis religion to that of protector of civil freedom. Murray's manner of restricting the socially significant meaning of religious freedom to an immunity right works well, if one considers the issue as applying to the interaction of the church hierarchy and the executive branch of civil government. Problems arise even within his own thought, however, when one considers the role of the laity in shaping governmental legislation. For his argument to still apply, one would have to presume that the laity could bring

no substantive content from their faith commitments to the laws that they shape—that their faith remains simply motivational. As discussed in the general introduction to this collection, some question whether Murray has adequately dealt with the laity's attempts to bring the gospel values to the juridical structures of the state, much less to what is called the world.

12. *AAS* 58 (1966) 10–11.

13. Pius XI, Letter to Card. Gasparri, May 30, 1929, on the Lateran Pacts, in J. B. Lo Grasso, S.J., *Ecclesia et status: De mutuis officiis et iuribus fontes selecti* (Rome: Gregorian University, 1939) pp. 326–27: " . . . la Religione cattolica è, e sol'essa, secondo lo Statuto ed i Trattati, la Religione dello Stato con le logiche e giuridiche conseguenze di una tale situazione di diritto costitutivo . . . ," that is, other cults are only "tollerati, permessi, ammessi."

14. This is the position stated in somewhat softened form in chapter 9 of the original schema of the Constitution on the Church, which emanated from the Theological Commission in November, 1962.

15. Encyclical *Immortale Dei,* Nov. 1, 1885 (Bonne Presse 2, 16).

16. Encyclical *Libertas praestantissimum,* June 20, 1888 (Bonne Presse 2, 192).

17. EDITOR NOTE: For a later discussion of these self-denying ordinances in a fuller ecumenical setting, see "The Declaration on Religious Freedom," 1966c, p. 10, and 1967n.

18. Encyclical *Sapientiae christianae,* Jan. 10, 1890 (Bonne Presse 2, 283).

4

Arguments for the Human Right to Religious Freedom[1]

The following article is the closest that the later Murray came to a "purely natural law" philosophical argument. As mentioned in the general introduction, Murray began his 1945 philosophical argument with "essential definitions" of key terms that he thought relevant to that debate—terms such as "conscience," "law," "state," and "God." Here he is defining the term "human dignity," which serves as the philosophical foundation for the right to religious freedom. In doing so, however, he is not delineating a timeless essence. Rather, he is making explicit a notion that, he contends, has emerged within Western societies. After the mid-1950s, natural law had become for Murray a developing tradition of ideas, commitments, and procedures that course through the social and political thought of a secular society that is continuously on the move.

In terms of the structure Murray established in "The Problem of Religious Freedom," this complex, secular notion of human dignity "converges" with the church's own theologically based judgments concerning the church's place in human history and its own freedom. That the secular society's and the church's judgments ought to converge is of course based in Murray's notion of Gelasian dualism (and *concordia*), as is his judgment that the church ought to affirm and defend human dignity as a social good. Since Murray is here simply trying to tone up *Dignitatis's* philosophical argument, the theological presuppositions of his earlier arguments recede into the background.

Here Murray strengthened his conciliar argument by adjusting the relative positions of the various principles that he had clarified in those conciliar discussions. The reader might especially note the positioning of the principle "as much freedom as possible" in this article, in contrast to its place in "Problem."

Yet a question remains: Is this what Western societies affirm when they proclaim commitments to human dignity? For Murray, the notion is intrinsically social and historical. It involves a view of the human person as constantly active within, and possessing responsibilities toward, the societies in which they live. Some criticisms of Western individualism do not find such a social notion of the human person at the heart of the Western experiment, while others find sociality there, but also a reticence to talk about those implied social commitments. Murray's understanding of human dignity also includes an intrinsic drive toward all that the human mind and heart can question, including the reality of God. Again, some criticisms of Western culture find at its core a constraining materialism. At the least, Murray's exposition perhaps can demonstrate that our alternatives are not simply between individualistic isolation and communitarian immersion, materialistic constriction and spiritualistic escapism. It might be possible to develop an understanding of the human person that preserves both the strong sense of personal integrity and worth of the individualist traditions, the social interdependence of more communitarian traditions, and a strong concern for material existence that is involved in commitments to social justice.

The Vatican Declaration "Dignitatis humanae personae" affirmed that the human person has a right to religious freedom. It showed that the concept of religious freedom is clear, distinct, and technically exact regarding both its ground and its object, and adequately developed concerning what it embraces. First I will reiterate what the Council meant and what generally is meant by religious freedom. Then I will address the more difficult question of how to construct the argument—whether derived from reason or from revelation—that will give a solid foundation to what the Declaration affirms. For nearly four years the conciliar Fathers and experts vigorously debated this justification, eventually completing the brief argument found in the Declaration (n. 2, 3). Even so, it is fair to say that this argument has pleased or pleases no one in all respects.

We can legitimately debate how better to construct the argument. For the Council's teaching authority falls upon what it affirmed, not upon the reasons it adduced for its affirmation. The Council did not intend that the Declaration establish an apodictic proof. The Declaration was merely to outline certain arguments, mainly to demonstrate that the affirmation of religious freedom is doctrinal.[2] The church's affirmation is based upon arguments drawn both from human reason and from Christian sources. Please allow me, then, what you have allowed others: to discuss this whole matter briefly.

Civil Religious Freedom

To begin with, it will be useful carefully to delimit what we must argue. This will not be difficult if we keep in mind that the concept of religious freedom includes a two-fold immunity from coercion.

First, in the sphere of religion no one is to be compelled to act against his conscience. Nowadays this principle is one upon which all persons of judgement agree, unshakably. Enough, then, to recall that for us Christians this principle derives its strongest argument from the necessary freedom of the act of Christian faith, a doctrine licitly and necessarily extended to the profession of every religion.

Second, in the sphere of religion no one is to be impeded from acting according to his conscience—in public or in private, alone or in association with others. It is around this second immunity that the conciliar debate turned. This second immunity had long been a historical problem; it remains a theoretical or doctrinal problem. It will help to clarify the problem.

Discussion of the human right to religious freedom calls for further inquiry into the foundations of the juridical relationship among human beings in civil society. The concept of a juridical relationship properly includes the notion of a correspondence between rights and duties. To one person's right there is a corresponding duty incumbent on others to do or give or omit something. In our case, the human person demands by right the omission of all coercive action impeding a person or a community from acting according to its conscience in religious matters. Therefore, the affirmation that every person has a right to such immunity is simultaneously an affirmation that no other person or power in society has a right to use coercion. On the contrary all others are duty-bound to refrain from coercive action. The second immunity, then, requires a compelling argument that no other person can raise, as a right or duty, a valid claim against that immunity or, put positively, that all are obliged to respect that immunity. The whole matter hinges on this argument for the juridical actuality of the second immunity.

To clarify this point, let us suppose that there does exist in human society a power that possesses the right to prohibit religious practice. Such a power could only be the public power (the state). Certainly a right of this kind could not be possessed by any private person or intermediate social group. One could argue—indeed, many have so argued—that the public power does possess such a right because of its duty toward the good of society and because it has a monopoly on coercive power that it must exercise for the good of society either by means of legislation or of administrative action.

To establish, then, that the human person enjoys a right to full religious freedom, one must first establish that the public power has no right to restrict religious freedom but has rather the duty to acknowledge and protect it.

Such being the case, clearly our inquiry, although of its nature ethico-juridical, is nevertheless finally and formally political, or what is called constitutional. By this I mean that it deals with the duties and rights of the public power—their nature, their extent, and their limits.

The classic difficulty in this matter is well known. It begins in the human person's obligation to act intelligently, i.e., according to his conscience. Yet it sometimes can and often does happen that someone who acts according to his conscience can act contrary to the objective order of truth—for example, by practicing a form of public worship not wholly in agreement with the divine ordinance or by disseminating religious opinions not in conformity with divine revelation. Surely spreading religious errors or practicing false forms of worship is per se evil in the moral order. About this there is no doubt. But our inquiry is not about the moral but about the juridical order. Does the public power have the duty and the right to repress opinions, practices, religious rites because they are erroneous and dangerous to the common good?

The Vatican Council's Declaration denies that such duty and such right fall within the competence of the public power. Yet we still must ask: On what justifying argument does this denial rest? Why may the limitation placed on the public power in matters of religion be considered just and legitimate? Thus is the state of our question. I will now evaluate the various arguments that were put forward to confirm the person's right to freedom in religious matters.

Arguments for Religious Freedom

First we must note that the doctrine of the Declaration is today supported by the sense and near unanimous consent of the human race. This is also intimated at the very beginning of the Declaration. The Declaration also suggests that this consent does not rely upon the laicist ideology so widespread in the nineteenth century but upon the increasingly worldwide consciousness of the dignity of the human person. It relies, therefore, upon an objective truth manifested to the people of our time by their own consciousness. Before adducing other arguments, then, the presupposition obtains and prevails that the teaching of the Declaration is also true. *Securus enim iudicat orbis terrarum.*[3]

From this it follows that the Council's sole purpose in adducing the argument in favor of the right to religious freedom is to clarify and strengthen under the light of both reason and Christian revelation the more or less confused contemporary consciousness of human dignity.

From Conscience

The first conciliar attempt to do so was laid out in the arguments of the first and second schemata.[4] The basis of that argument was the moral principle that in religious matters man is held bound to follow his conscience even if erroneous. From this moral principle the schema deduced, as if immediately, the moral-juridical principle that to man is due the right to be free in society to follow his conscience.

This moral argument if correctly expounded has its force. But ultimately it is defective because unable to demonstrate what, in line with our statements above, has to be demonstrated.

The moral principle is entirely valid that man is duty-bound always to follow his conscience. From this follows the moral-juridical principle that man has the right to fulfill his duty. No difficulty arises if the conscience in question is right and true. This is evident. But if the conscience in question is right but erroneous, it cannot give rise to a juridical relationship between persons. From one human being's erroneous conscience no duty follows for others to act or perform or omit anything. Some might insist that the first two schemata additionally presuppose that the public power lacks any right to prevent human beings in society from acting according to erroneous consciences. Perhaps it does, even though this is not immediately apparent from the text. Even so, the schemata's argument failed to demonstrate why the public power lacks this right.

This being the case, the argument fails to support that immunity upon which our whole inquiry hinges. Hence it is not surprising that the Council's third schema—entitled "corrected text"—abandoned this line of argument that would ground the right to religious freedom in the dictates of conscience. From the third schema down to the promulgation of the Declaration, the foundation for the right to religious freedom is placed in the dignity of the human person. Rightly and wisely.

I shall leave aside the justifying arguments found in the subsequent schemata and come at once to the final, definitive text. The text sets forth two main arguments and, to give completeness to the doctrine, a third additional argument based upon the faith.[5]

From the Obligation to Search After the Truth

In keeping with the wishes of many council Fathers, the first argument attempts ontologically to ground religious freedom in the fact that all men "are impelled by their nature and are bound besides by a moral obligation to seek the truth, especially truth regarding religion. They are also bound, once they have learned the truth, to adhere to it and to regulate their whole lives according to its demands" (no. 2). From this moral obligation the argument next deduces the human right to immunity from external coercion in fulfilling his obligations. The further assertion is made that "the exercise (of this right) cannot be impeded if the just public order is preserved."

Obviously this argument aims to vindicate the whole concept of religious freedom insofar as it imports the double immunity from coercion. What are we to think of this argument?

The argument is valid and on target. Undeniably the demand for freedom has its basis in man's intellectual nature, in the human capacity to seek, to embrace, and to manifest by his way of life the truth to which he is ordered. In no other way can he perform his duty toward truth than by his personal assent and free deliberation. What is more, from this single consideration it is already clear that no one is to be forced to act against his conscience or against the demands of the truth that he has in fact found, or at least thinks that he has found. If so forced, he would be acting against his intellectual nature itself.

Yet we may still ask whether this demand for freedom, which flows from the source just mentioned, has enough power to establish a true right in keeping with which no one is to be impeded from acting according to his conscience in religious matters. Put differently: Are man's natural and moral links to truth powerful enough to engender a political relationship between the human person and the public power so that the latter is duty-bound not to prevent the person from acting according to his conscience—whether the person acts alone or in association with others? It seems not.

Man is certainly impelled by his nature, and is obliged morally, to seek the truth so that he might conform his life to the truth, once found. Yet quite a few, either after searching for religious truth or not searching for it, actually cling to more or less false opinions that they wish to put into practice publicly and to disseminate in society. To highlight again the point upon which our investigation hinges, let us imagine public powers speaking to these erring people as follows:

"We acknowledge and deeply respect the impulse to seek truth implanted in human nature. We acknowledge, too, your moral obligation to conform your life to truth's demands. But, sorry to say, we judge you to be in error. For in the sphere of religion we possess objective truth. More than that, in this society we represent the common good as well as religious truth—in fact religious truth is an integral part of the common good. In your private and in your family life, therefore, you may lawfully act according to your errors. However, we acknowledge no duty on our part to refrain from coercion in your regard when in the public life of society, which is our concern, you set about introducing your false forms of worship or spreading your errors. Continue, then, your search for truth until you find it—we possess it—so that you may be able to act in public in keeping with it."

Is this proclamation imaginary? Hardly! Time and again over the centuries public powers have issued similar statements. And what answer can the poor people make who are thus judged to be living in error? None, certainly, if we stay within the principles laid down in the Declaration's first argument. For we can grant the premise of those principles: that those in error have an obligation to seek the truth in order to learn it and act in keeping with it. But we deny that from those principles the conclusion follows that those in error have the right not to be impeded from acting in public according to their consciences. It seems correct to deny this conclusion, since it appears to extend beyond its premises.

Assuredly those judged to be misguided would like to object that the public power has no right to issue judgements about objective truth in the religious sphere, that even less has it the right to transform those judgements into coercive legislation, thereby preventing its citizens from acting according to their consciences. This is as valid an objection as can be. But I ask: Does its validity proceed from the ontological basis of religious freedom as the Declaration claims and conceives that it does? It seems not.

For it may be said, and some at times have so claimed, that the right of civil power to repress false forms of worship or religious errors is compatible with man's moral obligation to seek the truth in order to act according to it. For such repression does not in the least prevent the quest for truth, nor does it prevent acting according to the truth. What it does prevent are public activities that proceed from a basis in error and that thus cause harm to the public good. This opinion is not to be scorned. It has even been widely received at times within the Church itself.

Admittedly it was mainly pastoral considerations that led the Fathers to accept this first argument in the Declaration, the argument that situates the ontological roots of religious freedom in the obligation to seek the truth. Some Fathers feared the establishment of a kind of separation between truth and freedom, or more exactly, a separation between the order of truth and the juridical order that equips man with rights against others. Of course this was an entirely legitimate concern. Still, the speculative question remains: Is it correct to place the ontological ground for religious freedom in man's natural and moral relationships to truth? On this point doubt may be allowed.

From the Person's Social Nature

The same pastoral uneasiness apparently controls the second major argument in the Declaration. This argument begins with the divine law to which every human being is subject and in which his nature makes him a participant. From this premise the argument at once concludes to man's moral obligation to investigate what the precepts of the divine law might be. The point is made that this investigation ought to be conducted in a social manner. The argument then lays down another moral principle—that man perceives the dictates of the divine law through the mediation of his conscience, which he is therefore always bound to follow. After positing these moral principles, the argument proceeds to a conclusion that is juridical: that not surprisingly man has a right to the two immunities that form the object of the right to religious freedom.

I acknowledge the value of this argument, provided the following distinction is made that always must be made. Indisputably the argument validly shows that no one is to be forced to act against his conscience, for by so acting a person would be doing wrong. But the second question recurs. Does it follow from this argument that no one is to be prevented from acting in public according to his conscience? To establish immunity from this kind of coercion—and this is specific to religious freedom in its modern meaning—the argument appeals to the necessary connection between internal acts of religion and those outward acts by which, in keeping with his social nature, a human being displays his religious convictions in a public way. Given this connection, the argument runs as follows: A purely human power cannot forbid internal acts; it is therefore equally powerless to forbid external acts.

But does not the fallacy of begging the question somehow lurk in this argument? It supposes that in society no power exists with authority reaching far enough to warrant its legitimately forbidding public acts of religion, even acts that transgress objective truth or divine law or even the common good. This must be established; it is the very heart of the matter under discussion. It is not proved by stating that persons are morally obliged to obey divine law as known by them through the mediation of their consciences. Nor is it proved by stating that human nature is social and requires that people profess their religion in a public and communitarian manner.

From the Limits of Public Power

Finally, there remains the third argument of the Declaration. It does concern the limits of the public power. This argument is introduced with the word *Praeterea* ["Furthermore"]. This suggests that the argument is added as a complement to the argument so far presented, a complement to an argument that is presumed in itself sufficient to justify the human right to religious freedom in its double sense.

But if the state of the question about this human right is examined thoroughly, it is at once evident that this political argument is of primary importance. Without it any other argument would not sufficiently settle the question. For the very question concerns the limits of public power in religious matters.

The Declaration makes the felicitous assertion that public power "must be said to exceed its limits if it should presume to direct or to impede religious acts" (n. 3). Felicitous, I repeat, and altogether true. But it is a simple assertion for whose truth no reasons are brought forward. May I be permitted, as long as time allows, to develop this political argument? I proceed in outline form, schematically, by enumerating the principles without further development. The intention of the argument I offer is the same as that prefixed to the Declaration: "to develop the teaching of recent Popes about the inviolable rights of the human person and about the juridical ordering of society" (n. 1).

The argument begins properly from a first principle: Every human person is endowed with a dignity that surpasses the rest of creatures because the human person is independent [in charge of himself, autonomous]. The primordial demand of that dignity, then, is that man acts by his own counsel and purpose, using and enjoying his freedom, moved, not by external coercion, but internally by the risk of his whole existence. In a word, human dignity consists formally in the person's responsibility for himself and, what is more, for his world. So great is his dignity that not even God can take it away—by taking upon Himself or unto Himself the responsibility for his life and for his fate. This in the Christian tradition, especially from the Greek Fathers on, is the dignity of the person conceived, fashioned in the image of God. The person's intellectual nature is a prior condition, the absence of which would render his assumption of responsibility impossible. Formally, however, human dignity consists in bearing this responsibility.

Now, from the first, ontological principle (the dignity of the human person), there follows a second principle, the social principle, which Pope Pius XII and later John XXIII began to develop somewhat fully. The social principle states that the human person is the subject, foundation, and end of the entire social life.[6]

For our purpose, the chief force of the social principle lies in its establishing an indissoluble connection between the moral and the juridical orders. This connection must not be conceived in some abstract manner but in a wholly concrete way. For the connection is the human person itself, really existing, in the presence of its God and Lord, in association with others in this historic world, but in such wise that it transcends by reason of its end both society and the whole world. The human person exists in God's presence as a moral subject bound by duties toward the moral order and toward the historical order of salvation established by Jesus Christ. The human person exists with others in society as a moral-juridical subject furnished with rights that flow directly and altogether from human nature, never to be alienated from that nature. The juridical order cannot be sundered from the moral order, any more than the human person can be halved.

Evidently, in this subordinate place we can and ought to collect and situate those things that the Declaration said so beautifully about the natural human impulse to seek truth and about the person's moral obligation to live according to the truth once found. They do illustrate the first ontological principle and the second social principle.[7]

Now, from the first and the second principles, the ontological and the social, taken together, there follows a third principle, the so-called principle of the free society. This principle affirms that man in society must be accorded as much freedom as possible, and that that freedom is not to be restricted unless and insofar as is necessary. By necessary I mean the restraint needed to preserve society's very existence or—to use the concept and terms of the Declaration itself—necessary for preserving the public order in its juridical, political, and moral aspects.

Parallel with the third principle, a fourth issues from taking the first two, the ontological and the social, together. This principle is juridical and maintains that all citizens enjoy juridical equality in society.[8] This principle rests upon the truth that all persons are peers in natural dignity and that every human being is equally the subject, foundation, and end of human society.

Finally, there follows a fifth principle, the political principle. It is admirably expressed in the following words of Pius XII, later quoted by John XXIII. "To protect the inviolable rights proper to human beings and to ensure that everyone may discharge his duties with greater facility—this is the paramount duty of every public power."[9] This constitutes for the public power its first and principal concern for the common good—the effective protection of the human person and its dignity. This definition of the paramount function of public power rests clearly upon the first four principles.

Further, all five principles cohere with one another in such a way that they form a kind of vision of the human person in society and of society itself, of the juridical ordering of society and of the common good considered in its most fundamental dimensions, and finally of the duties of the public power toward persons and society. Upon this vision, which recent pontiffs have newly elaborated while working within the tradition, rests the whole doctrine of the Vatican Declaration on Religious Freedom. In other words, the five principles just enumerated taken together finally bring our whole investigation to a point of decision. For they are sufficient to constitute that relationship between the human person and the public juridical power. Together they fully characterize the notion of religious freedom.

They are also sufficient to confirm the other human and civil freedoms with which John XXIII dealt in an eminent manner in his En-

cyclical *Pacem in Terris*. Along with these freedoms religious freedom
constitutes an order of freedoms in society. Religious freedom cannot be discussed apart from discussion of this whole body of freedoms. All human freedoms stand or fall together—a fact that secular
experience has made clear enough.

This said, it is not difficult to construct an argument for the human
right to religious freedom.

A Needed Argument

The first thing to note is that the dignity and the freedom of the
human person should receive primary attention since they pertain to
the goods that are proper to the human spirit. As for these goods, the
first of which is the good of religion, the most important and urgent
demand is for freedom. For human dignity demands that in making
this fundamental religious option and in carrying it out through every type of religious action, whether private or public, in all these
aspects a person should act by his own deliberation and purpose,
enjoying immunity from all external coercion so that in the presence
of God he takes responsibility on himself alone for his religious decisions and acts. This demand of both freedom and responsibility is the
ultimate ontological ground of religious freedom as it is likewise the
ground of the other human freedoms.

Now, this demand is grounded upon the very existence of the human person, or, if one prefers, in the objective truth about the human person. Therefore it is revealed as a juridical value in society, so
that it can impose upon the public power the duty to refrain from
keeping the human person from acting in religious matters according
to his dignity. For the public power is bound to acknowledge and to
fulfill this duty by reason of its principal function, the protection of
the dignity of the person. Once this duty is demonstrated and acknowledged, the immunity from coercion in religious matters demanded by human dignity becomes actually the object of a right. For
the juridical actuality of a right is established wherever a corresponding duty is established and is acknowledged, once the validity of the
ground for a right is assured and recognized.

Furthermore, the above mentioned principle of a free society—
taken together with the principle of the juridical equality of all citizens—likewise sets the outer limits on just how far the public power
must refrain from preventing someone from acting according to his

conscience. The free exercise of religion in society ought not be restricted save insofar as it is necessary, that is, save when a public act
ceases to be an exercise of religion because proven to be a crime
against public order.

The following considerations will clarify this. The foundation of
human society lies in the truth about the human person, or in its
dignity, that is, in its demand for responsible freedom. That which in
justice is preeminently owed to the person is freedom—as much freedom as possible—in order that society thus may be borne toward its
goals, which are those of the human person itself, by the strength and
energies of persons in society bound together with one another by
love. Truth and justice, therefore, and love itself demand that the
practice of freedom in society be kept vigorous, especially with respect to the goods belonging to the human spirit and so much the
more with respect to religion. Now this demand for freedom, following as it does from the objective truth of the person in society and
from justice itself, naturally engenders the juridical relationship between the person and the public power. The public power is duty-
bound to acknowledge the truth about the person, to protect and
advance the person, and to render the justice owed the person.

Again, from this follows the conclusion that no one is to be prevented in the matter of religion from acting according to the demands of his dignity or according to his inmost religious convictions.
Nor does this immunity cease except where just demands of public
order are proven to have the urgency of a higher force.

Quod erat demonstandum. Or rather, this argument from the five
principles mentioned is sufficient; nothing else is required.

The Question of a Theological Argument

Of course there remains the argument for religious freedom as
drawn from Christian revelation, but this is a lengthy question and
my discussion has already been too long.

Suffice it to say that the line of argument that the Declaration follows is entirely valid and sound. It embraces three major statements.
(1) The human person's right to religious freedom cannot itself be
proven from Holy Scripture, nor from Christian revelation. (2) Yet
the foundation of this right, the dignity of the human person, has
ampler and more brilliant confirmation in Holy Scripture than can be
drawn from human reason alone. (3) By a long historical evolution

society has finally reached the notion of religious freedom as a human right. And a foundation and moving force of this ethical and political development has been Christian doctrine itself—I use "Christian" in its proper sense—on the subject of human dignity, doctrine illuminated by the example of the Lord Jesus.

Difficult and important questions remain. The primary one concerns the relationship between the Christian freedom proclaimed in Holy Scripture, especially by St. Paul, and the religious freedom we have been speaking of, to which our contemporaries lay claim.[10] On this question no consensus exists. According to some, these two freedoms are so different from their inception that only a limited harmony can exist between them. According to others, of whom I am one, in the very notion of Christian and gospel freedom—or, better—in free Christian existence itself a demand is given for religious freedom in society. To demonstrate this is no mean task. Add to this the difficult historical question, as yet not investigated: Why has humanity had to travel so long a journey on so tortuous a course to reach at last a consciousness of its dignity and to bring to fulfillment in civil society all that that dignity demands?

Evidently these question belong to the ecumenical order. Equally evident and pressing is the need for us to enter into conversation with our separated brothers and even with our non-believing brothers. These have contributed much and still contribute toward the establishment and preservation in society of the full practice of freedom, including also religious freedom.

Notes

1. EDITOR NOTE: This was delivered as a talk on September 19, 1966, and published in Latin as "De argumentis pro iure hominis ad libertatem religiosam," in *Acta Congressus Internationalis de Theologia Concilii Vaticani II*, ed. A. Schönmetzer (Rome: Vatican, 1968), pp. 562–73 (English translation copyright 1993 Westminster/John Knox Press).

2. EDITOR NOTE: That is, the church did not affirm religious freedom because it was more expedient to do so in the modern world. The affirmation is based on principle.

3. EDITOR NOTE: "The whole world concurs in this judgement" is probably an allusion to Augustine, Contra ep. Parm., II, 10, 20. For a near parallel to this present article, see Murray's "The Declaration on Religious Freedom," 1966b. Certain points, such as the international political and ecclesiological

support given to religious freedom, are more fully spelled out in that latter article.

4. EDITOR NOTE: For a discussion of the various texts that preceded *Dignitatis,* see the introduction to "The Problem" in this volume. By Murray's count there were five such texts; the third and fourth were of Murray's creation.

5. EDITOR NOTE: The remainder of the article presents actually three philosophical arguments and a fourth based on faith. As we will see, Murray was unhappy with the first two "main arguments." (They both suggest an individualism (that often cloaks itself in abstraction) and an ahistoricity that he found in the "conscience" argument.) He will here present a third argument that he considers core to the church's affirmation and to contemporary affirmations of human dignity. This third line had been primary in the third and fourth drafts of the Declaration (the ones Murray wrote) and had been reduced to an ancillary position in subsequent drafts and in the final document.

Since Murray's own numbering is off, I felt free, by way of headings, to grant to the "conscience" argument the status of first in a line of arguments. In fact, the language of the "rights of conscience" argument was not limited to the first two drafts. There remains some residual "rights of conscience" terminology in the Declaration, a fact used by some who want to argue that the Council did not advance beyond the "conscience" argument.

6. Cf. Pius XII, *Nunt. radioph.* 24 dec. 1944, in *A.A.S.* [*Acta Apostolica Sedis*] 37 (1945) p. 12; Ioannes XXIII Litt. enc. *"Pacem in terris,"* in *A.A.S.* 55 (1963) p. 263; Dz.-S 3968.

7. EDITOR NOTE: By situating the drive for truth within the second, social pole of the human person, Murray apparently thinks that he has escaped the individualism and abstraction of the Declaration's main argument. Within that second pole, the argument must take account of the structures and forces that are active within historical societies as well as of the transcendental openness of the human person.

8. EDITOR NOTE: Just as the first two principles call up the individual/social aspects of human nature, similarly for Murray these third and fourth principles have individual/social references. The third points to the creative powers of persons and subgroups in society, while the fourth focuses on the largest social reality, the state. Murray has attempted to highlight the intrinsic social aspects of the human person throughout the various levels of this argument.

9. Pius XII, *Nunt. radioph.* 1 iun. 1941, in *A.A.S.* 33 (1941) p. 200; Ioannes XXIII *"Pacem in terris."* ed. cit., p. 274; Dz-S 3985.

10. EDITOR NOTE: Elsewhere Murray spelled out a broader list of freedoms that must be reconciled:

The Declaration therefore does not undertake to present a full
and complete theology of freedom. This would have been a far
more ambitious task. It would have been necessary, I think, to
develop four major themes: (1) the concept of Christian freedom—the freedom of the People of God—as a participation in
the freedom of the Holy Spirit, the principal agent in the history
of salvation, by whom the children of God are "led" (Rom. 8, 14)
to the Father through the incarnate Son; (2) the concept of the
freedom of the Church in her ministry, as a participation in the
freedom of Christ himself, to whom all authority in heaven and
on earth was given and who is present in his Church to the end of
time (cf. Matt. 28, 18. 20); (3) the concept of Christian faith as
man's free response to the divine call issued, on the Father's
eternal and gracious initiative, through Christ, and heard by man
in his heart where the Spirit speaks what he has himself heard (cf.
John 16, 13–15); (4) the juridical concept of religious freedom
as a human and civil right, founded on the native dignity of the
human person who is made in the image of God and therefore
enjoys, as his birthright, a participation in the freedom of God
himself. This would have been, I think, a far more satisfactory
method of procedure, from the theological point of view. In particular, it would have been in conformity with the disposition of
theologians today to view issues of natural law within the concrete context of the present historico-existential order of grace.
Moreover, the doctrine presented would have been much richer
in content. ("The Declaration on Religious Freedom," 1966c,
p. 4)

WORKS BY
JOHN COURTNEY MURRAY

All Murray Archive material can be found in Special Collections, Lauinger Library, Georgetown University, Washington, D.C.

1929. "Governmental Supervision of Schools in the Philippines." *Woodstock Letters* 58:48–53.

1932. "Crisis in the History of Trent." *Thought* 7 (December):463–73.

1937. *Matthias Scheeben on Faith: The Doctrinal Dissertation of John Courtney Murray*, edited by D. Thomas Hughson. Vol. 29, Toronto Studies in Theology. Lewiston, N.Y.: The Edwin Mellen Press, 1987.

1938. "Taken from Among Men." *Jesuit Seminary News* 12 (June):3–5.

1940a. "The Construction of a Christian Culture: I. Portrait of a Christian; II. Personality and the Community; III. The Humanism of God." Three talks given February 1940 at St. Joseph's College. Murray Archives, file 6-422.

1940b. "Necessary Adjustments to Overcoming Practical Difficulties." In *Man and Modern Secularism: Essays on the Conflict of the Two Cultures*, edited by the National Catholic Alumni Federation, pp. 152–57. New York: National Catholic Alumni Federation.

1941a. "The Christian Fulfillment." Murray Archives, file 5-577.

1941b. "Toward a Christian Humanism: Aspects of the Theology of Education." In *A Philosophical Symposium on American Catholic Education,* edited by H. Guthrie and G. Walsh, pp. 106–15. New York: Fordham University Press. Presented at the 17th Annual Convention of the Jesuit Philosophical Association of the Eastern States, September 4–6, 1940.

1942a. "Book Reviews: New Periodicals." *Theological Studies* 3 (May):290–93.

1942b. "Current Theology: Christian Co-operation." *Theological Studies* 3 (September):413–31.

1942c. Review of *The Layman's Call,* by William R. O'Connor. *Theological Studies* 3 (December):608–10.

1943a. "Current Theology: Co-operation: Some Further Views." *Theological Studies* 4 (March):100–111.

1943b. "Current Theology: Intercredal Co-operation: Its Theory and Its Organization." *Theological Studies* 4 (June):257–86. Also published as *Intercredal Co-operation: Principles.* Washington, D.C.: Catholic Association for International Peace, 1943.

1943c. "Descriptive Notes." *Theological Studies* 4 (September):466.

1943d. Review of *Principles for Peace: Selections from Papal Documents,* edited by Harry C. Koenig. *Theological Studies* 4 (December):634–38.

1943e. "To the Editor." *Theological Studies* 4 (September):472–74.

1944a. "The Juridical Organization of the International Community." *The New York Law Journal* (October 9):813–14. A sermon given at a Red Mass at St. Andrew. Also published as "World Order and Moral Law." *Thought* 19 (December 1944):581–86.

1944b. *The Pattern for Peace and the Papal Peace Program.* Washington, D.C.: Paulist Press. Pamphlet from the Catholic Association for International Peace. Another version of this article, with some alterations, can be found as "Co-operation Among All Men of Good Will," Murray Archives, file 12-769. This latter was in turn published as "La Cooperación Interconfessional Para la Pax," *Verbum* [Guatemala] (January 9, 1945) and in *Vida: Revista de Orientacion* 7 (1944):757–71.

1944c. "Toward a Theology for the Layman: The Pedagogical Problem." *Theological Studies* 5 (September):340–76.

1944d. "Toward a Theology for the Layman: The Problem of Its Finality." *Theological Studies* 5 (March):43–75. This and the preceding article appeared in a condensed form in "Toward a Theology for the Layman," *Jesuit Educational Quarterly* 11, no. 4 (March):221–28.

1944e. "Woodstock Wisdom." *Woodstock Letters* 73 (December 1944):280–84.

1945a. "Current Theology: Freedom of Religion." *Theological Studies* 6 (March):85–113.

1945b. "Freedom of Religion, I: The Ethical Problem." *Theological Studies* 6 (June):229–86. This was much later translated and published in *Relations* [Montréal] 22 (May 1962):118–20; (June 1962):151–53; (July 1962):179–82; (August 1962):207–10; (September 1962)234–38; (November 1962):301–04; (December 1962):33–35; 23 (January 1962):2–4. A further article, "Le droit à l'incroyance," *Relations* (April 1962):91–92, was part of this French series but not part of 1945b.

1945c. "God's Word and Its Realization." *America* 74 (December 8, supplement):xix–xxi.

1945d. "Memorandum" and April 30, 1945 letter to Zacheus Maher (Jesuit American Superior) on the racial issue at St. Louis University. Murray Archives, file 8-585.

1945e. "Notes on the Theory of Religious Liberty." Memo to Archbishop Mooney, April 1945. Murray Archives, file 7-555.

1945f. "On the Problem of Co-operation: Some Clarifications: Reply to Father P. H. Furfey." *American Ecclesiastical Review* 112 (March):194–214.

1945g. "The Real Woman Today." *America* 74 (November 3):122–24.

1946a. "How Liberal Is Liberalism?" *America* 75 (April 6):6–7.

1946b. "Operation University." *America* 75 (April 13):28–29.

1946c. "The Papal Allocution: Christmas." *America* 74 (January 5):370–71.

1946d. Review of *Religious Liberty: An Inquiry,* by M. Searle Bates. *Theological Studies* 7 (March):151–63.

1946e. "Separation of Church and State." *America* 76 (December 7):261–63.

1947a. "Admonition and Grace." In *The Fathers of the Church: Writings of St. Augustine II,* pp. 239–305. New York: Cima.

1947b. "The Court Upholds Religious Freedom." *America* 76 (March 8):628–30.

1947c. "Separation of Church and State: True and False Concepts." *America* 76 (February 15):541–45.

1948a. "Belief in Life." Three talks given on "The Catholic Hour" and published in pamphlet form with the specific titles: *The Assault of Fear,* March 7, 1948; *The Desert and the Garden,* March 14, 1948; and *The Supreme Sorrow,* March 21, 1948. Washington, D.C.: National Council of Catholic Men. Also published in *Catholic Mind* 80 (April 1982):2–7.

1948b. "Dr. Morrison and the First Amendment." *America* 78 (March 6):627–29; (March 20):683–86.

1948c. "Government Repression of Heresy." In *Proceedings of the Third Annual Convention of the Catholic Theological Society of America,* pp. 26–98. Bronx, N.Y.: Catholic Theological Society of America. This article and 1948i, 1949b, and 1951b were then collected as "A Church-State Anthology: The Work of Fr. Murray," *Thought* 27 (1952):6–43, then translated and reprinted as "Kirche und Demokratie" in *Dokumente: Zeitschrift für übernationale Zusammenarbeit* 12 (February 1956):9–16.

1948d. "On the Most Blessed Trinity." *The Summa Theologica of St. Thomas.* Vol. 3, pp. 3153–63. New York: Benziger Brothers.

1948e. "Religious Liberty: The Concern of All." *America* 78 (February 7):513–16.

1948f. "The Role of Faith in the Renovation of the World." *The Messenger of the Sacred Heart* 83 (March):15–17.

1948g. "The Roman Catholic Church." *The Annals of the American Academy of Political and Social Science* 256 (March):36–42. Also published as "What Does the Catholic Church Want?" *Catholic Digest* 13 (December):51–53 (abbreviated); and

"The Roman Catholic Church," *Catholic Mind* 46 (September):580–88.

1948h. "The Root of Faith: The Doctrine of M. J. Scheeben." *Theological Studies* 9 (March):20–46.

1948i. "St. Robert Bellarmine on the Indirect Power." *Theological Studies* 9 (December):491–535. This article and 1948c, 1949b, and 1951b were translated and reprinted as "Kirche und Demokratie," *Dokumente: Zeitschrift für übernationale Zusammenarbeit* 12 (February 1956):9–16.

1949a. "The Catholic Position: A Reply." *American Mercury* 69 (September):274–83; (November):637–39.

1949b. "Contemporary Orientations of Catholic Thought on Church and State in the Light of History." *Theological Studies* 10 (June):177–234. Also published in *Cross Currents* (Fall 1951):15–55. This article and 1948c, 1948i, and 1951b were translated and reprinted as "Kirche und Demokratie," *Dokumente: Zeitschrift für übernationale Zusammenarbeit* 12 (February):9–16.

1949c. "Current Theology: On Religious Freedom." *Theological Studies* 10 (September):409–32.

1949d. "Law or Prepossessions." *Law and Contemporary Problems* 14 (Winter 1949):23–43. Also published in *Essays in Constitutional Law,* edited by R. G. McCloskey (New York: Alfred A. Knopf, 1957), pp. 316–47.

1949e. "On the Idea of a College Religion Course." *Jesuit Educational Quarterly* (October):79–86.

1949f. "On the Necessity for Not Believing: A Roman Catholic Interpretation." *The Yale Scientific Magazine* 23, no. 5 (February):11, 12, 22, 30, 32, 34.

1949g. "Reversing the Secularist Drift." *Thought* 24 (March):36–46.

1949h. Review of *American Freedom and Catholic Power,* by Paul Blanshard. *The Catholic World* 169 (June):233–34.

1949i. Review of *Free Speech in Its Relation to Self-Government,* by Alexander Meiklejohn. *Georgetown Law Journal* 37 (May):654–62.

1950a. "The Natural Law." In *Great Expressions of Human Rights,* edited by Robert M. MacIver, pp. 69–104. New York: Harper. Also published as "Natural Law and the Public Consensus," in *Natural Law and Modern Society,* edited by John Cogley (Cleveland, Ohio: World Publishing, 1962; reprint Freeport, N.Y.: Books for Libraries Press, 1971), pp. 8–81. Forms the concluding chapter, "The Doctrine Lives: The Eternal Return of the Natural Law," of *WHTT,* pp. 295–336, with only slight revisions.

1950b. "One Work of the One Church." *The Missionary Union of the Clergy Bulletin* 14 (March):5–11. Also published in *Catholic Mind* 48 (June 1950):358–64.

1951a. "Paul Blanchard and the New Nativism." *The Month,* New Series 5 (April):214–25.

1951b. "The Problem of 'The Religion of the State.' " *The American Ecclesiastical Review* 124 (May):327–52. Also published as "The Problem of State Religion," *Theological Studies* 12 (June 1951):155–78. This article and 1948c, 1948i, and 1949b were translated and reprinted as "Kirche und Demokratie," *Dokumente: Zeitschrift für übernationale Zusammenarbeit* 12 (February 1956):9–16.

1951c. "School and Christian Freedom." *National Catholic Educational Association Proceedings* 48 (August):63–68.

1952a. "The Church and Totalitarian Democracy." *Theological Studies* 13 (December):525–63.

1952b. "For the Freedom and Transcendence of the Church." *The American Ecclesiastical Review* 126 (January):28–48.

1953a. "Christian Humanism in America." *Social Order* 3 (May-June):233–44. Slightly edited and republished as chapter 8, "Is It Basket Weaving? The Question of Christian and Human Values," in *WHTT,* pp. 175–96.

1953b. "Leo XIII on Church and State: The General Structure of the Controversy." *Theological Studies* 14 (March):1–30.

1953c. "Leo XIII: Separation of Church and State." *Theological Studies* 14 (June):145–214.

1953d. "Leo XIII: Two Concepts of Government." *Theological Studies* 14 (December):551–67.

1953e. "The Problem of Free Speech." *Philippine Studies* 1 (September):107–24.

1953f. Sermon given at Red Mass, Washington, D.C. February 1953. Murray Archives, file 2-294.

WORKS BY JOHN COURTNEY MURRAY   251

1954a. Correspondence with Robert MacIver, dating from 1952 through 1954. Murray Archives, file 2-147.

1954b. "Leo XIII: Two Concepts of Government: Government and the Order of Culture." *Theological Studies* 15 (March):1–33.

1954c. Notes to Murray's *Ci Riesce* talk at Catholic University. March 25, 1954. Murray Archives, file 5-402.

1954d. "On the Structure of the Church-State Problem." In *The Catholic Church in World Affairs*, edited by Waldemar Gurian and M. A. Fitzsimons, pp. 11–32. Notre Dame, Ind.: University of Notre Dame Press.

1954e. "The Problem of Pluralism in America." *Thought* 24 (Summer):165–208. Also published in *Commonweal* 60:463–68 and in *Catholicism in American Culture* (New Rochelle, N.Y.: College of New Rochelle, 1955). Republished, with less positive affirmation of American society, in *The Catholic Mind* (May-June 1959):201–15 and as chapters 1 and 2, "E Pluribus Unum: The American Consensus" and "Civil Unity and Religious Integrity: The Articles of Peace," in *WHTT*, pp. 27–78; and as "The Problem of Pluralism in America" *Thought* (Sesquicentennial Issue):323–59.

1955a. "Catholics in America—a Creative Minority—Yes or No?" *Epistle* (New York) 21:36–41. Also as "Catholics in America—a Creative Minority?" *Catholic Mind* 53 (October):590–97.

1955b. "The Christian Idea of Education." In *Eight Views of Responsibility in Government, Business, Education and the Church*, pp. 372–84. St. Louis: St. Louis University, 1955. Excerpts published as "The Unity of Truth," *Commonweal* 63 (January 13, 1956): 381–82. Also published as "The Christian Idea of Education," in *The Christian Idea of Education*, edited by Edmund Fuller (New Haven, Conn.: Yale University Press, 1957), pp. 152–63. Published with much editing and an entirely different conclusion as "The Catholic University in a Pluralistic Society," *Catholic Mind* 57 (May-June 1959): 253–60.

1955c. "Leo XIII and Pius XII: Government and the Order of Religion." Murray Archives, file 7-536.

1955d. "Special Catholic Challenges." *Life* 39–40 (December 26):144–46. Also published as "Challenges Confronting the American Catholic," *Catholic Mind* 57 (May-June 1959):196–200.

1956a. "The Bad Arguments Intelligent Men Make." *America* 96 (November 3):120–23. This and the Fischer article that provoked it were published as appendixes in *Catholic Viewpoint on Censorship*, edited by Harold C. Gardiner, S.J. (Garden City, N.Y.: Hanover House, 1958), pp. 157–92.

1956b. "Die Katholiken in der amerikanischen Gesellschaft." *Dokumente: Zeitschrift für übernationale Zusammenarbeit* 12 (August):287–92.

1956c. "Freedom, Responsibility and Law." *The Catholic Lawyer* 2 (July):214–23, 276. Reprinted in *Catholic Mind* 56 (September-October 1958):436–47.

1956d. "The Next Liberal Task for America." September 29, 1956. Murray Archives, file 3-295.

1956e. "The Quality of Reverence." *Journal of the Newman Club of the University of Minnesota* (June). A manuscript copy in Murray Archives, file 5-390.

1956f. "Questions of Striking a Right Balance: Literature and Censorship." *Books on Trial* 14 (June-July):393–95, 444–46. Reprinted as "Literature and Censorship," *Catholic Mind* 54 (December 1956):665–77; and slightly edited for chapter 7, "Should There Be a Law: The Question of Censorship," in *WHTT*, pp. 155–74. Translated and published as "Literatur und Zensur," *Frankfurter Hefte: Zeitschrift für Kultur und Politik* 17 (December 1962):824–33.

1956g. "Remarks on Theological Method." Murray Archives, file 4-324.

1956h. "The School Problem in Mid-Twentieth Century." In *The Role of the Independent School in American Democracy*, edited by William H. Conley, pp. 1–16. Milwaukee, Wisc.: Marquette University Press. Reprinted as "The Religious School in a Pluralistic Society," *Catholic Mind* 54 (September 1956):502–11, and slightly reedited for chapter 6, "Is It Justice? The School Question Today," in *WHTT*, pp. 143–54.

1956i. Sermon for a Red Mass, Boston College. September 1956.

1956j. "St. Ignatius and the End of Modernity." In *The Ignatian Year at Georgetown*. Washington, D.C.: Georgetown University Press.

1956k. "The Thesis Form as an Instrument of Theological Reflection." In *Proceedings of the Eleventh Annual Convention of the*

Catholic Theological Society of America, pp. 218–24. Bronx, N.Y.: Catholic Theological Society of America.

1957a. "Church, State and Political Freedom." *Modern Age: A Conservative Review* 1 (Fall):134–45. Also in *Catholic Mind* 57 (May-June 1959):216–29; as "The Freedom of Man in the Freedom of the Church," in *Modern Catholic Thinkers,* edited by A. Robert Caponigri (New York: Harper, 1960), pp. 372–84; and in *The Essentials of Freedom: The Idea and Practice of Ordered Liberty in the Twentieth Century,* edited by Raymond English (Gambier, Ohio: Kenyon College, 1960), pp. 151–166; and as chapter 9, "Are There Two or One? The Question of the Future of Freedom," in *WHTT,* pp. 197–217.

1958a. "America's Four Conspiracies." In *Religion in America,* ed. J. Cogley, pp. 12–41. New York: Meridian Books. Reprinted in *Catholic Mind* 57 (May-June 1959):230–41, and in *Readings in the Philosophy of Education,* edited by M. Carron (Detroit: University of Detroit Press, 1960), pp. 84–86. Also appeared as "Introduction: The Civilization of the Pluralistic Society," in *WHTT,* pp. 5–24.

1958b. "Church and State: The Structure of the Argument." Murray Archives, file 6-490.

1958c. "Confusion of U.S. Foreign Policy." In *Foreign Policy and the Free Society,* edited by John Courtney Murray and Walter Millis, pp. 21–42, with a discussion between Millis, Murray, and others, pp. 53–116. New York: Oceana Publications. This was sponsored by Fund for the Republic. Excerpt published as "Confusion of U.S. Foreign Policy," *Catholic Mind* 57 (May-June 1959): 261–73. Also published as chapter 10, "Doctrine and Policy in Communist Imperialism: The Problem of Security and Risk," in *WHTT,* 221–47.

1958d. "How to Think (Theologically) about War and Peace." *Catholic Messenger* 76 (December):7–8. Also as "U.S. Policy vis-à-vis the Soviet Union." Catholic Association for International Peace *News* 19 (December):8–10.

1958e. "The Making of a Pluralist Society." *Religious Education* 53 (November-December):521–28. Reprinted as "University in a Pluralist Society," in *Religion and the State University,* edited by Erich A. Walker (Ann Arbor, Mich.: University of Michigan Press, 1958), pp. 13–26. Reprinted as "State University in a

Pluralist Society," *Catholic Mind* 57 (May-June 1959):242–52. Edited for chapter 5, "Creeds at War Intelligibly: Pluralism and the University," in *WHTT,* pp. 125–39.

1958f.   Talk on religious knowledge and the university, given at Loyola. Murray Archives, file 6-423.

1959a.   "The Liberal Arts College and the Contemporary Climate of Opinion." November 1959. Murray Archives, file 6-480.

1959b.   *Morality and Modern War.* New York, N.Y.: The Church Peace Union. Pamphlet, from a paper delivered before the Catholic Association for International Peace, October 28, 1958. Printed as "The Morality of War," *Theological Digest* 7 (Autumn 1959):131–37; as "God, Man and Nuclear War," *Catholic Mind* 57 (May-June 1959):274–88; as "Remarks on the Moral Problem of War," *Theological Studies* 20 (March 1959):40–61; as "Theology and Modern War," in *Morality and Modern Warfare,* edited by William Nagle, pp. 69–91 (Baltimore, Md.: Helicon Press, 1960); as "Der Krieg als sittliches Problem," *Dokumente: Zeitschrift für übernationale Zusammenarbeit* 4 (August 1959):275–90; and slightly edited as ch. 11, "The Uses of a Doctrine on the Uses of Force: War as a Moral Problem," in *WHTT,* pp. 249–73.

1959c.   "The Next Task for America." Sermon for a Red Mass in Baltimore, Md., September 1959. Murray Archives, file 3-296.

1959d.   "Unica Status Religio." Murray Archives, file 7-558.

1960a.   "Morality and Foreign Policy, Part I & II." *America* 102 (March 19):729–32; (March 26):764–67. This two-part article appeared as chapter 12, "The Doctrine Is Dead: The Problem of the Moral Vacuum," in *WHTT,* pp. 273–94.

1960b.   "On Raising the Religious Issue." *America* 103 (September 24):702.

1960c.   *We Hold These Truths.* New York: Sheed & Ward. Made up of previously cited articles: Introduction, 1958a; chapters 1 and 2, 1954e; chapter 5: 1958d; chapter 6, 1956i; chapter 7, 1956f; chapter 8, 1953a; chapter 9, 1957b; chapter 10, 1958c; chapter 11, 1958e; chapter 12, 1960a; chapter 13, 1950a. Also including the new additions of chapter 3, "Two Cases for the Public Consensus: Fact or Need," pp. 79–96; and chapter 4, "The Origins and Authority of the Public Consensus: A Study of the Growing End," pp. 97–123.

1961a. "The American Proposition." *Commonweal* 73 (January 20):433–35. Transcription of an interview on "The Catholic Hour."

1961b. "Foreword." In *In a Spirit of Wonder: A Christmas Anthology for Our Age,* edited by M. L. Shrady, pp. ix–xi. New York: Pantheon Books.

1961c. "Hopes and Misgivings for Dialogue." *America* 104 (January 14):459–60. Also part of a pamphlet published as *One Fold, One Shepherd* (New York, N.Y.: America Press).

1961d. "What Can Unite a Religiously Divided Nation?" *Catholic Messenger* 79 (May 4):4. Republished as "The Return to Tribalism," *Catholic Mind* 60 (January 1962):5–12, and in *Readings in Social Theology,* edited by E. Morgan, (Dayton, Ohio: Pflaum Press), pp. 191–201.

1962a. "Le droit à l'incroyance." *Relations* [Montréal] 227 (April):91–92.

1962b. "Federal Aid to Church Related Schools." *Yale Political: A Journal of Divergent Views on National Issues* 1:16, 29–31.

1962c. "Foreword." In *The Encounter with God: Aspects of Modern Theology,* edited by Joseph C. O'Neill, pp. vii–x. New York: Macmillan & Company.

1962d. Letter to Archbishop L. J. Shehan, August, 1962. Murray Archives, file 18-1008.

1962e. "Remarks on Theological Method." Murray Archives, file 4-324.

1963a. "The Church and the Council." *America* 104 (October 19):451–53.

1963b. "The Elite and the Electorate: Is Government by the People Possible?" Center for the Study of Democratic Institutions, by the Fund for the Republic, Santa Barbara, California. An occasional paper on the role of political process in the free society; Murray comments on an article by J. William Fulbright.

1963c. *Encyclopaedia Britannica.* 11th ed. S.v. "Extreme unction," "Holy spirit," "Nuncio."

1963d. "Foreword." In *American Pluralism and the Catholic Conscience,* edited by Richard J. Regan, S.J., pp. xii–xv. New York: Macmillan & Company, 1963.

1963e. "Foreword." In *Religious Liberty and the American Presidency: A Study in Church-State Relations*, edited by Patricia Barret, pp. v–vii. New York: Herder.

1963f. "Good Pope John: A Theologian's Tribute." *America* 108 (June 15):854–55.

1963g. "Kirche und Staat in Nordamerika." *Dokumente: Zeitschrift für übernationale Zusammenarbeit* 19 (December):423–33. Republished as "Das Verhältnis von Kirche und Staat in den USA," in *Das Verhältnis von Kirche und Staat: Erwägungen zur Vielfalt der geschichtlichen Entwicklung und gegenwärtigen Situation* (Würzburg: Echter, 1965), pp. 51–71. English original in Murray Archives, file 11-703.

1963h. "Make the News Good News!" *Interracial Review* 36 (July):130–31, 134–35. Also published in *What Do They Want Now? Questions and Answers on Race*, edited by C. J. McNaspy (New York: America Press, 1964), pp. 33–39.

1963i. "On Religious Liberty." *America* 109 (November):704–6. Also published in *American Catholic Horizons*, edited by Eugene K. Culhane (New York: Doubleday, 1966), pp. 219–26. Also published as "Religionsfreiheit als Konzilsthema," in *Das Konzil: Zweiter Bild- und Textbericht*, edited by Mario von Galli and Bernard Moorburger (Mainz: Matthias-Grünewald), pp. 138–40; as "Liberté religieuse: la position de l'épiscopat américain," *Choisir* (1964):14–16; in *Etudes et Documents* [Secrétariat conciliaire de l'Episcopat Français, Paris] N.S. no. 2 (February 4, 1964); and as "En torno a la 'Libertad Religiosa,' " in *Libertad Religiosa: Una Solución Para Todos*, edited by Rafel López Jordan, S.J. (Madrid: Ediciones Studium, 1964), pp. 45–52; by Rafel López Jordan, S.J., in *Problematica della libertà religiosa (Milan*: Ancora, 1964), pp. 29–37; and as "Due documenti al Concilio sulla liberta religiosa," *Aggiornamenti sociali* 15 (1964):57–62.

1963j. "Things Old and New in 'Pacem in Terris' " *America* 108 (April 27):612–14. Also published in *American Catholic Horizons*, edited by Eugene K. Culhane (New York: Doubleday, 1966), pp. 188–94; and as "Key Themes in the Encyclical 'Pacem in Terris' " in the pamphlet *Peace on Earth* (New York: America Press, 1963), pp. 57–64.

1964a. "Information and the Church: The Function of the Catholic Press within the Catholic Church." *Social Survey* 13:204–8.

Expanded form of an address to the International Press Association, 1963. Also published as "The Social Function of the Press," *Journalistes Catholiques* 12 (January-April 1964):8–12.

1964b. "On the Future of Humanistic Education." In *Humanistic Education and Western Civilization,* edited by Arthur A. Cohen in honor of the sixty-fifth birthday of Robert M. Hutchins, pp. 231–47. New York: Holt, Rinehart, & Winston. Excerpted in *The Critic* 22 (February-March 1964):37–43.

1964c. "On the Structure of the Problem of God." *Theological Studies* 23 (March):1–26. Republished with significant editing as *The Problem of God, Yesterday and Today* (New Haven, Conn.: Yale University Press, 1964). Translated and published as *Il problema di Dio ieri e oggi* (Brescia: Morcelliana, 1971) and as *Le Problème de Dieu de la Bible á l'incroyance contemporaine* (Paris: Centurion, 1965)

1964d. "The Problem of Mr. Rawls' Problem." In *Law and Philosophy,* edited by Sidney Hooks, pp. 29–34. New York: New York University Press.

1964e. *The Problem of Religious Freedom.* Woodstock Papers, number 7. Westminster, Md.: The Newman Press. An earlier, briefer form was published as "The Problem of Religious Freedom," *Theological Studies* 25 (December 1964):503–75. Also published as "Le probleme de la liberté religieuse au Councile," in *La liberté religieuse: exigence spirituelle et problème politique* (Paris: Centurion, 1965), pp. 9–112; as "Die religiöse Freiheit und das Konzil," *Wort und Wahrheit* 20 (1965):409–30, 505–36; as "Il problema della libertà religiosa al concilio," *Il Nuovo Osservatore* 54 (1966):686–734; and as "La libertà religiosa: Un grave Problema di oggi ereditato dalla storia di ieri," in *Cattolicesimo e libertà,* edited by F. V. Joannes (Milan: Mondadori, 1969), pp. 157–254.

1964f. "The Schema on Religious Freedom: Critical Comments." Murray Archives, file 18-986.

1964g. "Today and Tomorrow: Conversation at the Council: John Courtney Murray, Hans Küng, Gustave Weigel, Godfrey Diekmann, and Vincent Yzermans." *American Benedictine Review* 15 (September):341–51. Also published in somewhat different form under the same title in *Ave Marie* 100 (1964):10–11.

1965a. *Acceptance Speech.* New York: Unitarian-Universalist Association. Pamphlet of a talk given on receipt of the Second Annual Thomas Jefferson Award, March 22, 1965.

1965b. "Commentary on the Declaration." Murray Archives, file 18-1005.

1965c. "The Conciliar History of the Declaration." No month cited. Murray Archives, file 18-1005.

1965d. "Foreword." In *Freedom and Man,* edited by John Courtney Murray, pp. 11–16. New York: P. J. Kenedy.

1965e. "Foreword." In *A Theology of Mary,* edited by Cyril Vollert, pp. 9–11, Saint Mary's Theology series number 3. New York: Herder & Herder.

1965f. Memo to Cushing on Contraception Legislation. No month cited. Murray Archives, file 1-43.

1965g. "Osservazioni sulla dichiarazione della libertà religiosa." *La Civiltà Cattolica* 116 (December):536–54. Also published as "La déclaration sur la liberté religieuse," *Nouvelle Revue Théologique* 88 (1966):41–67.

1965h. "Religious Freedom." In *Freedom and Man,* edited by John Courtney Murray, pp. 131–40. New York: P. J. Kenedy.

1965i. "Remarks on the Schema on Religious Liberty." Murray Archives, file 18-1000.

1965j. "This Matter of Religious Freedom." *America* 112 (January 9):40–43. Published as "La 'libertà religiosa': Materia di dibattito conciliare," *Aggiornamenti Sociali* 16 (April 1965):303–10.

1966a. "Conference on the Development of the Doctrine of Religious Liberty." In *Council Day Book,* edited by Floyd Anderson, pp. 14–17. Washington, D.C.: NCWC Press.

1966b. "The Declaration on Religious Freedom." In *Vatican II: An Interfaith Appraisal,* edited by John H. Miller, article, pp. 565–76, and discussion, pp. 577–85. Notre Dame, Ind.: Association Press. Translated and published as *La teologia dopo il Vaticano II,* edited by J. H. Miller (Brescia: Morcelliana, 1967), pp. 710–33.

1966c. "The Declaration on Religious Freedom." *War, Poverty, Freedom: The Christian Response,* pp. 3–10. New York: Paulist Press. *Concilium* 5, no. 2. Also published as "La Déclaration sur la Liberté Religieuse." *Concilium* 15 (1966): 7–18.

1966d. "The Declaration on Religious Freedom: A Moment in Its Legislative History." In *Religious Liberty: An End and a Beginning,* edited by John Courtney Murray, pp. 15–42. New York: Macmillan & Company.

1966e. "The Declaration on Religious Freedom: Its Deeper Significance." *America* 114 (April 23):592–93. Also published as "The Vatican Declaration on Religious Freedom: An Aspect of its Significance," in *The University in the American Experience* (New York: Fordham University Press, 1966), pp. 1–10.

1966f. "Fairfield Address." June 5, 1966. Murray Archives, file 6-463.

1966g. "Freedom, Authority, Community." *America* 115 (December 3):734–41. Also published in *Freedom and Authority in the West,* edited by G. Shuster, (Notre Dame, Ind.: University of Notre Dame, 1967), pp. 11–24; in *Christian Witness in the Secular City,* edited by E. Morgan (Chicago: Loyola University, 1970), pp. 118–30; and in *Catholic Lawyer* 15 (Spring 1969):158–68. Translated and published as "Libertà autorità e Communità Chiesa in un mondo in trasformazione," in *Verso il sinodo dei vescovi. I problemi* (Brescia: Queriniana, 1967), pp. 173–81.

1966h. "The Issue of Church and State at Vatican II." *Theological Studies* 27 (December):580–606.

1966i. "Religious Freedom." In *The Documents of Vatican II,* edited by Walter M. Abbot and Joseph Gallagher, introduction, pp. 673–74, and text with commentary, pp. 674–96. New York: America Press.

1966j. "The Status of the Nicene Creed as Dogma." *Chicago Studies: An Archdiocesan Review* 5 (Spring):65–80. Delivered as a talk on ecumenism in a Lutheran-Catholic dialogue, Baltimore, Md., July 1965.

1967a. "The Danger of the Vows: An Encounter with Earth, Woman and the Spirit." *Woodstock Letters* 116 (Fall):421–27.

1967b. "The Death of God." January 10, 1967. Address at the University of Connecticut. Murray Archives, file 6-462.

1967c. "Declaration on Religious Freedom: Commentary." In *American Participation at the Second Vatican Council,* edited by Vincent A. Yzermans, pp. 668–76. New York: Sheed & Ward.

1967d. "Freedom in the Age of Renewal." *American Benedictine Review* 18 (September):319–24. Also a talk given at St. John's, June 1965.

1967e. "Introduction." In *One of a Kind: Essays in Tribute to Gustave Weigel*, pp. 11–22. Wilkes-Barre, Pa.: Dimension Books.

1967f. "Mentalità moderna e problemi attuali dell'uomo nella Chiesa." In *Verso il sinodo dei vescovi. I problemi*, pp. 172–81. Brescia: Queriniana.

1967g. "Murray Says Church Was Too Sure." *Toledo Catholic Chronicle* 33, no. 29 (May 5):1, 5. Toledo address. See also National Catholic News Service, "Jesuit Priest Calls Minority Birth Control Report 'Classicism,' " *National Catholic Reporter* (May 17, 1967):3.

1967h. "Our Response to the Ecumenical Revolution." *Religious Education* 42 (March-April):91–92, 119.

1967i. "Religious Liberty and Development of Doctrine." *The Catholic World* 204 (February):277–83.

1967j. Review of *Academic Freedom and the Catholic University*, by Edward Manier and John W. Houch. *AAUP Bulletin* 53:339–42.

1967k. Review of *The Garden and the Wilderness: Religion and Government in American Constitutional History*, by M. D. Howe. *Yale Law Journal* 76 (April):1030–35.

1967l. *Selective Conscientious Objection*. Huntington, Ind.: Our Sunday Visitor, Inc. Pamphlet giving the text of an address at Western Maryland College, June 4, 1967. Published as "War and Conscience" in *A Conflict of Conscience*, edited by James Finn (New York: Pegasus, 1968), pp. 19–30.

1967m. "Vers une intelligence du développement de la doctrine de l'Église sur la liberté religieuse." In *Vatican II: La Liberté Religieuse*, edited by J. Hamer and Y. Congar, pp. 111–47. Paris: Cerf. Also published as "Zum Verständnis der Entwicklung der Lehre der Kirche über die Religionsfreiheit," in *Die Konzilerklärung: Über die Religionsfreiheit: Lateinischer und deutscher Text* (Paderborn: Bonifacius Druckerei, 1967), pp. 125–65. English original in Murray Archives, file 7-517.

1967n. "A Will to Community." In *Theological Freedom and Social Responsibility*, edited by Stephen F. Bayne Jr., pp. 111–16. New

York: Seabury Press. Also published as "We Held These Truths," *National Catholic Reporter* 3 (August 23, 1967):3.

1968. "De Argumentis pro Jure Hominis ad Libertatem Religiosam." In *Acta Congressus Internationalis de Theologia Concilii Vaticani II,* edited by A. Schönmetzer, pp. 562–73. Rome: Vatican.

1969. "The Unbelief of the Christian." In *The Presence and Absence of God,* edited by Christopher Mooney, pp. 69–83. New York: Fordham University Press.

1970. "La liberta religiosa e l'ateo." In *L'ateismo contemporaneo,* pp. 109–17. Torino: Società Ed. Internazionale. English original in Murray Archives, file 4-327.

Un-
dated. "Transcript of Rockefeller Project Conversation." Murray Archives, file 8-592.

Murray, John Courtney, and Millis, Walter. 1958. *Foreign Policy and the Free Society.* New York: Oceana Publications. This was a Fund for the Republic–sponsored exchange, with Murray's address, pp. 21–42, and then a discussion between Millis, Murray, and others, pp. 53–116. Excerpt published as "Confusion of U.S. Foreign Policy," *Catholic Mind* 57 (May-June 1959):261–73. Also published as chapter 10, "Doctrine and Policy in Communist Imperialism: The Problem of Security and Risk," in *WHTT,* pp. 221–47.

WORKS ON
JOHN COURTNEY MURRAY

The following vary in their use of, or appeals to, Murray. Some are simple obituaries. Some make passing reference to his attempts to reconcile (or challenge) the church and American society. Others are close textual analyses of his thought, while others consciously attempt to move beyond his work.

Allitt, Patrick. 1990. "The Significance of John Courtney Murray." In *Church Polity and American Politics: Issues in Contemporary American Catholicism*, edited by Mary C. Segers, pp. 51–65. New York: Garland Publishing, Inc.

Bacik, James J. 1989. "John Courtney Murray: Living as a Christian in a Pluralistic Society." In *Contemporary Theologians*. Chicago: Thomas More Association. Number 3.

Barr, Stringfellow. 1960. "A Review of *We Hold These Truths*." *New York Herald Tribune Book Review* (October 30):4.

Barrionuevo, Cristobal M. 1956. "La teoria del P. Murray sobre las Relaciones entre la Iglesia y Estado." Ph.D. diss., University of Granada, Granada, Spain.

Bennett, John Coleman. 1958. "A Protestant View of American Catholic Power." In *Christians and the State*, pp. 252–68. New York: Charles Scribner's Sons.

———. 1967. "John Courtney Murray." *Christianity and Crisis* 27 (September 18):198–99.

Brandt, Lawrence E. 1983. *John Courtney Murray and Religious Liberty: An American Experience*. Rome: Pontificia Università Lateranense.

Broderick, Albert. 1967. "From a Friend Who Never Met Him: Tribute to John Courtney Murray." *America* 117 (September 9):246–48.

Burgess, Faith E. R. 1971. *Ecclesia et Status: The Relationship Between Church and State According to John Courtney Murray, S.J.* Düsseldorf: Stehle.

Burghardt, Walter J. 1967. "A Eulogy." *Woodstock Letters* 96:416–20.

———. 1967. "He Lived with Wisdom: Tribute to John Courtney Murray." *America* 117 (September 9):247–48.

———. 1968. "A Tribute to John Courtney Murray." *Catholic Mind* 66 (June):29–31.

———. 1968. "Unity Through Ecstasy: A Tribute to John Courtney Murray." *Dominicana* 53 (Spring):3–5.

———. 1969. "From Certainty to Understanding." *Catholic Mind* 67 (June):13–27.

———. 1985. "Who Chilled the Beaujolais?" *America* 153, no. 16 (November 30):360–63.

———. 1989. "Consensus, Moral Witness and Health-care Issues: A Dialogue with J. Brian Hehir." In *Catholic Perspectives on Medical Morals,* edited by Edward Pellegrino et al., pp. 223–29. Boston: Kluwer Academic.

———. 1976. *Religious Freedom: 1965–1975.* New York: Paulist Press.

Burke, Eugene. 1980. "A Personal Memoir on the Origins of the CTSA." In *Proceedings of the Thirty-Fifth Convention* [of the Catholic Theological Society of America], vol. 35, pp. 337–45. Bronx, N.Y.: Catholic Theological Society of America.

Cahill, Lisa Sowle. 1987. "The Catholic Tradition: Religion, Morality, and the Common Good." *Journal of Law and Religion* 5, no. 1:75–94.

Canavan, Francis J., S.J. 1982. "Murray on Vatican II's Declaration on Religious Freedom." *Communio* 9 (Winter):404–5.

Carrillo De Albornoz, Angelo Francisco. 1965. "Religious Freedom: Intrinsic or Fortuitous?" *Christian Century* 82 (September 15): 1122–26.

"City of Man and God." 1960. *Time* 76 (December 12):64–70; see cover also.

Cogley, John. 1956. "In Praise of Father Murray." *Commonweal* 65 (December 7):253.

Coleman, John A. 1976. "Vision and Praxis in American Theology: Orestes Brownson, John A. Ryan, and John Courtney Murray." *Theological Studies* 37 (March):3–40.

————. 1978. "A Theological Link Between Religious Liberty and Mediating Structures." In *Church, State, and Public Policy: The New Shape of the Church-State Debate,* edited by Jay Mechling, pp. 22–48. Washington, D.C.: American Enterprise Institute for Public Policy Research.

Cox, Harvey. 1961. "Review of *We Hold These Truths.*" *Cross Currents* (Winter):79–83.

Cuddihy, John Murray. 1979. "John Courtney Murray, S.J." In *No Offence: Civil Religion and Protestant Taste,* pp. 64–100. New York: Seabury Press.

Curran, Charles E. 1982. "Civil Law and Christian Morality: Abortion and the Churches." In *Abortion: The Moral Issues,* edited by E. Batchelor, pp. 143–65. New York: Pilgrim Press.

————. 1982. "John Courtney Murray." In *American Catholic Social Ethics: Twentieth-Century Approaches,* pp. 172–232. Notre Dame, Ind.: University of Notre Dame Press.

Deedy, John. 1978. *Seven American Catholics,* pp. 125–53. Chicago: Thomas More Press.

Dionne, J. Robert. 1987. *The Papacy and the Church: A Study of Praxis and Reception in Ecumenical Perspective.* New York: Philosophical Library.

Dougherty, Jude. 1990. "II. Dean Dougherty on Separation of Church and State." *Wanderer* (October 25):6–7.

Drinan, Robert F. 1965. "A Review of Thomas T. Love, *John Courtney Murray: Contemporary Church-State Theory.*" *Journal of Church and State* 7 (Autumn):444–46.

Dumortier, François-Xavier. 1988. "John Courtney Murray revisité: La Place de l'Eglise dans le débat public aux Etats-Unis." *Recherches de Science Religieuse* 76, no. 4:499–531.

Faherty, William Barnaby, S.J. 1988. "American Freedom: John Courtney Murray (1904–1967)." In *Rebels or Reformers? Dissenting Priests in America,* pp. 91–97. Chicago: Loyola University Press.

Fallon, Thomas L., O.P. 1990. "A Review of *Matthias Scheeben on Faith,* by John Courtney Murray, ed. and with an introduction by D. Thomas Hughson, S.J." In *Critical Review of Books in Religion,* pp. 441–43. Atlanta: Scholars Press.

Ferguson, Thomas P. 1991. "Catholic and American: The Political Theology of John Courtney Murray." Ph.D. diss., University of Virginia.

Finn, James. 1983. "Pacifism and Just War: Either or Neither." In *Catholics and Nuclear War,* edited by P. Murnion, pp. 132–45. New York: Crossroads.

Flaherty, Daniel L. 1966. "Christian Marxist Dialogue." *America* 115 (December 17):805.

Formicola, Jo Renee. 1987. "American Catholic Political Theology." *Journal of Church and State* 29 (Autumn):457–74.

Gilby, Thomas. 1961. "Review of *We Hold These Truths.*" *Thomist* 24:111–13.

Goerner, Edward A. 1959. "John Courtney Murray and the Problem of Church and State." Ph.D. diss., University of Chicago.

——. 1965. *Peter and Caesar: Political Authority and the Catholic Church.* New York: Herder & Herder.

Gould, William J., Jr. "The Challenge of Liberal Political Culture in the Thought of John Courtney Murray." *Communio* 19 (Spring 1992): 113–144.

Gremillion, Joseph. 1982. "Religious Freedom and the Local Church's Responsibility for Mission: The Regional Church of North America." In *Mission in Dialogue: The SEDOS Research Seminar on the Future of Mission,* edited by Mary Motte and Joseph R. Lang, pp. 459–70. Maryknoll, N.Y.: Orbis.

Guroian, Vigen. 1987. "Between Secularism and Christendom: Orthodox Reflections on the American Order." *This World* 18 (Summer):12–22.

Harrison, Brian W. 1988. "Annexe: John Courtney Murray: sur l'Eglise et l'Etat." In *Le développement de la doctrine catholique sur la liberté religieuse,* pp. 166–79. Grez-en-Bour: Dominique Martin Morin.

Hastings, C. B. 1988. "Huges-Félicité Robert de Lamennais: A Catholic Pioneer of Religious Liberty." *Journal of Church and State* 30 (Spring):321–39.

Hehir, J. Bryan. 1976. "Issues of Church and State: A Catholic Perspective." In *Issues in Church and State: Proceedings of a Dialogue Between Catholics and Baptists,* edited by Claude U. Broach, pp. 81–95. Winston-Salem, N.C.: Ecumenical Institute.

——. 1985. "The Unfinished Agenda." *America* 153 (November 30):386–92.

——. 1989. "Religious Pluralism and Social Policy: The Case of Health Care." In *Catholic Perspectives on Medical Morals,* edited by Edward Pellegrino et al., pp. 205–21. Boston: Kluwer Academic.

Higgins, George G. 1969. "John Courtney Murray and the American Bishops." *Priest* 25 (March):175–79.

——. 1985. "Some Personal Recollections." *America* 153, no. 17 (November 30): 380, 382, 384, 386.

Hock, Raymond Anthony. 1964. "The Pluralism of John Courtney Murray, S.J., and Its Relationship to Education." Ph.D. diss., Stanford University.

Hollenbach, David. 1976. "Public Theology in America: Some Questions for Catholicism After John Courtney Murray." *Theological Studies* 37 (June):290–303.

————. 1985. "The Growing End of the Argument." *America* 153 (November 30):363–66.

————. 1987. "War and Peace in American Catholic Thought: A Heritage Abandoned?" *Theological Studies* 48:711–26.

Hollenbach, David, Lovin, Robin W., Coleman, John A., and Hehir, J. Bryan. 1979. "Theology and Philosophy in Public: A Symposium on John Courtney Murray's Unfinished Agenda." *Theological Studies* 40 (December):700–15.

Hooper, J. Leon, S.J. 1986. *The Ethics of Discourse: The Social Philosophy of John Courtney Murray.* Washington, D.C.: Georgetown University Press.

Hughson, D. Thomas, S.J. 1987. "Introduction." *Matthias Scheeben on Faith: The Doctrinal Dissertation of John Courtney Murray,* edited by D. Thomas Hughson, S.J. Vol. 29, Toronto Studies in Theology. Lewiston, N.Y.: Edwin Mellen Press.

Hunt, Robert P. 1989. "Murray, Niebuhr, and the Problem of the Neutral State." *Thought* 64 (December):362–76.

John Courtney Murray and the American Civil Conversation. 1992. Edited by Robert P. Hunt and Kenneth L. Grasso. Grand Rapids, Mich.: Eerdmans.

"J.C.M.—R.I.P." 1967. *Commonweal* 86 (September):540.

"John Courtney Murray." 1967. *Ave Maria* 106 (September 2, 1967):4.

"John Courtney Murray, S.J.: Obituary." 1967. *Tablet* 221 (August 26):915.

Kerwin, Jerome G. 1960. *Catholic Viewpoint on Church and State.* Garden City, N.Y.: Doubleday & Company.

Komonchak, Joseph A. 1992. "The Coldness of Clarity, the Warmth of Love: The Measure of John Courtney Murray." *Commonweal* (August 14):16–17.

————. 1993. "Vatican II and the Encounter Between Catholicism and Liberalism." In *Catholicism and Liberalism: Contributions to American Public Philosophy.* Woodstock Theological Center Symposium. New York: Cambridge University Press.

Kossel, Clifford George, S.J. 1984. "Religious Freedom and the Church: J.C. Murray." *Communio* 11 (Spring):60–74.

Krause, Edward C. 1975. "Democratic Process in the Thought of John Courtney Murray and Reinhold Niebuhr." Ph.D. diss., Boston University.

Larrey, Martin F. 1972. "John Courtney Murray: A Reappraisal." *Triumph* 7 (December):20–23.

Lawler, Peter Augustine. 1982. "Natural Law and the American Regime: Murray's *We Hold These Truths.*" *Communio* 9 (Winter):368–88.

"Life Issues After the Election." 1984. *America* 151 (November 10):285.

Lindbeck, George A. 1961. "John Courtney Murray, S.J.: An Evaluation." *Christianity and Crisis* 21 (November 13):213–16.

Little, David. 1989. "Conscience, Theology, and the First Amendment." *Soundings: An Interdisciplinary Journal* 72 (Summer-Fall): 356–78.

Love, Thomas T. 1965. "Contemporary Conservative Roman Catholic Church-State Thought." *Journal of Church and State* 8:18–29.

———. 1965. *John Courtney Murray: Contemporary Church-State Theory.* New York: Doubleday.

———. 1965. "John Courtney Murray: Liberal Roman Catholic Church-State Theory." *Journal of Religion* 45 (July):211–24.

———. 1966. "Review of John Courtney Murray, *The Problem of Religious Freedom.*" *Journal of Church and State* 8:475–77.

———. 1967. "John Courtney Murray." In *Modern Theologians: Christians and Jews,* edited by T. E. Bird, pp. 18–39. Notre Dame, Ind.: University of Notre Dame Press.

Lovin, Robin W. 1978. "The Constitution as Covenant: The Moral Foundations of Democracy and the Practice of Desegregation." Ph.D. diss., Harvard University.

———. 1979. "The Constitution as Covenant: The Moral Foundations of Democracy and the Practice of Desegregation." *Harvard Theological Review* 72 (July-October):318.

Marquez, Antonio. 1959. "Catholic Controversy on Church and State." *Theology Today* 15 (January):531–41.

Marshner, William H. 1983. "*Dignitatis humanae* and Traditional Teaching on Church and State." *Faith & Reason* 9 (Fall):222–48.

Marty, Martin. 1960. "Review of *We Hold These Truths.*" *Christian Century* 77:1315.

May, Joseph R. 1958. "The State and the Law of Christ." Rome: Ponta Grossa.

McCann, Dennis P. 1987. "The Good to be Pursued in Common." In *The Common Good and U.S. Capitalism*, edited by O. Williams and J. Houck, pp. 158–78. Lanham, Md.: University Press of America.

———. 1990. "Natural Law, Public Theology and the Legacy of John Courtney Murray." *Christian Century* 107 (September 5–12): 801–3.

McDonough, Peter. 1990. "Metamorphoses of the Jesuits: Sexual Identity, Gender Roles and Hierarchy in Catholicism." *Comparative Studies in Society and History* 32, no. 2 (April): 325–56.

———. 1992. *Men Astutely Trained: A History of the Jesuits in the American Century.* New York: Free Press/Macmillian.

McElroy, Robert. 1988. "Revisiting John Courtney Murray: The Question of Method in Public Theology." *New Catholic World* (July/August):179–83.

———. 1989. *The Search for an American Public Theology: The Contribution of John Courtney Murray.* New York: Paulist.

McEvoy, Raymond Owen. 1973. *John Courtney Murray's Thought on Religious Liberty in Its Final Phase.* Rome: Pontifical Lateran University.

McManus, Robert Joseph. 1987. *Ecclesial Loyalty in Political Responsibility: A Critical Reading and Evaluation of the Discussion in the American Arena from 1960 to 1985.* Rome: Pontifical Gregorian University.

McManus, William E. 1985. "Memories of Murray." *America* 153, no. 16 (November 30):366–68.

McNearney, Clayton Leroy. 1970. "The Roman Catholic Response to the Writings of Paul Blanshard." Ph.D. diss., University of Iowa.

Miller, William Lee. 1987. *The First Liberty: Religion and the American Republic.* New York: Alfred A. Knopf.

Moser, Mary Theresa. 1988. "Revising the Constitution: The Problem of Religious Freedom." *Journal of Religious Ethics* 16, no. 2 (March):325–44.

Most, William G. 1983. "Religious Liberty: What the Texts Demand." *Faith & Reason* 9 (Fall):196–209.

"Murray Dies of Heart Attack in Taxi at 62." 1967. *National Catholic Reporter* 3 (August 23):1–2.

Neuhaus, Richard John. 1984. *The Naked Public Square: Religion and Democracy in America.* Grand Rapids, Mich.: Eerdmans.

———. 1987. *The Catholic Moment: The Paradox of the Church in the Postmodern World.* San Francisco: Harper & Row.

Novak, Michael. 1983. *Moral Clarity in the Nuclear Age*. Nashville: Thomas Nelson.

———. 1984. *Freedom with Justice: Catholic Social Thought and Liberal Institutions*. San Francisco: Harper & Row.

———. 1985. "Economic Rights: The Servile State." *Catholicism in Crisis* (October):8–15.

O'Brien, David J. 1972. "American Catholicism and American Religion." *Journal of the American Academy of Religion* 40 (March): 36–53.

O'Collins, Gerald, S.J. 1984. "Murray and Ottaviani." *America* 151 (November 10):287–88.

Palmer, T. Vail. 1965. "Eschatology and Foreign Policy in the Thought of Reinhold Niebuhr, William Ernest Hocking, and John Courtney Murray." Ph.D. diss., University of Chicago Divinity School.

Pavlischek, Keith J. 1990. "The Real John Courtney Murray." *First Things* (October):46–49.

Pawlikowski, John T. 1979. "Human Rights in the Catholic Tradition: Some Theological Reflections." In *The Annual of the Society of Christian Ethics, Selected Papers*, edited by Max Stackhouse, pp. 145–66. Newton Centre, Mass.: American Society of Christian Ethics.

———. 1989. "Catholicism and the Public Church: Recent U.S. Developments." In *The Annual of the Society of Christian Ethics 1989*, pp. 147–65. Washington, D.C.: Georgetown University Press.

Pelotte, Donald E. 1976. *John Courtney Murray: Theologian in Conflict*. New York: Paulist.

Regan, Richard J., S.J. 1967. *Conflict and Consensus: Religious Freedom and the Second Vatican Council*. New York: Macmillan.

"Religious Liberty: A Jesuit View." 1945. *Christian Century* 62:878–80.

Rielly, J. E. 1961. "Contemporary Catholic Thought on Church and State: An Analysis of the Work of Jacques Maritain and John Courtney Murray." Ph.D. diss., Harvard University.

Rohr, John A. 1966. "Murray and the Critiques." *Continuum* 4 (Spring):147–50.

———. 1978. "John Courtney Murray's Theology of Our Founding Fathers' 'Faith': Freedom." In *Christian Spirituality in the United States: Independence and Interdependence*, edited by Francis A. Eigo, pp. 1–30. Villanova, Pa.: University of Villanova Press.

———. 1985. "John Courtney Murray and the Pastoral Letters." *America* 153 (November 30):373–79.

Sanders, Thomas G. 1958. "A Comparison of Two Current American Roman Catholic Theories of the American Political System with Particular Reference to the Problem of Religious Liberty." Ph.D. diss., Columbia University.

————. 1965. *Protestant Concepts of Church and State.* Garden City, N.Y.: Doubleday.

Scharper, Philip. 1967. "Grace Under Pressure: A Salute to John Courtney Murray, S.J." *Catholic Mind* 65 (February):29–31.

Scharper, P. 1977. "John Courtney Murray: Belated Hero." *Commonweal* 104 (March 4):150–52.

Schuck, Michael J. 1991. "John Courtney Murray's Problematic Interpretations of Leo XIII and the American Founders." *Thomist* 55, no. 4 (October):595–612.

Sebott, Reinhold. 1977. *Religionsfreiheit und Verhältnis von Kirche und Staat: Der Beitrag John Courtney Murrays zu einer modernen Frage.* Rome: Università Gregoriana Editrice.

Segers, Mary C. 1990. "American Catholicism: The Search for a Public Voice in a Pluralistic Society." *Conscience* 9 (May/June):1–7.

Sheridan, Michael P. 1967. "Honor to Fr. John Courtney Murray." *America* 117 (September 2):208.

Shrady, Maria. 1967. "John Courtney Murray, S.J., Some Memories." *Thought* 42 (Winter):485–87.

Smith, E. A. 1969. "Fundamental Church-State Tradition of the Catholic Church in the United States." *Church History* 38 (December):486–505.

Spann, Edwin Russell. 1956. "The Freedom of the Church and the Freedom of the Citizen." *Bibliography for Religious in Life* 25, no. 2 (Spring):205–16.

Sullivan, Andrew. 1987. "Cross Purposes: A Review of: Eric O. Hanson, *The Catholic Church in World Politics* (Princeton University Press); George Weigel, Jr., *Tranquillitas Ordinis: The Present Failure and Future Promise of American Catholic Thought on War and Peace* (Oxford University Press); John Courtney Murray, S.J., *We Hold These Truths: Catholic Reflections on the American Proposition* (Sheed and Ward)." *New Republic* 196 (June 1):30–34.

Tinnelly, J. T. 1961. "The Challenge of John Courtney Murray: Can an American Public Philosophy Be Stated." *Catholic Lawyer* 7:270–96.

Traffas, John Raymond. 1983. "John Courtney Murray's Theology of Political Right: An Analysis of Murray's Theory of Religious Liberty in Terms of the Teaching of Dignitatis Humanae." Master's thesis, University of Dallas.

Van Allen, Roger. 1982. "Review Symposium: *American Catholic Social Ethics: 20th Century Approaches,* by Charles E. Curran." *Horizons: The Journal of the College Theology Society* 9 (Fall):323–47.

Villaroel Carmona, A. 1967. *Libertad religosa signo de nuestro tiempo.* Santiago, Chile.

Wallace, Marilyn. 1988. "The Right of Religious Liberty and Its Basis in the Theological Literature of the French Language (1940–1988): An Analysis and Critique of the Contributions of Guy de Broglie, René Coste, Philippe Delhaye and Louis Janssens." Ph.D. diss., Catholic University, Washington, D.C.

Weigel, George S. 1985. "John Courtney Murray & The American Proposition." *Catholicism in Crisis* (November):8–13.

———. 1986. "John Courtney Murray and the Catholic Human Rights Revolution." *This World* 15 (Fall):14–27.

———. 1987. *Tranquillitas Ordinis: The Present and Future Promise of American Catholic Thought on War and Peace.* New York: Oxford University Press.

———. 1987. "The National Interest and the National Purpose: From Policy Debate to Moral Argument." *This World* 19 (Fall): 75–100.

———. 1989. *Catholicism and the Renewal of American Democracy.* New York: Paulist.

Weston, William. 1987. "Michael Novak's Pluralistic Religion." *This World* 19 (Fall):14–26.

Whelan, Charles M. 1985. "The Enduring Problems of Religious Liberty." *America* 153 (November 30):368–72.

Wolf, Donald J., S.J. 1966. "American Catholic Theories of Church-State Relations." In *Current Trends in Theology,* edited by Donald Wolf and James Schall, pp. 191–210. Garden City, N.Y.: Doubleday Image Books.

———. 1968. "Historical Consciousness and the Contemporary Church-State Problematic." In *Toward Consensus: Catholic and Protestant Interpretations of Church and State,* pp. 3–35. New York: Doubleday.

Yanitelli, V. R. 1951. "A Church-State Controversy." *Thought* 26:443–51.

———. 1952. "A Church-State Anthology: The Work of Father Murray." *Thought* 27:6–42.

INDEX

The following index tracks various concepts, distinctions, and sources across the four Murray arguments contained in this volume. Murray's frequent appeals to a narrow range of sources (mostly papal) and his tight control over his own language complicate the assembly of an index that might be useful to the reader. For example, Leo XIII appears as a subject or a source on nearly every page of the first two articles, leaving few consistent handles for distinguishing between those citations. I have chosen to list the source documents for the Leonine appeals, while giving little or no document citation for authors that Murray used only sparingly. Further, the term "human dignity" best exemplifies the problem we encounter with Murray's terminological choices. "Human dignity" permeates Murray's conciliar and postconciliar arguments (in fact, the last article in this collection is in its entirety a complex exposition of that term). Yet the first article barely mentions the term. Slight familiarity with Murray's work suggests that his rich concept of human dignity appeared in his earlier articles under terms such as the "jurist," the "authorization principle," and "constitutionalism" as "active moral agency." Where possible I have tried to point out some of these links of later terms with their forerunners. Finally, this is an index of Murray's work. However, I have included references to my own editorial additions within brackets at the end of each entry for my own general discussions of key terms and relations.